Additional p
Shark's Fin and S

"Since her first Sichuan cookbook came out several years ago, Fuchsia Dunlop has been a particular hero of mine, on par with Paula Wolfert and David Thompson—part anthropologist, part gourmet."

—Jonathan Kauffman, *Seattle Weekly*

"Delightful."

—Jeffrey Steingarten, *Vogue*

"What makes it a distinguished contribution to the literature of gastronomy is its demonstration . . . that food is not a mere reflection of culture but a potent shaper of cultural identity."

—Dawn Drzal, *New York Times Sunday Book Review*

"This charming, informative textbook/memoir/travelogue . . . [is] one of the more noteworthy recent food studies. Readers definitely won't be hungry an hour after finishing this satisfying history from a witty Chinese food authority."

—*Kirkus Reviews*

"With Fuchsia Dunlop as your lively guide you'll learn more about Chinese food than you can possibly digest. . . . Food study serves as a useful vehicle for grasping cultural and historical diversity and Dunlop does this with humor, skill and timing."

—Kendra Nordin, *Christian Science Monitor*

"Literary, entertaining and almost anthropological. . . . illuminating even for those who would touch neither shark's fin nor Sichuan pepper."

—Rebekah Denn, *Seattle Post-Intelligencer*

"A lively new memoir."

—Andrea Thompson, NewYorker.com

"An autobiographical food-and-travel classic." —*Publishers Weekly*

"Painstakingly researched, beautifully written and impossible to put down, Dunlop takes us on a tantalizing tour of China in what's sure to be the gastronomic book of the year." —Eric Vellend, *Inside Toronto*

"Dunlop's grasp of Chinese culture and cuisine run deep . . . she is as comfortable researching Confucian philosophy as she is stir-frying a duck." —Sasha Chapman, *Toronto Globe and Mail*

"A wonderful and engaging book. . . . Dunlop's enthusiastic writing makes you want to run out and get some Chinese." —Bookdwarf.com

"A historical (and often hysterical) glimpse at . . . fascinating facets of Chinese cooking." —Bruce Tierney, *Bookpage*

"Marvellous and mesmerising. . . . To those of us who relish the occasional special fried rice and sweet and sour pork balls, Dunlop's fascinating book will be a revelation." —Val Hennessy, *Daily Mail*

"As much a memoir and a superlative example of travel writing as it is a book about food. . . . a funny, honest and illuminating account of her education in Chinese food and Chinese mores . . . should be mandatory reading for anyone who considers themselves a fan [of Chinese food]." —Jacqueline O'Mahony, *London Lite*

"An inspiring read." —Michelle Stanistreet, *Sunday Express*

"This journey through the intricacies of Chinese cuisine is one of the most fascinating food books I have ever read. Not only is she a gifted storyteller, but Fuchsia's experience is so authentic that the reader gets to know the real China. . . . Highly recommended." —*Sunday Tribune*

"From one of the leading experts in the West, this is a fascinating account of Fuchsia's love of the food and culture of China."
                    —*Sainsbury's Magazine* (Book of the Month, March 2008)

"Much more than just a book that helps explain Chinese food (which it does *par excellence*), this is also a brilliant travelogue."
                    —Guy Dimond, *Time Out London*

"The enthusiasm that award-winning Fuchsia Dunlop brings to her memories of eating in China is infectious. . . . [This book is] impossible to put down . . . a fascinating, informative and very honest book."   —*Oxford Times*

"An absorbing adventure."   —Matt Rudd, *Sunday Times*

"Compelling . . . it is testament to how well she writes that . . . she manages to make caterpillars sound distinctly underrated as a snack. She makes you hungry for more."   —Robert Douglas-Fairhurst, *The Telegraph*

"More than just a memoir: it is a fascinating piece of travel writing in its fullest sense, not simply a record of sights, sounds and tastes, but a sympathetic and passionate attempt to explain another people's way of seeing the world."   —Press Association (UK)

"Succeeds triumphantly because Dunlop tells such a compelling story—how, as a young Englishwoman, she was seduced by the spicy food of Sichuan Province."   —Bee Wilson, *Sunday Times*

"Dunlop is now an expert on Chinese cuisine, but she's also a fantastically witty storyteller. . . . Dunlop will charm and delight you with her enthralling anecdotes."   —*Wanderlust*

"If you are remotely interested in China and the social history of her people, you should read this book. If you enjoy travelers' tales, you will be delighted. And if you eat or cook for the sheer pleasure of doing so . . . lick your lips, and dive in. . . . Flawless."　　　　　　—Lesley Mason, TheBookbag.co.uk

"More than just a delicious memoir of extraordinary meals . . . an erudite, nuanced look at Chinese culinary culture, its history, and China's development over the last decade."　　　　　　　　　　　—*China Daily* (Beijing)

"[Dunlop] writes of China's familiar culinary faces . . . with an outsider's eye, an insider's palate, and a lover's affection. The best food book I've read so far this year."　　　　　　　　　　　　　　　—*Straits Times* (Singapore)

"A sensual feast of a book. . . . Fuchsia Dunlop is a star in the world of food writing, but she's never preachy in this Oriental food odyssey."
　　　　　　　　　　　　　　　　　　　　　—*The Times* (South Africa)

SHARK'S FIN AND SICHUAN PEPPER

SHARK'S FIN AND SICHUAN PEPPER

A sweet-sour memoir of eating in China

FUCHSIA DUNLOP

W. W. Norton & Company
New York · London

Note from the author: Some names and details in this book have been changed to protect the identities of various people. I have also played fast and loose with chronology in a few places, for the sake of narrative structure.

Copyright © 2008 by Fuchsia Dunlop
First published by Ebury Publishing, one of the publishers in
The Random House Group Ltd.
First American Edition 2008

For information about permission to reproduce selections from this book, write to Permissions,
W. W. Norton & Company, Inc., 500 Fifth Avenue, New York, NY 10110

For information about special discounts for bulk purchases, please contact
W. W. Norton Special Sales at specialsales@wwnorton.com or 800-233-4830

Manufacturing by RR Donnelley, Bloomsburg

Library of Congress Cataloging-in-Publication Data

Dunlop, Fuchsia.
Shark's fin and Sichuan pepper : a sweet-sour memoir of eating in China /
Fuchsia Dunlop.—1st American ed.
p. cm.
Originally published: London : Ebury, 2008.
Includes index.
ISBN 978-0-393-06657-9 (hardcover)
1. Cookery, Chinese. 2. Food habits—China. 3. Dunlop, Fuchsia—Travel—China.
4. China—Description and travel. I. Title.
TX724.5.C5D868 2008
641.5951—dc22

2007050283

ISBN 978-0-393-33288-9 pbk.

W. W. Norton & Company, Inc., 500 Fifth Avenue, New York, N.Y. 10110
www.wwnorton.com

W. W. Norton & Company Ltd., Castle House, 75/76 Wells Street, London W1T 3QT

1 2 3 4 5 6 7 8 9 0

CONTENTS

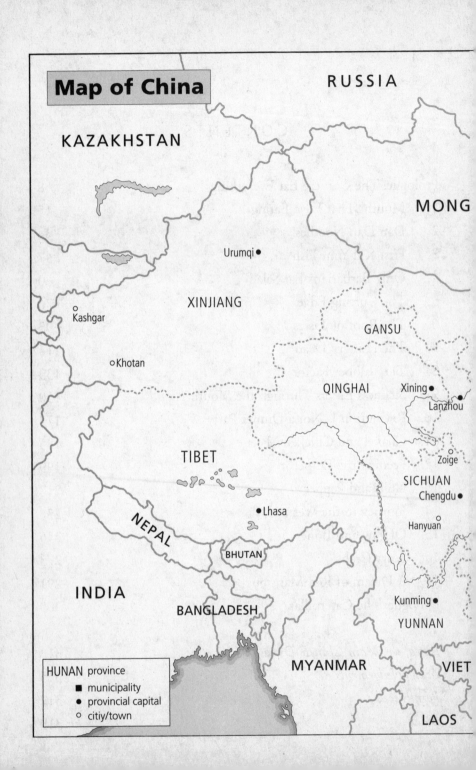

Map of China

RUSSIA

KAZAKHSTAN

MONG

Urumqi

XINJIANG

GANSU

Kashgar

QINGHAI   Xining
Khotan   Lanzhou

Zoige

TIBET   SICHUAN
                              Chengdu

Lhasa   Hanyuan

NEPAL

BHUTAN

INDIA

BANGLADESH   Kunming

MYANMAR   YUNNAN

VIET

LAOS

HUNAN province
■ municipality
● provincial capital
○ citiy/town

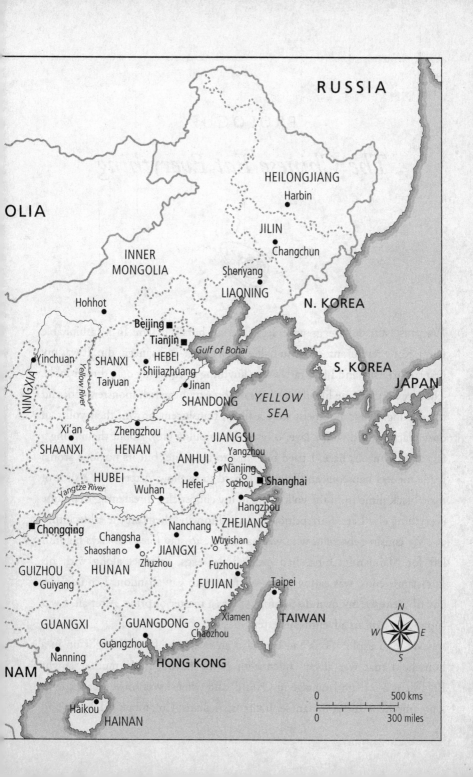

RUSSIA

HEILONGJIANG
Harbin

OLIA

JILIN
Changchun

INNER
MONGOLIA

Shenyang

LIAONING

N. KOREA

Hohhot

Beijing ■
Tianjin ■

Gulf of Bohai

S. KOREA

JAPAN

Yinchuan

SHANXI

HEBEI
Shijiazhuang

Yellow River

Taiyuan

Jinan

NINGXIA

SHANDONG

YELLOW
SEA

Xi'an

Zhengzhou

JIANGSU

SHAANXI

HENAN

Yangzhou

ANHUI

Nanjing

Hefei

Suzhou

Shanghai ■

HUBEI

Yangtze River

Wuhan

Hangzhou

Chongqing ■

Nanchang

ZHEJIANG

Changsha

Wuyishan

Shaoshan

JIANGXI

Zhuzhou

GUIZHOU

HUNAN

Fuzhou

Guiyang

FUJIAN

Taipei

GUANGXI

GUANGDONG

Xiamen

TAIWAN

Guangzhou

Chaozhou

Nanning

HONG KONG

NAM

Haikou

HAINAN

N

W ✦ E

S

0   500 kms
0   300 miles

PROLOGUE

The Chinese Eat Everything

The preserved duck eggs were served as an hors d'oeuvre in a fashionable Hong Kong restaurant, sliced in half, with a ginger-and-vinegar dip. It was my first trip to Asia, and I had rarely seen anything so revolting on a dinner table. They leered up at me like the eyeballs of some nightmarish monster, dark and threatening. Their albumens were a filthy, translucent brown, their yolks an oozy black, ringed with a layer of greenish, mouldy grey. About them hung a faintly sulphurous haze. I tried one, just to be polite, but its noxious aroma made me feel nauseous and I found it hard to swallow. Afterwards, a slick of toxic black slime from the yolk clung to my chopsticks, threatening to pollute everything else I ate. Surreptitiously, I tried to wipe them on the tablecloth.

My cousin Sebastian, who was having me to stay for a few days before I left for Mainland China, had ordered the eggs, and he, along with his Eurasian friends, was eating pieces of them with gay abandon. I couldn't let any of them see my own discomfort. It was a matter of pride. After all, I was supposed to be an adventurous eater.

My food explorations had begun at an early age. I was brought up in a household that was always filled with exotic flavours. My mother taught English as a foreign language in Oxford, and when I was small, her students – among them Turks, Sudanese, Iranians, Sicilians, Colombians, Libyans and

Japanese – often took over our kitchen to cook up feasts that reminded them of home. Our Japanese au pair girl made riceballs for my sister and me for breakfast, and our Spanish au pair boy telephoned his mother for the details of her famous paella. As for my mother, she cooked curries she'd been taught by my unofficial Hindu godfather, Vijay, while my father experimented with surrealist dishes like purple mashed potatoes with green scrambled eggs. When my Austrian grandfather visited, he prepared recipes he'd learned during his time as a wartime commando in Burma and Ceylon. At a time when most English people were living on toad in the hole, corned-beef hash and macaroni cheese, we were eating hummus, lentil curry, cacik and caponata. I certainly wasn't the kind of girl who would blanch at the sight of a snail or a kidney.

Yet Chinese food was something different. Of course I'd had the occasional Chinese takeaway as a child, deep-fried pork balls served with a bright-red sweet-and-sour sauce, chicken with bamboo shoots and egg-fried rice. Later, I had visited a few Chinese restaurants in London. But nothing had prepared me for the gastronomic assaults of that first trip to Hong Kong and China in the autumn of 1992.

I went there because of my job. I was working in the Monitoring department of the BBC, sub-editing news reports from the Asia-Pacific region. After a few months of immersion in the strange, twilight world of Chinese politics, I had decided I wanted to see the country for myself, and Hong Kong, where I had a few friends, was my first port of call. I was immediately drawn to the food. Sebastian, who was working in the territory as a graphic designer, showed me around the wet markets of Wanchai on Hong Kong Island. Other expatriate friends took me out to restaurants and ordered their favourite dishes. There were many delightful surprises: exquisite roast goose, sparklingly fresh seafood and myriad delicate *dim sum* dumplings. Even the cheapest and most nondescript restaurants served stir-fries and soups more delicious than any I had tasted in England, and the sheer variety of the food on offer was dazzling. But I was also faced with many new ingredients that I found disconcerting – or disgusting.

Soon after that dinner with Sebastian and his friends, I crossed the border into Mainland China and took the slow train to Guangzhou. There I visited the notorious Qingping market, where badgers, cats and tapirs languished in cages in the meat section, and the medicine stalls displayed sacks filled with dried snakes and lizards, scorpions and flies. For dinner, I was offered 'roasted piggy', frog casserole and stir-fried snake, its flesh still edged in reptilian skin. Some of these things – such as that stir-fried snake – turned out to be unexpectedly palatable. Others, like the loathsome preserved duck eggs (or 'thousand-year-old eggs' as they are called in the West), had tastes or textures that made my flesh crawl.

But I have never been one to turn down a taste of something new. Although in some ways I'm a cautious person, I have a streak of recklessness that tends to land me regularly in situations outside my zone of comfort. By the time I reached China, I had travelled widely in Europe and Turkey, and I was used to being shocked and challenged. My parents had also brought me up to eat whatever I was offered, in that polite English way, and it would have seemed unforgiveably rude to leave anything in my ricebowl in China, even if it had six legs or a sulphurous aroma. So from the beginning of that first trip, almost without thinking about it, I braced myself to eat whatever the Chinese might put in front of me.

Since the first European merchants and missionaries began recording their impressions of life in China, foreigners have been astounded by the Chinese diet. In the late thirteenth century, Marco Polo noted with distaste that Chinese people liked eating snakes and dogs and even, in some places, he claimed, human flesh. The French Jesuit historian Jean-Baptiste du Halde adopted a tone of wonder in his description of the exotic Chinese diet in 1736: 'Stags-Pizzles ... Bears-Paws ... nay they do not scruple eating Cats, Rats, and such like animals.' Chinese banquets have always been a cause for trepidation for outsiders because of the use of shark's fin, sea cucumbers and other rubbery delicacies, and because so many of the ingredients are simply unrecognisable. The British surgeon C. Toogood Downing, writing in the nineteenth century, described British sailors in the trading port of Guangzhou picking carefully at their food, 'lest they should detect themselves in the act of devouring an earthworm, or picking the delicate bones of a cat.'

Nearly two centuries later, in the early twenty-first century, Chinese food has become part of the fabric of British and American life. In Britain, even the smallest towns have Chinese restaurants; supermarket shelves are lined with Chinese ready meals and stir-fry sauces; and 65 per cent of British households now own a wok. In 2002, Chinese food even overtook Indian as the country's favourite 'ethnic' cuisine. Yet still a dark, muscular fear of the unknown lurks beneath the surface. In a notorious article published in 2002 under the head-line 'Chop Phooey!', the *Daily Mail* denounced Chinese food as 'the dodgiest in the world, created by a nation that eats bats, snakes, monkeys, bears' paws, birds' nests, sharks' fins, ducks' tongues and chickens' feet.' Echoing the fears of the early European travellers, it said you could never be sure what the 'oozing Day-Glo foodstuff balanced between your chopsticks' actually was.

There is nothing the British press prefers to publish or, apparently, the public to read, than a juicy story about a Chinese restaurant serving dog hotpot or penis stew. These disgusting delicacies seem to exert an irresistible pull. A story about a penis restaurant in Beijing was one of the most popular on the BBC news website for a long period in 2006. The following year, British television broadcast a four-part series about the comedian Paul Merton's travels in China. One of the aspects of Chinese culture the series covered was food, and what delicacies did they feature? Dog meat and penises! Seven centuries after Marco Polo wrote about the Chinese penchant for dog, nearly three centuries after Du Halde exclaimed at stags' pizzles, Westerners remain fixated, obsessed even, with the weird fringes of Chinese gastronomy.

Chinese communities have, on the whole, been strangely silent in the face of these disparaging stereotypes. Perhaps it's because they see 'eating every-thing' as unremarkable. Although a typical Chinese meal consists largely of grains, pork and vegetables, with a bit of fish or seafood thrown in, depending on the region, there is little that can't be considered a *potential* ingredient. Most people eat dog meat and donkey penis rarely, if at all, but there is no taboo in China about the *idea* of eating them.

The Chinese don't generally divide the animal world into the separate realms of pets and edible creatures: unless you are a strict Buddhist (and bearing in mind certain regional preferences), you might as well eat them all. Likewise, there is no conceptual divide between 'meat' and 'inedible rubbery bits' when butchering an animal carcass: in China they traditionally favour the kind of nose-to-tail eating of which restaurateur Fergus Henderson, the notorious English purveyor of offal, could only dream. As the poet Christopher Isherwood memorably wrote during his travels in China in the late 1930s: 'Nothing is specifically either eatable or uneatable. You could begin munching a hat, or bite a mouthful out of a wall; equally you could build a hut with the food provided at lunch.'

For me, the height of Chinese omnivorousness is to be found in a cookery book written by a chef and restaurateur I know from Hunan Province. It is a nice-looking, full-colour book that cheerfully enacts the worst nightmares of every foreigner who might be squeamish about Chinese food. The heads and feet of various fowl loll over the rims of soup tureens and serving dishes. Ten fishheads peer up out of a 'sea' of mashed beancurd and eggwhite, their open mouths stuffed with fishballs made from their own cooked flesh. Eleven lizards have been partially skinned and then deep-fried, so their bodies, golden and crisp like chicken nuggets, are sandwiched between scaly tails and heads in which the ruined eyeballs have been replaced by fresh green peas. One grand platter holds ten whole turtles which look as though they might wake up and shuffle away at any moment.

My favourite photograph in the book depicts a whippy egg-white pudding decorated with maraschino cherries and chocolate sprinkles. How unfortunate, I thought, that it has been photographed in such a way that the sprinkles look like ants – until I peered at the small print and discovered the 'pudding' was in fact sprinkled with ants, which, the notes say, are good for dispelling rheumatism. And then, on page forty-five, the *pièce de résistance*, a whole puppy, roasted crisp, splayed out on a plate after having been attacked with a cleaver, so its skull is split in half, an eye and a nostril on each side, served with an elegant garnish of coriander, and flowers made from pink radish. Could any racist cartoonist have created a better stereotype of the disgustingly omnivorous Chinese?

That first visit of mine to China in 1992 was a revelation. The country was so vibrant and disorganised, so unlike the monochrome, totalitarian place I'd been expecting – those indelible images of crowds in Mao suits brandishing Little Red Books. Through train windows I gazed out at vivid landscapes of rice paddies and fish ponds, where farmers worked and water buffalo grazed. I visited an incredible circus in Guangzhou where people put snakes up their noses and danced barefoot on broken glass. I cycled along the beautiful Li River near Guilin; and discussed the Cultural Revolution with a group of elderly political delegates on a passenger ship sailing through the Three Gorges of the Yangtze River. I was charmed and enthralled by almost everything I saw. Back in London, I enrolled in evening classes in Mandarin and started writing quarterly round-ups of Chinese news for the magazine *China Now*. I even began to experiment with a few Chinese recipes, from Yan-Kit So's *Classic Chinese Cookbook*. All this was just the beginning of a fascination with China that would take over my life. And as my involvement with China gained pace, so did my explorations of Chinese food.

It is not an easy thing for a traveller to go completely native in her tastes. What we eat is an essential part of who we are and how we define ourselves. Keeping up cultural traditions when abroad is no trivial matter; it is a deeply felt way of protecting ourselves from the threat of the unknown. We take holiday vaccinations to shield our bodies from the risk of invasion by foreign diseases; similarly, we may eat familiar foods while abroad to shield ourselves from the threat of exposure to different cultures. It wasn't just for their amusement that the British colonialists who lived in Asia in the late nineteenth and early twentieth centuries dressed for dinner and drank cocktails every evening. They knew that if they didn't, they risked losing themselves, like those English eccentrics in India who threw themselves so wholeheartedly into the local culture that they forgot where they really belonged.

In the nineteenth century, many of the British residents in Shanghai and the other treaty ports avoided Chinese food as far as possible, living on 'metallic' meals of tinned and bottled foods imported from home. *The Anglo-Chinese Cookbook*, published in the 1920s (in two volumes, one in English for the mistress, one in Chinese for the cook), lists classic recipes for lobster bisque and pigeon pie, and though it includes some exotic dishes such as 'Hungarian Goulasch' and 'Indian Curry', it makes no mention whatsoever of Chinese cuisine. The authors' fear of the omnivorous Chinese, hovering in the shadows, waiting to pounce, is almost palpable.

Somehow, it seems that the more foreign a country, and the more alien the diet of its natives, the more rigidly expatriates living there want to adhere to the rituals of their homelands. It's safer that way. Even now, many of my expatriate European friends in China live largely on European food at home. You take on the food of another country at your peril. Do it, and you inevitably loosen your own cultural moorings, and destabilise your fundamental sense of identity. It's a risky business.

So this is a book about the unexpected wonders of Chinese cuisine. It is also the tale of an English girl who went to China, ate everything, and was sometimes surprised at the consequences.

CHAPTER 1

Mouths That Love Eating

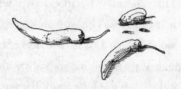

Crawling out of bed on a damp October morning, in my small shared room in the Foreign Students' Building of Sichuan University. My Italian room-mate, Filomena, is already up and out. Sleepily, I pull on a padded jacket and look out of the window. As usual, the sky is a muffled grey ('Sichuanese dogs bark' – in surprise – 'at the sun', goes the old saying). Over the wall that is sup-posed to keep foreign students in and curious Chinese people out, I can see a row of wutong trees and, beyond them, the Brocade River, where a cormorant fisherman is trying his luck in the murky water. His birds, their great black wings flapping, have rings around their necks. When they catch a fish too big to slide down their constricted throats, they offer it to the fisherman, who drops it into his basket, and gives them a smaller fish in exchange. I watch, captivated by yet another of the endlessly fascinating little events that mark my daily life in Chengdu.

When the cormorant fisherman has drifted past and I can no longer see his birds at work, I shower, dress, and go off in search of breakfast. I say good morning to the elderly watchman at the gate of the Foreign Students' Building, and wander out past a row of plantain trees. Students and lecturers on bicycles ride past me, ringing their bells. Laundry and birdcages hang on the balconies of the low-rise apartment blocks. Everything is softened slightly by the gentle touch of the Sichuan mist. The campus is a quiet, leafy place, an oasis of tranquillity in a city where the taxis honk their horns incessantly and the street vendors shout and clatter.

Not far away, just behind the university offices, there's a snack stall, which I can find just by following my nostrils. The heavenly scent of *guo kui*, twirly flatbreads stuffed with minced pork, spring onion and Sichuan pepper, drifts out across the campus. They are made by an elderly couple who don't speak much as they go about their business. The woman kneads her dough and rolls it into balls on an oiled wooden board. With the heel of her hand, she smears each ball into a long tongue of pastry which she rubs with lard and a smattering of spicily seasoned pork. Then she rolls it up, flattens it into a round and passes it to her husband. After frying them golden in oil, he tucks the *guo kui* under the griddle, where they bake crisp at the side of the charcoal brazier. Eaten hot, they are crunchy and chewy and savoury, and the Sichuan pepper makes your lips dance and tingle. Could there be anything more delicious for breakfast on a damp autumn day?

It wasn't food that originally lured me to go and live in China, or at least that's what I told myself. I was supposed to be researching Chinese policy on ethnic minorities. A year after my first visit to China in 1992, I had flown to Taipei for a two-month summer course in the Chinese language, and then spent a month travelling around Mainland China and Tibet. On my way home from Lhasa, I called in on the Sichuanese capital, Chengdu, arriving on one of those rare, balmy days when the sun shines brightly, only slightly blurred by the perennial Sichuan haze. With me I had the crumpled namecard of a Sichuanese *er hu* (Chinese two-stringed violin) player called Zhou Yu, whom I had met on the streets of my hometown, Oxford, spellbinding a crowd with his melodies. 'Look me up if you ever visit Chengdu,' he had told me. So I checked into the Traffic Hotel, hired a bicycle, and went off in search of him at the Sichuan Conservatory of Music.

Zhou Yu was as warm and engaging as I had remembered. He and his exuberant wife Tao Ping, another musician, welcomed me as an old friend, and took me on a bicycle tour of the sights of the city. We went for a walk in the grounds of the poet Du Fu's 'thatched cottage', and then they invited me for lunch at a modest restaurant near the bus station. It was a single room on the ground floor of a timber-framed cottage, tiled in white like a bathroom, with a few tables and chairs and nothing to adorn the walls. Zhou Yu ordered some food, and we waited for the dishes to emerge from the tiny kitchen at the back, amid the sounds of furious sizzling. The room filled up with the most marvellous aromas.

I can still remember every detail of that delicious meal. The cold chicken tossed in a piquant dressing of soy sauce, chilli oil, and Sichuan pepper; a whole carp, braised in chilli-bean paste laced with ginger, garlic, and spring onions; pig's kidneys cut into frilly, dainty morsels and stir-fried, fast, with celery and pickled chillies. And so-called 'fish-fragrant' eggplant, one of the most scrumptious dishes I'd ever tasted: the golden, buttery fried eggplant cooked in a deep-red, spicy sauce, with no actual fish but seductive hints of sweet and sour. This was Chinese food as I had never known it before. It was a revelation.

A few months later, a colleague at the BBC suggested I apply for a British Council scholarship to study in China. She helped me devise a worthy plan to investigate Chinese policy on ethnic minorities, a subject that had interested me for some time. Filling in the scholarship form, I came up with various academically convincing reasons for basing my research in Chengdu. I wanted to avoid the expatriate centres of Beijing and Shanghai, so that I had a chance to immerse myself in Chinese life and the Chinese language – never mind that Sichuan dialect is a notoriously distorted version of Mandarin. Then there was Sichuan's location on the fringes of Han Chinese China, near the borderlands inhabited by Tibetans, Yi, Qiang, and countless other minorities. It all sounded quite plausible. But as I filled in the boxes on the form and composed my personal declaration, I must confess that I was thinking also about sweet and spicy eggplant, of a fish lazing in chilli-bean sauce, of frilly pig's kidneys and Sichuan pepper. Fortunately, the British Council and the Chinese government agreed that Chengdu was a suitable place for me to study, and they gave me my grant, a golden ticket to explore China for a year, with no strings attached.

In the autumn of 1994, the foreign affairs office of Sichuan University held a meeting to welcome the new cohort of foreign students to Chengdu. We gathered in the main hall of the Foreign Students' Building, where a stern member of the local Public Security Bureau read us the national regulations on 'aliens', with a teacher translating into stilted English. We were told that 'subversive actitivities' would get us into trouble, and that if our offences were serious enough, we might be expelled from the country. When the policeman had finished, the teacher added that medical staff would soon be coming to the university to draw our blood, which would be tested for HIV. Given that we had all been required to have exhaustive physical examinations before entering China, including HIV tests, we were indignant (my own doctor had laughed heartily at the Chinese state's medical demands of a healthy young woman, especially the electrocardiogram). It was a reminder that, however nervous we might feel about going to live in China, China – opening up gradually after decades of Maoist introversion – was equally nervous about us.

In the mid-nineties, the expatriate community in Chengdu was tiny. We foreign students numbered about 120 in all. Besides us, there were just a few American consulate workers, foreign teachers and aid workers, and a mysterious businessman from Peru. The forty or so Japanese students at the university were cliquey and exclusive. The rest of us, Italian, French, Mongolian, Russian, Ethiopian, Polish, Jordanian, Laotian, Ghanaian, German, Danish, Canadian and American, lived sociably together.

The protected enclave of the campus we inhabited was known by the Chinese students as the Panda Building, because it seemed to them that we were treated like some rare and endangered species. Our Chinese counterparts lived in concrete dormitories where they were crammed together, eight to a room, with no heating in winter and no air-conditioning in summer, and distant communal showers that were available only at certain hours of the day.

We lived in carpeted twin rooms with heaters and air-conditioners, and every floor of our building had its own kitchens, washing machines and bathrooms. Our dining room offered à la carte Sichuanese food much better (and much more expensive) than that served in the Chinese students' canteen. There was a watchman at the gate of our compound, and an office from which the sinister staff of the foreign affairs office kept an eye on our activities.

But if we lived in luxurious isolation, we had only to step outside the dormitory to be overwhelmed by the hubbub of Sichuanese life. Just around the corner from the side gate of the university was a market overflowing with fresh and seasonal produce. Fish leapt and eels wriggled in tanks of water, ducks and chickens squawked in their pens. Vegetables and fruits were piled up in great bamboo trays: water spinach and bamboo shoots, garlic stems and bitter melons, seasonal treats like three-coloured amaranth, loquats, and 'spring shoots', the tender leaves of the Chinese toon tree. One stall sold a dozen different types of beancurd. Farmers sat on tiny stools behind woven bamboo baskets heavy with produce, ready to weigh them out by the *jin* or the *liang* with their old-fashioned, hand-held balances, and tot up the bill on an abacus.

Everyone in Chengdu shopped in markets like this on a daily basis. There were no real supermarkets, yet. From time to time I would run into one of my teachers from the university, struggling through the crowd, bicycle basket overflowing with green onions, beansprouts, spinach and ginger, a recently killed fish hanging from the handlebars in a plastic bag, still twitching.

Very quickly, the stallholders became familiar to me. The squint-eyed old woman in white overalls who sat before her bags and jars of spices: blood-red dried chillies, whole and ground; dusky-pink Sichuan pepper. The handsome flower-seller, smart in a dark business suit, slumped in his tiny bamboo chair, leaning back against the brick wall in a peaceful sleep, surrounded by a sea of brilliant roses and carnations. When a customer appeared and roused him with a gentle word, his eyes would blink open, and he would smile good-naturedly, light a cigarette and take money for one of his rainbow bouquets.

Although the market was busy in the mornings and the late afternoons, there was a period after lunch when the *xiu xi*, or siesta, took over, especially when the weather was warm. Then, not only the flower-seller, but everyone else too, seemed to be asleep. Rural women snoozed over their squashes and aubergines, cradling their heads in circled arms. Tomato and bean sellers drooped over crouched-up knees. The fishmonger lay back against the wall, snoring gently. And beyond the market, the entire city appeared also to be suffused with drowsiness. Rickshaw drivers lounged in their empty passenger seats, feet up on the saddles of their tricycles. Office workers lay down on fake leather sofas, sprawled like cats.

Despite the immediate charms of Chengdu, I spent my first weeks there in a state of misery and confusion. I didn't really have a clue what I was doing in China. My life until then had been like a conveyor belt that had carried me, almost unthinking, from my academic hothouse of a high school to Cambridge University, and then to the BBC. For a long time I had nurtured the idea of becoming a professional cook, but I left university with debts, and the short-term BBC contract I took to pay them off led to the offer of a permanent post, which I lacked the courage to refuse. By my early twenties, I was stuck in a dry, academic job that didn't suit me at all, and exhausted by a daily commute from London to Reading. So when my colleague brought up the idea of a British Council China scholarship, I seized the chance to escape.

Now that the world is besotted with China, it is hard to remember how marginal it seemed in the early nineties. No one, then, would have considered going to Shanghai for a glamorous holiday or *shopping*. Few British universities offered Chinese courses; the idea of Mandarin being taught in schools would have seemed laughable. In London, my friends saw my Chinese studies as eccentric, if not hilarious. Even to me, Mandarin seemed a fairly irrelevant language.

From the moment I arrived in China, I was almost completely cut off from the rest of the world. Email and the Internet were, for the majority of people, no more than unlikely rumours; an exchange of letters with a friend in England could take several weeks. There were only three places in Chengdu where cross-continental telephone calls were possible, and, if you found one, the cost of a call was astronomical (you could host a dinner party in a restaurant for the price of three minutes' conversation with Europe). Outside the glitzy sophistication of the city's two international hotels, Western food hardly existed, and the only foreign cultural activity available was watching pirated videos in a row of illegal cinema shacks near the university. Even news was hard to access, and censored when it came from official sources. My classmates and I were stranded in China, like it or not, and outside the cocoon of the Foreign Students' Building we had little choice but to throw ourselves into Sichuanese life.

My own supposed studies offered me little sense of direction. My Chinese was too poor for any serious academic research, and, besides, I had chosen a research subject fraught with political sensitivities. The books and journals in the university library were filled with propaganda – fairy stories about ethnic harmony and the gratitude of the Tibetans for the benevolent overlordship of the Chinese state. University lecturers became twitchy when the conversation veered towards uncomfortable subjects, and tried to steer it back to the safety of platitudes. I didn't know how to begin my work. China was not the totalitarian state of my London friends' imagination, but neither was it open, and for a newcomer it was impossible to gauge the boundaries. Even the locals found it confusing. The juddering old framework of the state economy was falling apart, along with the political controls of the Maoist era. No one really knew the rules. The whole country, waking up after the nightmare of Maoism, was making it up as it went along.

Socially and culturally, China was challenging, too. As outsiders, my fellow students and I were still unusual enough to be treated as freaks or celebrities. We were interviewed by journalists, and invited to give speeches about nothing in particular at prestigious events. Crowds gathered to scrutinise our most trivial actions, even buying a bus ticket. A simple bicycle ride across town would provoke a Mexican wave of attention, as passers-by dropped what they were doing to watch us, and shout out 'Hello!' or '*Lao*

wai!' (foreigner). People were almost unfailingly nice to us, but it was difficult living under a microscope, and it took months to begin to understand
what was really going on. You couldn't just parachute into China and start
achieving – after half a year, perhaps, you might be able to start fumbling your
way through the political and social system.

And then there was the slow, insinuating lethargy of the place itself.
Chengdu was a city where it was virtually impossible to have any plans, let
alone fulfil them. Since the Tang Dynasty it had been renowned for its easy
life, the fruit of a gentle climate and soil of legendary fecundity. The inhabitants of Chengdu didn't have to work particularly hard to eat well and enjoy
themselves. Their city had a southern, almost Mediterranean feel about it.
People there moved more slowly than they did in Beijing or Shanghai. They
sat in teahouses all afternoon and evening, playing Mah Jong or cards,
exchanging banter in the honeyed cadences of Sichuan dialect, with its long,
drawn-out vowels and burred 'r's. '*Bai long men zhen*' they called it, this
leisurely Sichuanese habit of conversation. And the most expressive word in
Sichuanese must be '*hao suanr*' (good fun), said lazily, with a broad grin, the
creak of a bamboo chair in the background. 'Those coastal people,' one taxi
driver told me, speaking of the Cantonese and Fujianese, 'they are ambitious
and hardworking; that's why they've been the first to get rich. We Sichuanese
just want to earn enough to fill our bellies with good food.'

I wasn't the only foreign student finding it hard to concentrate. My classmates and I heard from friends in Beijing and Shanghai about tough
attendance regulations at other universities; miss a few lessons in those places
and you might lose your scholarship. But in Sichuan, nobody cared. A few of
us, mostly those with prior experience of China, settled down to some serious
study. Otherwise, one by one, gradually and inexorably, we all dropped out of
our official classes. My roommate Filomena spent most of her time playing
Mah Jong. A young Danish student, Sören, hung around in the park, learning martial arts from a frail, elderly master. Volker, a German who was taking
a break from his successful career as a film production manager in Los

Angeles, idled away his days and weeks in conversation. The rest played rugby, fell in love, got drunk, and went travelling, here and there.

As for me, I spent the first month trying to be a conscientious student, and beating myself up about my lack of academic progress. But I found myself caring less and less about my scholarship, and my career. And so, after a few dark weeks of depression, I decided, like most of my classmates, to abandon my preconceptions, simply to be in Sichuan, and to let the place take me as it would. Loosed of my disabling mental moorings and opening my eyes, finally, to the enchanting city around me, I allowed Sichuan to work its slow, sweet magic on me. And that was the beginning of the most wonderful period of my life.

Mention Chengdu to any Chinese person and the first thing they will say in response is almost certainly that the food is very spicy: 'Are you afraid of chilli heat?' (*Ni pa bu pa la?*) is the customary warning for travellers on their way to Sichuan. But give them a moment more and they are likely to smile with remembered pleasure, and murmur something about the magnificence of the local cuisine. 'I never raise my chopsticks without remembering my dear Sichuan,' sighed the Song Dynasty poet Lu You. 'Go to China for food, but for flavour, you must go to Sichuan,' is the mantra of modern gourmets.

Convention carves China into four great regional cuisines. In the north there is the grand, stately culinary school of Beijing and Shandong Province (*lu cai*). This is the food of emperors and courtiers, famed for its roast meats, unbelievably rich soups, and expensive delicacies like shark's fin and sea cucumber. In the east, you have the refined and subtle cooking of the literati, who mused about the pleasures of eating in cultural centres like Yangzhou and Hangzhou (it is known as *huai yang cai*). Think, here, of sweet, soy-dark braises; 'drunken' shrimps steeped in old Shaoxing wine; fresh aquatic vegetables like water chestnuts and lotus; and steamed freshwater crabs dipped in fragrant Zhenjiang vinegar.

In the south, there is the notoriously fresh food of the Cantonese (*yue cai*), so fresh it is almost alive. In this region, chefs apply seasonings with a gentle touch – just a little salt, sugar, wine and ginger to enhance the natural flavours of their raw ingredients. Cooking is precise, intervention minimal: a steamed fish, treated lightly with ginger, green onion and soy; translucent shrimp dumplings; a stir-fry of slivered ingredients in which everything is perfectly crunchy or tender, according to its own particular nature. And they adore to eat wild things here, too: snakes and frogs, civet cats and orioles.

Sichuanese food (*chuan cai*) is the spice girl among Chinese cuisines, bold and lipsticked, with a witty tongue and a thousand lively moods. 'Each dish has its own style,' they say, 'and a hundred dishes have a hundred different flavours.' Sichuanese cooking doesn't require extravagant raw ingredients like Cantonese or Shandong. Yes, you can fashion a Sichuanese banquet out of such things if you must; but you can, equally, work wonders with the most humble ingredients, dazzle the tastebuds with a simple repast of pork and aubergines. This is the greatness of Sichuanese cuisine, to make the ordinary extraordinary.

They were eating spicy food in the Sichuan region at least as far back as sixteen hundred years ago, when the historian Chang Qu remarked on local people's liking for bold and interesting flavours. Go to Sichuan and you realise that this isn't so much a matter of choice as of environmental determinism. The Sichuan basin has a humid climate: in winter, a creeping dampness penetrates every layer of clothing; summers are insufferably hot and sultry, with the sun hidden behind a haze of mist. In terms of Chinese medicine, the body is an energetic system, in which damp and dry, cold and hot, yin and yang, must be balanced; if they are not, illness is sure to follow. And although the moist Sichuan air keeps the skin of the women soft and youthful, it can destabilise the body as a whole. Therefore the people of this region have, for as long as anyone can remember, felt obliged to doctor their diets with dry, warming foods to counter the unhealthy humours of the climate. Until the first chillies arrived from the Americas, however, the only warming ingredients they had at their disposal were a few ancient imports from Central Asia, and native spices like Sichuan pepper.

Sichuan pepper is the original Chinese pepper, used long before the more familiar black or white pepper stole in over the tortuous land routes of the old Silk Road. It is not hot to taste, like the chilli, but makes your lips cool and tingly. In Chinese they call it *ma*, this sensation; the same word is used for pins-and-needles and anaesthesia. The strange, fizzing effect of Sichuan pepper, paired with the heat of chillies, is one of the hallmarks of modern Sichuanese cookery.

The first chillies were seen in China in the sixteenth century, when Portuguese traders, newly returned from South America, sailed their galleons into the eastern ports. The Chinese of the coastal regions admired the chilli plant first as an ornament, with its delicate white flowers and vibrant scarlet fruits. It was only later that they began to use the piquant fruits as a seasoning. Merchants took the chilli up the waterways of the Yangtze Delta to the central province of Hunan, and from there to Sichuan, a little further westwards along the river. It was in these two warm, humid provinces that the chilli found its spiritual home. They were all but waiting for it; there was a place ready in their medical and culinary cosmologies. Its blazing colour lit up the grey mistiness of their skies, and its fiery heat drove out the dampness in people's bodies, bringing a delicious equilibrium to their lives.

The canteen in the Foreign Students' Building at Sichuan University was a dull place, serving food that was fresh but soulless. With our meagre allowances and the teeming market just outside, we scholarship students might therefore have taken advantage of the cooking facilities in the Foreign Students' Building and made our own food. Some did, like Areej, the young Jordanian woman who kept house for her husband Taizer and baby Motaz in a single room in the dormitory, but most of us were too lazy. Besides, we quickly discovered that the food available outside the campus was so thrilling and plentiful that it would have been senseless to waste our time fighting for space in the communal kitchens. So every day, at lunchtime, we trooped out to a favourite noodle shop and guzzled bowlfuls of noodles with a variety of toppings. In the evenings, we pitched up at one of half a dozen little restaurants in wooden cottages near the university. Our Chinese student friends found our constant dining-out extravagant, but to foreigners it seemed ridiculously cheap. A noodle lunch set us back a few *kuai* (30p), while one person's share of an abundant group dinner with plenty of beer rarely amounted to more than 12 *kuai* (about £1).

After a few weeks in Chengdu we knew the names of all the essential dishes. *La zi ji*, dry, crisp, sizzling pieces of chicken buried in an improbable mound of seared chillies; *yu xiang qie bing*, a pile of succulent eggplant fritters stuffed with minced pork and bathed in a luxuriant sweet-sour-spicy sauce; *hui guo rou*, fat pork stir-fried with Chinese leeks in an indescribably delicious chilli bean sauce... actually there were chillies everywhere: as a dip for aromatic duck hearts and livers, in the chilli oil drizzled over our chicken slivers; in the sauces for our pork and our eggplant. Whole, chopped, red, green, fresh, dried, ground, pickled, steeped in oil, the variety was infinite. Yet the spicy cooking of Chengdu never lived up to the fiendish reputation that so terrified visitors from other parts of China. For a taste of that, you had to travel a few hours by bus to Sichuan's second city, the great Yangtze metropolis of Chongqing.

I went there once, soon after my arrival in Chengdu, to pay a visit to my musician friend Zhou Yu's parents. It had a filthy magnificence, that city, in the early nineties. Its buildings, tainted by the pollution from factory chimneys, were scattered on steep slopes that fell away to the broad sweep of the Yangtze and Jialing Rivers where they met in a fork far below. It was a fierce, hard-working river port, where people spent their days trudging up and down hills and battling with a humidity so stifling that, in summer, it was known as one of China's 'furnace' cities. Even in Sichuan, Chongqing was infamous for the *ma la* (numbing-and-hot) punchiness of its food.

Zhou Yu's parents invited me out, on a sweltering evening, for a hotpot supper by the river. We took our seats around a wok in which an inconceivably large mass of dried red chillies, Sichuan peppercorns and other spices were stuck in a thick, pasty layer of fat. A waiter bent down and ignited a gas flame underneath the table. As the wok warmed up, the fat began to melt, and soon the chillies were bobbing around in it. The waiter brought plates of raw ingredients: beef offal and mushrooms, beancurd and greens. We used our chopsticks to cook them in the fiery broth. Every morsel emerged from the pot in a slick of fiery oil, studded with spices; even a single beansprout came out embroiled with a mouthful of chilli. By the end of the meal, I was almost delirious with heat. My mouth burned and tingled, my body ran with sweat. I felt ragged and molten; pain and pleasure were indistinguishable.

No one would decide to go and live in Chongqing after such a baptism of fire. But Chengdu is a gentle city. Life there is not a battle against the elements and the gradient of hills, it is a sweet, idle dream. Chillies are used not in violence, but to awaken and stimulate the palate, to make it alive to the possibilities of other tastes. They are melded with an undercurrent of sweetness, a robust beany savouriness, or a splash of mellow vinegar-sour, to seduce and delight. In Chengdu, Sichuanese cuisine is not the assault course of international stereotype, it is a teasing, meandering and entirely pleasurable journey.

I quickly became a regular at the Bamboo Bar, one of the restaurants near the university that was known for its hearty flavours and friendly atmosphere. It was a simple place, housed in a ramshackle wooden cottage, but the food was sensational and I never tired of it. By six o'clock every evening, it was already noisy and jam-packed with people. Customers sat on low bamboo stools around square wooden tables, tucking into fragrant stir-fries and steaming soups. The waitresses, young peasant girls from the countryside who slept like sardines in the low-ceilinged attic upstairs, bustled around with bottles of beer. *Po po* ('Granny'), the owner's mother, presided over the abacus at a counter by the door.

A few cottages down, on the opposite side of the street, was 'The Italian', which was actually nothing of the kind. Named after a long-forgotten group of Italian students who used to frequent it, the restaurant served the usual

Sichuanese food and became our favourite venue for special dinners and birth-day parties. On such occasions we would take over one of its two rooms and feast at a table laden with dishes. We would drink copious quantities of spirits that seared our throats and gave us rotten hangovers and listen to Jay – a Canadian English teacher – make one of his speeches, which were always deliberately pompous, peppered with random phrases of Chinese, and side-splittingly funny, especially after a few rounds of the local firewater.

On warm evenings we would drift down to the riverbank outside the university, where a rash of *al fresco* restaurants had sprung up under the wutong trees. We would sit for hours under their branches, sipping beer in the uneven light of hanging lightbulbs and candles stuck into the necks of beer bottles, nibbling pig's ear, lotus-root slices, and fresh green soybeans squeezed out of their pods. All around us, people lounged around in bamboo chairs, laughing and chatting in Sichuan dialect, shouting in excitement as they played *hua quan*, a noisy finger-guessing game that was all the rage. Cicadas hummed in the trees overhead.

In those days the restaurants we visited didn't even have fridges, and the beer was kept cool by being stored in a bucket of water. Meat and vegetables were bought daily from the markets; if you wanted an ingredient the restaurant didn't have, one of the girls might be despatched to buy it outside. Fish and eels lived in tanks in the kitchens. And everything, apart from the slow-braised soups and stews, was freshly cooked. Hygiene inspectors would no doubt have blanched at the cooked offal sitting around in unchilled cabinets, the reusable wooden chopsticks, and the poor facilities for washing up, but we almost never fell ill.

Sitting in the Bamboo Bar, watching grand platters of fish and mysterious claypot soups being brought to neighbouring tables, wafting their aromas under my nose, I became frustrated. Two years of Chinese evening classes in London and two months of study in Taipei had failed to give me the most rudimentary tools for deciphering restaurant menus. The Sichuan university textbooks I'd encountered in my few weeks of class were deathly dull and totally impractical. Instead of introducing us to useful words like 'stir-fry' and 'braise', 'bamboo shoot' and 'quail', they had required us to learn by rote long lists of largely irrelevant Chinese characters: the names, for example, of the heroes and villains in the ancient epic *The Three Kingdoms*; the words for an ancient kind of chariot, weapon or musical instrument.

Learning Chinese characters is a painful process anyway; it nearly breaks you. They say that, to read a newspaper, you need to know two or three thousand, and that's only a fraction of the number of characters in existence. So you cram them into your head, writing them out, again and again, in rows of squares marked out on special paper, or on little cards that you paste to the wall or read over breakfast. Yet, however hard you try to keep them in your head, most of them fall out again, like flour through a sieve. It's a Sisyphean labour, thankless and frustrating, which is why so many foreigners who learn Chinese end up speaking it quite well, but largely unable to read or write. I resented wasting hours memorising the vocabulary of the classic romances, and so I stopped going to my language classes as well as my lessons on 'minorities history'. Instead I took a few private Chinese lessons, and spent the rest of my time hanging around markets and restaurants, or sitting in teahouses, poring over dictionaries and photocopies of local restaurant menus.

Ever since I was a child, I have loved to cook. After every family holiday in Europe, I tried to recreate foreign recipes that I had found particularly exciting. At university I spent one long summer vacation immersed in Turkish cookery. I had been invited to spend two months with a family friend, a Turkish porcelain mogul who lived in central Anatolia. As a young, unmarried woman staying in a Muslim family, I had little freedom to explore his old-fashioned hometown or the surrounding region, and spent most of my time at home with his extended family. Naturally, I gravitated towards the kitchen, and my diary filled up with recipes for stuffed vegetables, köfte and purslane salad. From my mother I had picked up the habit of guessing the ingredients and cooking methods of dishes in restaurants, picking up traces of herbs and spices, forensically analysing the food on my plate. By the age of eleven I already wanted to be a chef. But the conveyor belt of my education took me further and further away from food.

Students who get good grades at school are not encouraged to run away and work in restaurants. I remember one middle-school teacher laughing at me, incredulous, when I told him of my ambition. So I carried on passing exams, working hard and doing what was expected of me. It was in China, thousands of miles away from home and almost completely cut off from my past, that I was able to do what I really wanted. Finally, I was able to admit to myself that I was no socio-economic analyst, not even really a journalist, but a cook. It was in the kitchen, chopping vegetables, mixing a dough in my hands or seasoning a soup, that I felt most completely myself. Growing up in Oxford, studying in Cambridge, working in London, I had been propped up by a string of academic and professional credentials that had seemed to define me in the eyes of other people. But in China none of that mattered. I was just one of a bunch of homesick and culturally disorientated foreigners, trying to find our feet in a country about which, despite all our studies, we actually knew very little. It took me some time to accept this, but in the end it was the best thing that could have happened to me.

For someone with a natural curiosity about food, Chengdu in the mid-nineties was a kind of paradise. It was all there, under your nose. In the backstreets, people cooked dinner for their families on charcoal braziers outside their cottages. The aromas of chilli-bean paste, Sichuan pepper and jasmine tea hung in the air on warm autumn nights. The most humble shack of a restaurant would often be serving Chinese food better than any you could find in London. Almost everyone in Sichuan seemed to love talking about cooking and eating. Surly taxi drivers waxed lyrical as they recounted to me, in great detail, their favourite recipes. Middle-aged couples slurping their lunchtime noodles would reminisce about the great beancurd chefs of the past. And I remember once listening to a radio broadcast in which a young female presenter recited the pleasures available at various city restaurants in tones that dripped with sensuality and greed. She murmured her way through an endless litany of dishes, lovingly describing their flavour and textures ('Oh, the ox tripe, so crisp and snappy!'), her words interspersed with breathy sounds of appreciation and excitement. She could barely contain herself. And she was typical of the people I met. As a chef friend once said to me, Chengdu people have '*hao chi zui*' – 'mouths that love eating'.

Within weeks of arriving in Chengdu, I was writing down my impressions of the food. Even on the first few pages of my first Sichuan notebook, dated September 1994, there are lists of fruits and vegetables on sale in the markets, and accounts of conversations about food. And once I had divested myself of my academic responsibilities, my casual food investigations took over my life. It was just irresistible. Every day brought new gastronomic discoveries: perhaps a street vendor specialising in a type of snack I'd never seen before, or a peasant scurrying along with baskets slung from a bamboo shoulderpole, bearing some unusual fruit or herbal tea. I leapt at every chance to spend time with Sichuanese friends and acquaintances in their kitchens. My friendship with Zhou Yu and Tao Ping, the couple whose hospitality had lured me to Chengdu in the first place, deepened. Now I went regularly to their small flat near the music conservatory for supper. Tao Ping's grandmother, a ninety-year-old woman who was still walking up and down twelve flights of stairs every day with bags full of ingredients from the nearest market, invited us over for a feast of dry-fried beans and braised duck with wild yam jelly. My private Chinese teacher, Yu Weiqing, welcomed me into her home from time to time for a slap-up dinner: she taught me just as much about cookery as about the Chinese language.

The Sichuanese are famously warm and relaxed, as different from their buttoned-up northern compatriots as the Neapolitans are from the British. I lost count of the number of chance encounters that led to invitations to dinner from strangers. I spent a memorable afternoon chatting to a roast-duck vendor in a backstreet near the Minshan Hotel, as he primed his birds with malt-sugar syrup and vinegar, and then roasted them in a domed oven made from bricks and clay. We talked as the ducks roasted, and soon he was inviting me to dine in a restaurant where he had an interest. For years afterwards (until his duck shop was demolished by city developers), whenever I cycled past, he would rush out for a chat, and press into my hands a jar of some spicy pickle or fermented beancurd that he had been keeping for me.

One public holiday, Zhou Yu and Tao Ping invited me to go with them on a trip out of town, to share a home-made hotpot with some friends. When we arrived, we went to the local market to buy ingredients, and then returned to the friends' apartment to set up a potful of spicy broth over a gas burner on the kitchen floor. Sitting around it on little stools, we cooked our own lunch, dipping into the pot strands of enoki mushrooms, ribbons of beancurd, sweet-potato noodles and crunchy pieces of tripe. There was a tangible shift in mood as the meal progressed. In the beginning we were lively and animated, but gradually a deep stupor overcame us all, and we drifted off and fell asleep on armchairs, sofas, anywhere. It was only later, after a long, blissful siesta had restored me to my senses, that I noticed the enormous poppyheads bobbing around in the broth.

Actually, though, you didn't need poppyheads to unwind and lose your inhibitions in Sichuan. There was something in the air, in the dialect, in the people, and above all in the food: a warmth and a languor that melted away any English stiffness, like butter in the sun. My heart was clenched like a fist when I moved to Chengdu. I could barely communicate, except through food. But as the weeks drifted past, I felt myself softening. For the first time in my life I was freed of all duties and expectations; life was a blank slate.

Fish-fragrant eggplant

魚香茄子

21–25 oz (600–700 g) eggplant
Salt
Peanut oil for deep-frying
1¹/₂ tbsp Sichuanese chilli bean paste
3 tsp finely chopped fresh ginger
3 tsp finely chopped garlic
²/₃ cup (150 ml) stock
1¹/₂ tsp white sugar
¹/₂ tsp light soy sauce
³/₄ tsp cornstarch, mixed with 1 tbsp cold water
1¹/₂ tsp Chinkiang vinegar
4 spring onions, green parts only, sliced into fine rings
1 tsp sesame oil

1. Cut the eggplant in half lengthwise and then crosswise. Chop each quarter lengthwise into 3 or 4 evenly sized chunks. Sprinkle generously with salt and leave for at least 30 minutes to drain.

2. In a wok, heat oil for deep-frying to 356–392°F (180–200°C). Add the eggplant in batches and deep-fry for 3–4 minutes until slightly golden on the outside and soft and buttery within. Remove and drain on kitchen paper.

3. Drain off the deep-frying oil, rinse the wok if necessary, and then return it to a medium flame with 2–3 tablespoons of oil. Add the chilli bean paste and stir-fry until the oil is red and fragrant; then add the ginger and garlic and continue to stir-fry for another 20–30 seconds until they too are fragrant.

4. Add the stock, sugar and soy sauce and mix well. Season with salt to taste if necessary.

5. Add the fried eggplant to the sauce, bring to the boil and then let them simmer gently for a few minutes to absorb some of the flavours. Then sprinkle the cornstarch mixture over the eggplant and stir in gently to thicken the sauce. Next, stir in the vinegar and spring onions and leave for a few seconds until the onions have lost their rawness. Finally, remove the pan from the heat, stir in the sesame oil and serve.

CHAPTER 2

Dan Dan Noodles!

'*Sa zi mian*? What noodles d'you want?' Xie Laoban gave me his usual surly look as he glanced up from the conversation he was having with one of his regulars.

'Two *liang* of sea-flavour noodles, one *liang* of Dan Dan noodles,' I replied, dumping my schoolbag on the ground and perching on an unsteady stool, just inches from the stream of passing bicycles. There was no need to look at the blackboard, chalked up with the names of a dozen or so noodle dishes, because I knew it by heart, having eaten at Xie Laoban's almost every day since I had arrived in Chengdu. Xie Laoban yelled my order out to his staff of three or four young blokes, who were scurrying around inside the noodle shop behind the coal-burning stove. A glass cabinet held bowls of seasonings: darkly fragrant chilli oil, ground roasted Sichuan pepper, sliced green onions, soy sauce and vinegar, salt and pepper. Nearby, potfuls of stocks and stews simmered away on an electric cooker, and skeins of freshly made noodles lay snakily in deep trays of woven bamboo. At the front of the shop, in full view of the street, steam drifted up from two enormous wokfuls of boiling water.

Resuming his conversation, Xie Laoban slumped back in his bamboo chair, smoking a cigarette as he recounted some grimly amusing tale. There was always an embittered look about his face, an edge of hostility and suspicion, and if he smiled at his acquaintances, his smile was tinged with a sneer of sarcasm. In his forties, he had a face pitted with the legacy of acne, sundarkened yet wan and drawn. He seemed world-weary and cynical, though my foreign student friends and I never knew why. He fascinated us, but while we speculated incessantly about his life, wondering where he lived and with whom, what he did in the evenings, and whether he had ever been happy, in the end it was hard to imagine Xie Laoban being anywhere else but in that bamboo chair in the backstreets around the university, taking orders for noodles and barking at his staff. The bolder among us – Sasha and Pasha from Vladivostock, Parisian Davide – greeted him heartily, trying to engage him in conversation or cracking jokes in a vain attempt to raise the glimmer of a smile. But he remained stony-faced and deadpan, simply asking, as he always did, '*Sa zi mian?*'

I could see the young men assembling my lunch, trickling spices and oils into the tiny bowl for my Dan Dan noodles, sprinkling a little salt and pepper into the larger bowl for the sea-flavour noodles. The appropriate weight of noodles (one *liang* is about fifty grammes) were flung into the wok to cook, and before long steaming bowls were brought to my table. The sea-flavour noodles were, as always, richly comforting in their seafood broth, with a topping of stewed pork and bamboo shoots, mushrooms, dried shrimps and mussels. And the Dan Dan noodles – well, they were undoubtedly the best in town, the best anyone had ever tasted. They looked quite plain: a small bowlful of noodles topped with a spoonful of dark, crisp minced beef. But as soon as you stirred them with your chopsticks, you awakened the flavours in the slick of spicy seasonings at the base of the bowl, and coated each strand of pasta in a mix of soy sauce, chilli oil, sesame paste and Sichuan pepper. The effect was electrifying. Within seconds, your mouth was on fire, your lips quivering under the onslaught of the pepper, and your whole body radiant with heat. (On a warm day, you might even break out into a sweat.)

Xie Laoban's Dan Dan noodles were a potent pick-me-up, a cure for hangover or heartache, and the perfect antidote to the grey humidity of the Chengdu climate. As students, we were slavishly addicted to them. Many, like me, ordered a gentler meal of soup noodles with fried egg and tomatoes or sea-flavour stew, with a small shot of fiery Dan Dan noodles as a chaser, while the fast-living, hard-drinking Russians and Poles invariably ordered a full three *liang* of '*dan danr*'. We devoured them at one of the wobbly tables in the street, brushed by bicycles, assaulted by the honk of taxis and their sour aftermath of exhaust fumes. When we had finished, we asked Xie Laoban for the bill, and he would add up the paltry sums, take our crumpled notes, and rootle around in the little half-open wooden drawer for some change.

Dan Dan noodles are the archetypal Chengdu street snack. Their name comes from the bamboo shoulderpole that street vendors traditionally use to transport their wares: the verb '*dan*' means to carry on a shoulderpole. Elderly residents of the city still remember the days when the cries of the noodle sellers – '*Dan dan mian! Dan dan mian!*' – rang out in all the old lanes. The vendors would lay down their shoulderpoles wherever they found custom, and unpack their stoves, cooking pots, serving bowls, chopsticks and jars of seasonings. Servants would hear their call and rush out to the gateways of the old wooden houses to order noodles for their masters. Mah Jong players, clattering their tiles in a teahouse, would interrupt their game for a bowlful. Passers-by would slurp them in the street. The noodles were served in tiny bowls, a *liang* at a time, just enough to take the edge off your hunger, and so cheap that almost anyone could afford them.

The noodle sellers weren't the only traders on the move; they were part of a thriving and colourful street life for which Chengdu was renowned. At the end of the Qing Dynasty, in the early twentieth century, a guide to the city by Fu Chongju included descriptions and illustrations of some of its many street traders, including itinerant barbers and pedicurists, water-carriers and flower-sellers, menders of parasols and fans, vendors of chicken-feather dusters, knife sharpeners, and snack makers. The old city was a maze of alleys lined with timber-framed houses, their walls made of panels of woven bamboo that were packed with mud and straw, then whitewashed. Stone lions stood on pedestals at either side of imposing wooden gateways. There was a teahouse on almost every street, where waiters with kettles of boiling water scurried around, refilling china bowls of jasmine-scented tea. And amidst the cacophony of the markets and the bustling streets, no sound was more welcome than the cry of a snack-seller, advertising the arrival of some delicious *xiao chi*, or 'small eat'.

The late nineteenth and early twentieth centuries are remembered as the heyday of Chengdu snacks. Street vendors lived or died by the quality of their cooking, so the secrets of their methods were jealousy guarded. In an atmosphere of fevered competition, individual traders devised new recipes, some of which still bear their names. One man, Zhong Xiesen, invented the divine 'Zhong boiled dumpling' (*zhong shui jiao*), a tender pork-filled crescent bathed in spiced, sweetened soy sauce and chilli oil, and finished off with a smattering of garlic paste. Another, Lai Yuanxin, left to posterity his squidgy glutinous rice balls (*lai tang yuan*), stuffed with a paste of toasted black sesame seeds and sugar. A married couple who roamed the streets with their cooking equipment had a relationship so famously harmonious that their speciality – slices of beef offal tossed with celery and roasted nuts in a fiery dressing of spiced broth, chilli oil and Sichuan pepper – is still known as 'Man-and-wife lung slices' (*fu qi fei pian*). The more successful traders often went on to open their own restaurants, usually named after their most celebrated snack.

The eyes of the older generation tended to mist over when they recalled the street food of their childhoods. One elderly man I met in a teahouse sat with me for an hour, writing out in meticulous detail a list of dozens of kinds of dumplings, categorised according to their cooking method and main ingredients. A portly and jovial chef in his fifties smiled wistfully as he reminisced: 'Oh, they were all out there on the streets, sold from the shoulderpole, Dan

Dan noodles, "Flower" beancurd and toffee.' And he sang for me a long-remembered street vendor's chant: 'I got sweet ones, crispy ones, sugared dough twists!'

During the Cultural Revolution, any kind of private enterprise was banned. The teahouses of Chengdu were forced to close, and snack-sellers were banished from the streets. Yet soon after the end of China's 'Decade of Chaos', the old street-food culture heaved itself back into life. Its resurgence was partly a symptom of the 'smashing of the iron ricebowl' – the post-Mao dismantling of the old socialist system that had guaranteed jobs and incomes for life. Middle-aged workers suddenly found themselves 'laid-off' on subsistence wages, and were forced to find other ways to make money. So some of them would fry up a basketful of *ma hua* (dough twists) in the mornings, or put together some *zong zi* (glutinous rice wrapped in bamboo leaves), which they took out into the streets to sell. And there were peasants making a bit on the side in the slack farming season.

In the mid-nineties, Chengdu was still a labyrinth of lanes, some of them bordered by grey brick walls punctuated by wooden gateways, others lined with two-storied dwellings built of wood and bamboo. The grand old houses had been divided up into more humble living quarters, plastic signs had been hoisted up above the open shopfronts, and the stone lions had disappeared from their pedestals. But if you closed your eyes to these signs of change, you could imagine yourself walking through a more distant Chinese past.

The old streets of the city were endlessly fascinating, and I spent much of my time exploring them. In shady corners, barbers hung mirrors on tree trunks or the walls of convenient buildings, and set up bamboo chairs for their clients, who lay back to be frothed and shaved with cut-throat razors in full view of the street. Knife sharpeners wandered past in dirty aprons, carrying their wooden stools and long, grey whetstones, ready to bring a keen edge to anyone's cleaver. There were mobile haberdasheries, carried on bicycles that were pegged all over with zips, buttons and reels of cotton. Some pedlars sold their own handiwork – colanders woven from strands of bamboo, or black cotton shoes with padded white soles.

In March, when the spring winds whipped up, there was a kite vendor on every thoroughfare, displaying colourfully painted birds and insects made from bamboo and tissue-thin paper (the whole wide sky was full of them, too, like a swarm). When it rained, sellers of foldaway waterproofs appeared as if by magic; in the soupy summer heat, old men laid out rows of fans on the pavement. I even saw, once, a bicycle stacked with hundreds of tiny cages woven from thin strips of bamboo. Each one contained a live cricket, a potential pet; together, they hummed like a small orchestra.

In the alleys there were wine shops, with strong grain spirits sold from enormous clay vats. Some of the wine was steeped with medicinal wolfberries, some – for the gentlemen, of course – with assorted animal penises. Flute-sellers wandered among the crowds with bamboo pipes slung all over their bodies, playing a melody as they went. And it was hard to go more than a few yards without being tempted to eat. I might be waylaid by an old man selling sesame balls; distracted by someone selling glutinous rice dumplings wrapped in tangerine leaves from a steamer on the back of a bicycle; or arrested by the scent of eggy pancakes stuffed with jam, fresh from the griddle.

The notes *ding ding dang, ding ding dang,* beaten out on two ends of a piece of metal, signified the arrival of the Ding Ding toffee man, selling his pale, malt-sugar sweetmeat, which melted stickily in your hand if you didn't eat it quickly. Best of all was the shouted '*Dou huar! Dou huar!*' of the Flower beancurd vendor. I would rush to catch up with him, and he would put down his shoulderpole and the two red-and-black wooden barrels suspended from either end, and set about making me up a bowl of beancurd. It was still warm from the stove, as soft and tender as crème caramel, with a zesty topping of soy sauce, chilli oil, ground Sichuan pepper and morsels of preserved mustard tuber.

I never saw street vendors selling Dan Dan noodles. Like the famous Zhong dumplings and Mr Lai's glutinous riceballs, they had disappeared from their original habitat, and were served instead in specialist snack canteens, or as a kind of *amuse-bouche* in more glamorous restaurants. On the streets, they'd been replaced by newly fashionable titbits: Shanghai fried chicken, Xinjiang potatoes or barbecue skewers. Every few months a new street-eating craze arrived, and a rash of identical stalls would jostle for position with the dispensers of more established fare.

Although the name Dan Dan noodles refers only to the way in which the snack was sold from a shoulderpole, over time it has become associated with a particular recipe, in which the noodles are topped with minced meat and *ya cai*, a famous vegetable preserve whose dark crinkly leaves add salt and savour. Every restaurant serving traditional Sichuanese food has Dan Dan noodles on its menu, and you can now buy Dan Dan noodle sauces in the supermarkets that have sprung up since I first lived in Chengdu. I've lost count of the different versions of the recipe I've tried over the years. Yet in all my wanderings, I have never come across Dan Dan noodles as delicious as those made by Xie Laoban in his modest noodle shop near Sichuan University.

Of course I tried to persuade him to give me his recipe, but he would never divulge it in its entirety: instead, he tantalised me with fragments. On one occasion, he grudgingly let me watch his staff assemble the seasonings in the bowls; another time he let me taste his oils and sauces; finally, he told me me the ingredients of his *niu rou shao zi*, the marvellous minced-beef topping. Eventually, with a great sense of relief and achievement, I managed to put together the pieces of the puzzle, and to reproduce his recipe at home.

For years afterwards, whenever my Sichuan University classmates and I returned to Chengdu from Paris, London, Munich, Verona or Krakow, we would go to Xie Laoban's for a nostalgic bowl of Dan Dan noodles. And whatever ends of the earth we had come from, and however many hundreds or even thousands of bowls of noodles we had eaten in his shop in the past, he would look at us without a smile or the merest flicker of recognition, and simply ask in the same deadpan Sichuan dialect, '*Sa zi mian?*' If we were lucky, he might give us a perfunctory nod as we left, bidding him goodbye for another year or so. It became a bittersweet joke among us, this refusal to acknowledge who we were.

It was like that until my final visit to his shop, sometime in 2001. This was during the architectural reign of terror of city mayor Li Chuncheng (or Li Chaiqiang – 'Demolition Li' – as he was popularly known). Li was a man determined to make his mark on the era by demolishing the old city in its entirety, and replacing it with a modern grid of wide roads lined with concrete high-rises. Great swathes of Chengdu were cleared under his command, not only the more ramshackle dwellings, but opera theatres and grand courtyard houses, famous restaurants and teahouses, and whole avenues of wutong trees. Chengdu hadn't known such ruin and destruction since the Cultural Revolution, when Red Guards dynamited Chengdu's own 'Forbidden City', a complex of courtyards and buildings dating back to the Ming Dynasty (a statue of a waving Mao Zedong now stands in its place).

The lanes around Xie Laoban's noodle shop lay in ruins, bony cadavers of wood and bamboo, and his restaurant clung to one or two other little shops in a precarious island amongst them. When I wandered up for a lunchtime bowl of noodles, Xie Laoban gave me a sunny look and, to my amazement, almost smiled. And as he took orders, settled bills and chatted with his regulars, he seemed mellower and less spiky in his movements. By his own standards, he was radiant with bonhomie. What was behind this miraculous transformation? Had he fallen in love, or won a fortune at Mah Jong? Or had the obliteration of the city, and the impending destruction of his business, just filled him with a sense of the lightness of being? I shall never know. I sat there and ate my noodles, which were as fabulous as ever, and then it was time to go. I never saw Xie Laoban again. Later that year, I went to look for him. I wanted to tell him that I had described him and his shop in my Sichuanese cookery book, and published his recipe for Dan Dan noodles, which was now being read and perhaps cooked by a network of Sichuanese food fans all over the world. But the place where his noodle shop had stood was a moonscape of debris, a great plain of rubble, scattered here and there with shattered pickle jars and ricebowls. And none of the passers-by knew where I could find him.

Of course, in my first year in Chengdu, the idea of writing a Sichuanese cookery book hadn't even occurred to me. And it would have been hard, then, to believe that such a vibrant old city would disappear in just a few short years. I passed my time there in pleasure and idleness. One day I might spend hours in a teahouse, memorising Chinese characters; on another I might decide to visit a nearby fishing village to see what people there were cooking for lunch. Some friends and I began taking Qi Gong lessons from a retired Chinese doctor in the shady gardens of the Qing Yang Gong Taoist Temple, where we learned to sense and control the energy flowing around our bodies. The Russians, Sasha and Pasha, persuaded one of the illegal cinemas to hold a special screening of *Pulp Fiction* (a bootleg copy), which turned into a riotous party. With my German friend Volker and eight other foreign students I hired a bus for a wild trip to eastern Tibet. But on many days, I simply meandered around the old streets of Chengdu on my bicycle, waiting for something to happen. And it usually did.

In one of my favourite teahouses, I befriended an ear-cleaner called Xiao Chang'an. I was familiar with the sound of him before we ever met. I liked to lie back in my bamboo chair, eyes closed, a bowl of jasmine tea by my side, listening out for the street vendors as they passed. A sharp, metallic twang heralded the arrival of the ear-cleaner, his shirt pocket filled with a terrifying array of instruments: little knives, copper spikes and tiny scoops, and a few delicate goose-feather brushes. Xiao Chang'an was a regular in this particular teahouse, and I had often watched him poking his instruments into the ears of teahouse customers, who lounged in their chairs with expressions of extreme bliss on their faces. One day we struck up a conversation, and he told me about his trade. He explained about the acupressure points that he stimulated with his little prongs and knives, and told me that the art of ear-cleaning dated back to the Song Dynasty. 'These days,' he said, 'some women use ear-cleaning as a cover for prostitution. They may carry the right tools, but they have no idea how to pleasure an *ear*.' I was intrigued by everything he told me, but much too scared to let him give me a practical demonstration of his art.

One sunny afternoon, however, after I'd known him for a while, my resistance crumbled. I settled back nervously in my chair and let him have his way with me. He began by gently drawing back my hair, and stroking the skin around my ear with a small blunt knife, sending shivers of pleasure all over my body. Silent and concentrated, he then began to scrape and probe inside my ear with his little scoops and copper prongs, and to twirl around a series of feather brushes. The most thrilling sensations came when he placed a brush in my ear and then touched its handle several times with his humming tuning fork. The vibrations sent a rhythmic sound like the buzz of a grasshopper into the depths of my ear.

Life in Chengdu often seemed surreal. The most extraordinary things happened on a daily basis. It was impossible for any of us foreign students to have a 'normal' life there, anyway. Whatever we did was inherently eccentric and fascinating in the eyes of the locals. We were recruited to appear in advertisements and films; images of our faces were printed on packets of soap. I spent a day at a theme park, dressed up in a Spanish flamenco costume and full stage make-up, chosen for a role in a commercial on account, said the director, of my 'mysterious eyes'. If we had striven to go about our lives in a discreet and boring manner, we would still have drawn crowds and gasps of amazement wherever we went. In practice, this gave us licence to do just about anything.

One night, I took a taxi with my Italian friends Francesca and Katya to a dinner party in another part of town. We hadn't gone far when the taxi broke down in the middle of a vast open junction (there were few private cars then, and no traffic lights, so vehicles just wove their way across these massive intersections in an ad hoc manner). Our driver got out to tinker with the engine. We were in a stupid, drunken mood, giddy with hilarity, so we shoved a rock cassette into the car stereo, turned the volume up to the maximum, stepped out into the road and began to dance. Our driver smiled at us indulgently, as people tended to do. Soon another taxi ground to a halt beside us, and its driver leapt out to gawp at the spectacle of three laughing foreign girls dancing in the middle of the road. It was followed by another, and another, until the whole space was gridlocked with a crazy zigzag of abandoned taxis, twenty or thirty of them. At that point our driver got the engine running again, so we jumped back in, wove our way out of the chaos of parked cars and zoomed off, looking back at a sea of astonished faces.

In such a bizarre context, it wasn't surprising that my own tastes were becoming ever more adventurous. At first, like most foreigners, I steered away from the wilder waters of Chinese cuisine. Dining out with my classmates, I would order chicken or pork rather than frog or loach, and always choose flesh over offal. But as I made more Chinese friends, it became impossible to continue with such fastidiousness, if only because of my English good manners. Some well-meaning Chinese person was always plopping a bit of pig's intestine or cartilage into my ricebowl, as a special favour.

I remember one hair-raising lunchtime when Zhang Changyu, a kindly scholar of culinary history whom I had met through my Chinese teacher, invited me out for hotpot, and ordered a whole dishful of expensive pig's brains, just for me. He scooped them up in a little wire sieve, which he dipped into the simmering broth. And then he turned the brains into my seasoning bowl, where they sank gently into the sesame oil and chopped garlic. At first I tried to hide them under the garlic, and to flip them on to the waste plate with the fishbones, distracting him with lively conversation. But it just didn't work. Every time I 'lost' some brains by my feeble subterfuge, he would tip some more into my bowl. In the end, I just ate them, with a sense of grim resignation. They were as soft as custard, and dangerously rich.

Sometimes my reticence over a particular food was overcome through simple drunkenness. The Chengdu equivalent of the late-night *döner* kebab in 1994 was fried rabbit-heads, a snack I'd heard about from a Canadian friend. I'd seen the rabbit-heads sitting ominously in glass cabinets, earless and skinless, staring out with beady rabbit eyes and pointy teeth. The idea of eating one was utterly revolting. But one night, after a long dancing session, I fetched up at a street stall bedraggled and hungry. My reason befuddled by alcohol, I ate my first rabbit-head, cleft in half and tossed in a wok with chilli and spring onion. I won't begin to describe the silky richness of the flesh along the jaw, the melting softness of the eyeball, the luxuriant smoothness of the brain. Suffice it to say that from that day on I ate stir-fried rabbit-heads almost every Saturday night. (Later I learned that a Sichuanese slang term for snogging is *chi tu lao kenr* – eating rabbit-heads.)

Affection, too, played a part in my growing omnivorousness. Affection for my Chinese friends, who would offer me wobbly morsels of dubious-looking food with expressions of such eager and expectant kindness that I couldn't refuse. And a growing love also for Chengdu, for Sichuan, and for China. Sometimes the most disgusting things can taste delicious when they are associated with a familiar and beloved place. Aside from the offal and the weird delicacies, certain unlikely snacks became part of my Chinese gastronomic landscape. *Huo tui chang*, pale pink 'sausages' made from an unspeakable mix of reconstituted pork and cereal squirted into a red plastic sheath, were sold on every railway platform in China. Eating them became part of the ritual of long train journeys. They still make me nostalgic and I can't resist buying them occasionally, even though nothing would induce me to eat that kind of thing in England. I also became addicted to *ta ta* bubblegum, which was sold as a long, spiralling pink ribbon in a flat round box: this is probably why, having had perfect teeth until the age of twenty-five, I went home to England after my time in Sichuan and had to have seven fillings.

Xie Laoban's Dan Dan noodles

牛肉擔擔面

Feeds 2 for supper, 4 for a street snack

7 oz (200 g) dried Chinese flour-and-water noodles
For the meat topping:
1 tbsp peanut oil
3 Sichuanese dried chillies, snipped in half, seeds discarded
$^1/_2$ tsp whole Sichuan pepper
0.9 oz (25 g) Sichuanese *ya cai* or Tianjin preserved vegetable
3.5 oz (100 g) minced beef
2 tsp light soy sauce
Salt to taste
For the sauce:
$^1/_2$ tsp ground roasted Sichuan pepper
2 tbsp sesame paste
3 tbsp light soy sauce
2 tsp dark soy sauce
4 tbsp chilli oil with chilli sediment
Salt to taste

1. Heat 1 tablespoon of peanut oil in a wok over a moderate flame. When the oil is hot but not yet smoking, add the chillies and Sichuan pepper and stir-fry briefly until the oil is spicy and fragrant. Take care not to burn the spices. Add the *ya cai* or preserved vegetable and continue to stir-fry until hot and fragrant. Add the meat, splash in the soy sauce and stir-fry until the meat is brown and a little crisp, but not too dry. Season with salt to taste. When the meat is cooked, remove the mixture from the wok and set aside.

2. Divide the sauce ingredients among the serving bowls and mix together.

3. Cook the noodles according to the instructions on the packet. Drain them and add a portion to the sauce in each serving bowl. Sprinkle each bowl with the meat mixture and serve immediately.

4. Before eating, give the noodles a good stir until the sauce and meat are evenly distributed.

CHAPTER 3

First Kill Your Fish

Feng Rui slapped the fish, hard, on the edge of the bath. Then he took a knife and started scraping away its scales, which flicked into the air in a glassy scatter. But the fish was still alive. It flexed violently, and jumped out of his hands. Feng Rui snorted in exasperation, seized it and then whacked it, harder this time, against the enamel. The fish, stunned, became still, allowing him to scale it clean, rip out its blood-red gills, slit its belly open and finger out the bulging slickness of its guts. By now the small bathroom was a mess of scales and slime, but, unconcerned, Feng Rui simply gathered up the debris and threw it into the bin. Back in the kitchen, he made a few incisions in the fish's side, rubbed it with salt and wine, smashed a clod of ginger and a couple of spring onions and stuffed them into its belly. Then he lit a cigarette and inhaled deeply. 'You know, you won't believe this, but in Guangdong they actually eat fish intestines! Imagine! How disgusting. Those Cantonese, they eat *anything*.' I cast my eye to the kitchen counter, where a bowlful of chicken intestines were marinating, ready for our lunch, and smiled to myself.

Feng Rui had tried to pick me up the night before in the Reggae Bar, the only 'cool' nightclub in Chengdu, run by the only 'Rastafarian' in China, a Sichuanese artist with laboriously contrived dreadlocks, a fine CD collection and an obsession with Bob Marley.

It was late and the dance floor was nearly empty. As I sashayed away with my friends, I noticed a dishevelled Chinese man trying to catch my eye. He looked vaguely familiar, so when the track ended I wandered over to investigate. Standing unsteadily, his hair rumpled, he thrust out a cigarette packet and offered to buy me a beer.

'You're the one who likes cooking, aren't you?' he said, slurring his words. Already, I was becoming known in the university district for my interest in food. I had pleaded my way into the kitchens of several restaurants, and was regularly seen in conversation with street vendors and market traders. But this was the first time I'd had my culinary investigations used in a chat-up line. I agreed with the drunken man that, yes, I was the *lao wai* who was an aspiring Sichuanese cook.

'Well, I wouldn't be a true Sichuanese if I didn't offer to give you a cooking lesson,' he replied, 'And I've got these friends, top chefs who used to work at the Jinjiang Hotel. We're cooking together tomorrow. Want to come?' Normally I wouldn't accept invitations from strangers in nightclubs, but when he mentioned red-oil chicken and twice-cooked pork, I felt ready to agree to almost anything. And then, when I realised that he was actually the owner of the Bamboo Bar, my favourite restaurant, I told him I'd love to come.

'Great,' he said. 'How about bringing along a couple of female friends?'

'What's this,' I laughed, 'a cooking lesson or a seduction?'

Grinning tipsily, he professed innocence. 'Ah, you see, for perfect food you have to balance the *yin* and *yang*.'

It was the beginning of a wonderful friendship. Over the next few months, Feng Rui and I spent many happy hours together in the kitchen. I soon learned, however, that his cooking lessons were not for the squeamish. Like any good Chinese chef, Feng Rui insisted on using extremely fresh ingredients, which he chose for himself in the local market. So I went shopping with him, and began to learn the tolerance for slaughter that I needed if I was to learn to cook seriously in China.

Around the eel stall alone, there was always a bloodbath. The eels were paddy eels, their shiny skins a dark grey-green, thin as a finger, a yard-or-so long, coiled like snakes in tubfuls of water. Preparing them for sale was a simple but messy business. The vendor, seated on a low wooden stool, cigarette on his lip, grabbed a specimen by its neck, and, as it flicked and flailed, impaled its head on a spike at the top of a strip of wood propped up between his knees (a crunchy, squelching sound). Fag still in mouth, he took a small dirty knife, slit the twitching creature from neck to tail, and scraped the mess of its spine and guts into a bucket at the base of the board. A few stray bits of intestine or internal organ splattered to the ground. Finally, he chopped off and discarded its head and tail, and tossed the blood-streaked body into another plastic pail. 'You have to eat them fresh,' said Feng Rui, 'Leave them for an hour and their flavour spoils.'

I'd been to many Chinese markets before that outing with Feng Rui, and had at first been amazed – and appalled – by the cruelty I witnessed. It was the sheer nonchalance of it, the way people scaled fish as though they were simply peeling potatoes, skinned live rabbits while smoking a cigarette, joked with a friend as the blood drained from the throat of a bewildered duck. They didn't kill animals before they cooked and ate them. They simply went about the process of preparing a creature for the pot and table, and at some random point it died. But there, perhaps, is the crux of the matter, embedded almost invisibly in those last two sentences. In English, as in most European languages, the words for the living things we eat are mostly derived from the Latin *anima*, which means air, breath, life. 'Creature', from the Latin for 'created', seems to connect animals with us as human beings in some divinely fashioned universe. We too are creatures, animated. In Chinese, the word for animal is *dong wu*, meaning 'moving thing'. Is it cruel to hurt something that (unless you are a fervent Buddhist) you simply see as a 'moving thing', scarcely even alive?

Culture shock hit me hardest when I was invited to lunch by a motherly middle-aged woman in her special rabbit restaurant, not long after I had arrived in Chengdu. 'Come into the kitchen and watch,' she urged me. When we entered, the main ingredient for our stew was sitting sweetly in the corner of the room, nibbling lettuce. The following is an extract from my diary, written in the kitchen that day as I watched:

Death of a rabbit
Hit rabbit over the head to stun it.
Hang up by foot.
Slit its throat.
Immediately peel off skin.
Chop brutally into small pieces with a cleaver.
[...]
From live rabbit to dish on table in less than ten minutes.

Still reeling from the brutality of what I had just witnessed, I was led into the dining room and presented with a steaming bowlful of rabbit stew. I didn't want to eat it. But Mrs Li looked at me with such proud anticipation, such sweet and generous eagerness, that I did.

Some of the cruellest tales of Chinese eating are apocryphal. A late-nineteenth-century account of life in Beijing by a Dr D.F. Rennie included a description of cooking a live turtle. The special pot used, he said, had a hole for the turtle's head in its lid, so the poor creature, growing thirsty with heat, could be fed with spiced wine, which perfumed its flesh as it cooked. He also recounted how live ducks were stood on a hotplate over a fire in order to cook just their feet. Were they true, these ghoulish stories? Dr Rennie admitted that they were secondhand, told to him by a Shanghai merchant. An elderly Buddhist monk once described to me with wide eyes and a solemn manner a Cantonese dish called 'san jiao' (three cries): 'The first cry,' he told me, 'is when they pick up the wriggling new-born mouse in their chopsticks, the second when they dip it in the sauce, and the third when they bite off its head.' I wasn't sure whether to believe that they really ate live mice in southern China, or simply that this gentle monk, a lifelong vegetarian, was trying to put me off my meat.

All over the world, people have heard of that notorious Chinese delicacy, live monkey brains. The monkey, so they say, is strapped to the table, its head immobilised in some kind of vice. Then the waiter slices off the top of its skull, and you eat its brains with a spoon, like pudding. But has anyone actually seen this practice? A journalist writing in the *Japan Times* in 2002, Mark Schreiber, said his own exhaustive investigations had produced no first-hand accounts, and suggested that the legend might be traced back to a tongue-in-cheek newspaper column on Chinese eating habits written in 1948.

But if the most infamous examples of Chinese culinary cruelty are urban myths, the everyday cruelty of Chinese cooking can be shocking. Once I was served with a dish called 'sauna prawns' in a smart hotel in Chengdu. The waitress brought in a tabletop burner, and a potful of hot water covered by a grill and a perspex lid. When the water was boiling, she took off the lid, threw in a plateful of live prawns, and then replaced it. We watched through the perspex as the prawns writhed and flicked on the grill in their 'sauna' steam. When they were cooked, we were supposed to remove the lid and eat them, with a soy sauce dip. I didn't find the dish very appetising. But I couldn't say there was anything sadistic about the enthusiasm of my Chinese companions, because, although they were amused by the agonising display on the table before us, as far as they were concerned, the prawns were just moving, not feeling.

As time went by, of course, I dirtied my own hands in the blood of the markets: I insisted on seeing my fish and chickens killed in front me so that I knew they were fresh; I watched nonchalantly as the eel vendor wreaked carnage for my lunch. Although the Chinese attitude to *dong wu* continued to disturb me, at least it was honest, I thought. Back at home in Britain, the stench of death hung in the background of a carnivorous meal like a guilty secret; people bought their meat safe and sanitised, while the animals languished in battery pens. In China, you saw what meat meant, there was no avoiding it. You chose to eat it, with your eyes open.

That morning at the market, Feng Rui took me to a poultry stall where toffee-coloured chickens stood around in a woven bamboo pen, mobile and jittery. The ducks lay more serenely on the ground, their feet bound with bunches of rice straw. Every day the city's duck sellers brought in clumps of ducks on carts attached to three-wheeled bicycles; their heads and necks swayed elegantly above their anchor of straw as the sellers negotiated their way through the maelstrom of bicycles and buses. Like the eels, the chickens and ducks met a bloody, public end. 'Let's have a look at that one,' said Feng Rui. So the vendor snatched the chicken by the scruff of its neck and held it up for his approval. Feng Rui prodded it and peered at its feet. 'You can tell its age by the feet,' he told me, 'This one, you see, its thumb has scarcely developed, that means it's quite young, its flesh will be tender. If the thumb is long and gnarled, it's an old bird, best for making soup. Yes, I'll take this one,' he told the vendor.

So the vendor drew back the head of the bird and slit its throat with a knife. He shook the blood into a plastic bag, plunged the fowl into a potful of hot water that sat on a charcoal stove. The bird was still twitching as he sat down on his stool and began to strip off its feathers. Then he dipped it into a potful of bubbling tar that clung to it like rubber, set the tar in cold water, and peeled off the sticky black shroud with all the stubby quills and remaining tiny feathers, like a leg wax. Working quickly, he slit open its belly and disembowelled it, discarding the stomach and gall bladder in a shambles on the ground, keeping the prized gizzard, liver, heart and intestines, which he handed over to Feng Rui with the small bagful of blood. The other live birds hung around nearby, stupidly.

Feng Rui and I ambled back to his friend's flat with our purchases, the chicken with all its inner accoutrements safely bagged up; a live carp, flapping around; a hunk of pork rump; bunches of onions. The two top hotel chefs he had mentioned the night before were waiting for us inside. One of them was sitting in an armchair, smoking a cigarette. The other was chopping a flattened smoked rabbit into small chunks. Feng Rui rinsed the chicken's intestines, cut them into sections with a sharp cleaver, and sprinkled them with a little salt. Then, having dispatched the carp in the bathroom, he put the whole chicken and the chunk of pork into a panful of water, and set them to boil on the stove. 'Your "European chickens" (*ou zhou ji*),' he said with disdain, 'They may be tender but they're completely tasteless. It's all that artificial feed, it plumps them up, but it makes their flesh unhealthy. Our Chinese birds, they are fed on leftover rice and stuff, and they run around in the farmyard, so they have much more flavour.' He continued to talk as he put the bagful of chicken blood into a panful of simmering water, where it set to a jelly, and blanched the intestines to clean them. And then he prodded his taciturn friend to give me the recipe for smoked rabbit, which involved skinning the animal alive, rubbing it in a marinade of salt and spices, flattening its body between two heavy stones, crucifying it on a cross of wooden sticks, and then smoking it over a smouldering fire of pine, camphor and cypress leaves. I wasn't sure how easy it would be to reproduce that particular recipe in London, but I took notes assiduously, eager to miss nothing.

A former chef, Feng Rui owned two or three modest restaurants and bars in Chengdu. He was a small-time businessman, taking advantage of the new economic liberalisation to escape the inferno of the Chinese restaurant kitchen. But he was fascinated by the art and science of cookery; it was his passion as well as his profession. I understood this from his perfectionist attention to detail, the tenderness with which he talked about food and his obvious pride in passing on some of his knowledge to a curious foreigner. But this pride, and his pleasure, were always tinged with bitterness.

'These cultured people,' he would say, his face clouding, 'they despise cookery. They think it's low status. It's so unreasonable.'

As I came to know Feng Rui better over the next few years, I learned about his own, troubled family background. His father, Feng Mang, had been a military man, an engineer in the Nationalist air force, and when the Nationalists were defeated in the Chinese civil war, he found himself on the wrong side of history. During the Cultural Revolution, Feng Mang was 'struggled against' because of his political background, and imprisoned for seven long years, during which time he never saw his family. In the eyes of the revolutionary state and its brainwashed society, his six children were all contaminated by the seeping stain of their father's ideological misdeeds. Feng Rui, only four when the Cultural Revolution started, was bullied at school, and lost a year of his education. Later, he was excluded from military service. 'We had no political prospects, no future, and no "face" in society,' he told me. 'We were always under pressure.'

But Feng Rui found his solace in the kitchen. As a child, he hovered around the family stove, learning from his parents. At the age of only eight or nine, eager to develop his culinary skills, he began helping out at wedding banquets. People were poor then: it was the height of the Cultural Revolution; food was rationed, and life was harsh. But at weddings the chefs had a rare chance to show off their skills. 'I have loved cooking for as long as I can remember,' Feng Rui told me one day, 'and by the time I was twenty I wanted to be recognised as a chef.' In 1984 he qualified as a 'Chef of the Second Rank' in the official Chinese culinary hierarchy, and was the envy of those around him, because people knew, in those hard times, that chefs were guaranteed a decent diet. Yet in the eyes of the educated, cooks like him were little more than servants.

Cooking is traditionally a lowly profession in China. The development of a refined palate and an appreciation of food was part of the education of the Confucian gentleman, but the actual cookery fell to the lot of the uneducated masses. Boys from poor households went into service in restaurants or private kitchens, often simply because their families knew they would be given three square meals a day. Many were illiterate, and they passed on their skills from one generation to another without the use of written manuals. They were known, disparagingly sometimes, as the 'fire-head army'. Snobbery about kitchen work has its roots, perhaps, in the writings of Mencius, one of the great Confucian philosophers, who lived in the fourth century BC. Mencius saw a chasm between mental and manual work, and famously said that 'the gentleman keeps his distance from the kitchen'.

This is not to say that there aren't a few chefs in the Chinese history books. Yi Yin, a legendary cook of the Shang Dynasty, impressed the King of Tang so much with his knowledge of cooking that he was made prime minister. In the Zhou Dynasty, another chef, Yi Ya, was promoted at court after enrapturing the Duke of Qi with a series of midnight feasts. In a dark twist to the tale, he also steamed his own son to satisfy the Duke's desire to taste the flesh of an infant. Despite this monstrous act, he is still fondly remembered for the brilliance of his cooking. Chefs in Hunan province still revere Yi Ya as the ancestor of their profession: until the Cultural Revolution they made offerings to his image in a dedicated cooks' temple. Most of the famous names in Chinese culinary history, however, are those of gourmets, members of the literati who enjoyed eating, and who wrote about it in prose or poetry.

Perhaps the most famous among them is Yuan Mei, an eighteenth-century essayist and poet. He retired early from the civil service, and based himself for the rest of his life in the southern city of Nanjing, where he bought a piece of land and built the 'Garden of Contentment', a series of gracious pavilions laid out in a romantic landscape. Among his writings, Yuan Mei left to posterity a remarkable cookery book, *The Food Lists of the Garden of Contentment*. In it, he wrote of culinary theory and technique, advising on hygiene and the selection of ingredients, outlining his own food taboos, suggesting which flavours went harmoniously together, and offering hints on menu planning. He also recorded some three hundred recipes, ranging from simple vegetable stir-fries to elaborate duck preparations. But Yuan Mei never sullied his own hands in the kitchen. He was an observer, standing at the shoulder of his skilled personal chef, Wang Xiaoyu, tasting, taking notes, and asking questions.

Yuan himself gave due credit to the man who worked such magic for his dinner parties. After Wang died, Yuan missed him so much that he wrote his biography, an account of the life of a 'lowly person' that sat somewhat uneasily alongside his more conventional biographies of literary and upper-class figures. Two and a half centuries later, however, the name of Wang Xiaoyu has faded into obscurity, while Yuan Mei's lives on in the memories of all those who are interested in Chinese culinary culture. It's a similar story with other notable gourmets: the dishes they loved bear their names, but the men who worked so hard to feed them are forgotten. One of the few exceptions is the Song Dynasty poet Su Dongpo, who wrote so lovingly about pork that he was immortalised in the name of the Hangzhou dish 'Dongpo Rou', but who also liked personally to prepare food for his wife and his favourite concubine. Mostly, though, it was the masters who ate and pontificated, while their nameless chefs slaved away over the stove and the chopping board.

In the post-reform era, highly skilled chefs in China can command lofty salaries. One I know wears designer clothes, has two cars, two apartments and various investments, and likes to go on holiday to the wild places of Tibet. Cooking has become a more attractive career, particularly since it offers the possibility of working abroad. Yet the prejudice against it as a respectable profession runs deep in Chinese society. One of my mentors, the Cantonese cookery writer Yan-kit So, who began her career as a first-class historian, had to defy the disapproval of her well-educated and well-heeled friends when she turned her attention to food. It just wasn't the kind of thing a nice girl should do. And my own Chinese friends have always been baffled by the fact that I choose to associate with dumpling makers and beancurd sellers as well as 'intellectuals'.

But, for Feng Rui and countless other people throughout Chinese history, the pleasures of food have also been a refuge from the difficulties of personal and professional life. Eating was the solace of the exiled and the excluded; it offered sweet respite from the bitterness of life. In a society fraught by political danger, where individuals were subject to the arbitrary rule of their imperial or communist masters, and careers and reputations could be broken on a whim, it was a safe pleasure, one in which you could lose yourself without fear. The poet Su Dongpo started growing his own vegetables and experimenting in the kitchen only after the collapse of his official career and the start of an impoverished exile. Feng Rui, ostracised in his formative years, his father persecuted and imprisoned, found joy in the colours and flavours of the kitchen. It gave him his freedom, and it unleashed his creativity.

Despite his lingering bitterness and resentment of society's wrongs, Feng Rui put the best of himself into his food. That first morning in the kitchen with him, I was impressed by his skill and his serenity. I stood at his side, notebook in hand, breathing in the aromas that filled the kitchen. There was the smell of the fresh shiitake mushrooms he added to the chicken's cooking broth to make a simple soup; the overwhelming, citrussy scent of Sichuan peppercorns, slow-roasted in the wok; the gentler exhalations of warm chicken and pork.

One of the dishes Feng Rui chose to make for lunch that day was just an afterthought. It was *chao ji za*, stir-fried chicken miscellany, a concoction that would have seemed more at home in the kitchen of a country cottage than on a restaurant menu. It was made with all the parts of the chicken that most European cooks would throw away: the blood, set to a jelly, the gizzard, the heart, the liver, and the intestines. They were all cooked in the wok with pickled red chilli and ginger, and batons of slender, fragrant Chinese celery. Each innard was prepared in a way that would make the most of its particular qualities of taste or texture.

It was typical of the careful economy of Sichuanese home cooking that almost nothing of Feng Rui's chicken was wasted. And it was the same with the fish that I'd seen slaughtered in the bathroom (apart from its intestines – fit only, as Feng Rui had told me so disparagingly, for the foul-feeding Cantonese). Virtually every edible morsel was to be savoured: even, and especially, the silky strands around the eye, the tender flesh in the cheek, the eyeball. We would leave only bones and fins on the plate.

I had had some, limited acquaintance with this kind of cooking at home in Oxford. My mother brought me up knowing how to joint chickens, roast bacon rinds as a snack, make bones into stocks, reuse leftovers to make tomorrow's supper. And we did eat offal, too, on occasion: mostly liver and kidneys, although once my mother made brain croquettes, serving them with some sleight of hand. But this was nothing compared to China.

There, in the mid-nineties, memories of famine and rationing were still fresh and raw, at least for the older generation. Children were told, as Chinese children had been told since time immemorial, that every grain of rice was produced by the sweat of a peasant. Their parents, many of them, had spent years in the countryside during the Cultural Revolution, eking out a hard living from the land. There was a sense that food was precious, and that you should make the most of it.

As the months slipped by in Chengdu, I too learned to appreciate the bits of fish and fowl that I would have left on my plate in England or never seen at all (mostly, they are spirited away before the meat reaches the butcher's counter or the supermarket shelf). Feng Rui's stir-fried chicken miscellany was delicious, as was his twice-cooked pork, served in a sumptuous sizzle of chilli-bean paste and garlic leaves. The fish, whose journey from tank to table I had watched with trepidation, was steamed and then scattered with shreds of ginger and spring onion. He finished the dish with a libation of fizzing-hot oil that awakened the fresh fragrances of the onion and ginger, and then a slow, dark trickle of soy sauce. Lastly, Feng Rui placed a bowlful of winter melon and mushroom broth on the table. There was rice too, he said, if we wanted it later. We raised our chopsticks, and ate.

So Feng Rui fulfilled what he saw as his duty, and gave a nosy foreign girl a lesson in Sichuanese cookery. After that, he let me study in the kitchen of the Bamboo Bar whenever I wanted, and he took me out for various amazing dinners. I don't imagine he had any idea what he had started. In a sense, you could say he was my first Sichuanese *shi fu* (cooking master).

Twice-cooked pork

回鍋肉

Serves 2 as a main dish served with plain rice, 4 with two or three other dishes
as part of a Chinese meal

12 oz (350 g) pork belly, with skin still attached
6 baby leeks
2 tbsp peanut oil or lard
1¹/₂ tbsp chilli bean paste
1¹/₂ tsp Sichuanese sweet wheaten paste or sweet bean paste
2 tsp fermented black beans
1 tsp dark soy sauce
1 tsp white sugar
Salt

1. Bring a good panful of water to the boil. Add the pork, return to the boil
and then simmer at a gentler heat until just cooked – this should take 20–25
minutes, depending on the thickness of the pork. Remove the pork from the
water and allow to cool. Refrigerate the meat for at least a couple of hours to
firm up the flesh – this makes it easier to cut.

2. When the meat is completely cold, slice it thinly – ideally, each piece should
be a mixture of fat and lean, with a strip of skin at the top.

3. Chop the leeks diagonally at a steep angle into thin slices.

4. Heat 2 tablespoons oil or lard in a wok over a medium flame, add the pork
pieces and stir-fry until their fat has melted out and they are toasty and slightly
curved. Push the pork to one side of the wok and tip the chilli bean paste into
the space you have created. Stir-fry it for 20–30 seconds until the oil is richly
red, then add the sweet paste and black beans and stir-fry for another few seconds until they too smell delicious. Mix everything in the wok together and add
the soy sauce and sugar, seasoning with a little salt if necessary.

5. Finally, add the leeks and stir and toss until they are just cooked. Turn on to
a serving dish and eat immediately, with plained steamed rice.

CHAPTER 4

Only Barbarians Eat Salad

One of the things that really annoyed me about China in those days was how extremely rude everyone I met was about 'Western food'. There was I, unfailingly polite and diplomatic, trying to look on the bright side of their grisly slaughter practices, accommodating their penchant for gristly innards, forcing myself to eat pig's brains – and no one, absolutely no one, was prepared to treat *me* with equal good manners.

Whenever the subject of 'Western food' came up in conversation, people would dismiss it out of hand with a few barbed stereotypes: '*Xi can hen dan diao*!' (Western food is very monotonous) or '*Xi can hen jian dan*!' (Western food is very simple). My own compatriots had a habit of talking about 'Chinese food' as if it were a single tradition, collapsing the diverse regional cuisines of this vast country into a dull set menu of spring rolls, sweet-and-sour pork and egg-fried rice, or writing it off as 'junky' and 'gloopy'. Similarly, Chinese people all viewed 'Western food' as a single, rather boring, school of cookery. It didn't occur to them that you might eat differently in, say, Naples or Helsinki, Alabama or Paris. Often, I found myself having to remind people that France alone was the size of Sichuan Province, and that *some people* thought its cuisine was as distinctive and complex as the Sichuanese.

This might have been hilarious, but it didn't seem so on the many occasions when I went to great trouble and expense to cook Western food for my Chinese friends. My delightful Chinese teacher, Yu Weiqin, for instance, persuaded me once to make a traditional English dinner for a party she was arranging. Even deciding what to cook was a challenge, because it was impossible to obtain ingredients for most of the dishes I might have chosen. There were no fresh herbs or non-Chinese spices in the markets; and no supermarkets stocking tinned ingredients from abroad (in fact, there were no supermarkets at all). The only 'chocolate' one could buy was some revolting Chinese brand that consisted mainly of vegetable fat; cream was unheard of; and olive oil was sold in tiny bottles as a beauty product, as expensive by local standards as Chanel No 5 was in London. To add to my problems, Teacher Yu's kitchen, like every other domestic kitchen in China, lacked an oven. In the end, I clubbed together with some other foreign students to buy a small portable oven, and decided to make roast beef with potatoes and an apple crumble.

Afterwards, I wondered why I had bothered. Teacher Yu's friends found what I had cooked so outlandish that they saw no need to be polite in their comments. They roared with laughter at the menu, barely able to comprehend that I would offer my guests a meal consisting of only three or four dishes. '*Xi can hen dan diao!*' (How bland Western food tastes!) they crowed, demanding chilli sauce to liven up the roast beef. 'Where's the rice?' they asked after the meal, filled with disbelief at the idea that we would make do with potatoes *instead* (in China, only starving peasants eat potatoes as a staple food). One middle-aged lady toyed with a piece of beef and then ate no more. Her husband curled his tongue at the revolting flavours of my apple crumble. And because Chinese people lacked the concept of dessert as a separate course, they all piled up their bowls with roast beef, buttered carrots, potatoes and apple crumble, all at the same time.

'Western food' was at that time a distant and exotic concept for most Chinese. In 1994, in the whole of Chengdu, a cultural centre and provincial capital of some eight million people, there was a single restaurant specialising in foreign food, the Yaohua Canting. It called itself a 'Western food restaurant', and had been established in 1943, when it served chic foreign dishes like curry chicken, ice cream, salad, fried jam sandwiches and the acclaimed *lao mian*, a concoction of pasta covered in a thick eggy sauce and baked in an oven. In the forties, it was the trendiest place in town, frequented by well-heeled and well-educated youths, and it had somehow survived nationalisation in the fifties and the Cultural Revolution in the sixties to limp into the nineties in a new location on Dong Da Street. I visited it once, although I never ate there because the menu and atmosphere were so weird and alien. The place was decorated in what the managers clearly believed was cutting-edge Western style, with framed images of cigars and cocktail glasses in heightened graphics, and lurid photographs of scantily clad Western women, pouting provocatively. The tables were laid ostentatiously with knives, forks and spoons. The menu, as I remember, featured old-fashioned European-style dishes: heavy soups, steaks and cutlets drowned in murky sauces.

Apart from the Yaohua, there were two smart, five-star hotels in Chengdu that catered for visiting Westerners. The Minshan hotel offered a regular evening buffet that included extraordinary exotica like sliced cheese and salad, and on one occasion I ate a mushroom vol-au-vent and a steak in the swanky dining room at the top of the Jinjiang Hotel. Mostly, though, homesick foreign students and backpackers had to content themselves with occasional breakfasts at the city's only travellers' café, the Flower Garden, which served muesli with yoghurt and banana pancakes, and kept plastic packages of sliced processed cheese locked up in a glass cabinet like caviar or truffles (twelve rubbery and tasteless slices cost the equivalent of about ten bowls of noodles).

Outside the rarefied atmosphere of these hang-outs for foreign businessmen and students, such delicacies were hard to find. The most dedicated foreign students at the university cycled for miles across town to buy a spongey version of French bread and margarine, just so they could avoid the local breakfast of watery rice porridge, fried peanuts and spicy pickled vegetables. Other than that, we had little alternative but to eat Sichuanese food all the time. This wasn't exactly a hardship, as you've probably gathered, but we did miss some things, like decent chocolate. Most of all, though, we longed for cheese. We fantasised about it, discussed it, and begged anyone coming to see us from Europe to bring some. My own father has always loathed cheese. He refuses to eat it, and flinches if you wave some under his nose. But in an act of stupendous generosity, he carried a boxful of slowly maturing and increasingly smelly cheeses (including Roquefort, Cheddar, and Camembert) around China for a week, before he finally arrived in Chengdu for a visit. I was almost as pleased to see the cheeses as I was to see him.

If it was difficult for us to eat 'Western food', it was almost impossible for the average Chengdu resident. The prices in the hotel restaurants were astronomical; no one on a local wage could afford them. And the whole eating environment was unfamiliar and intimidating, as I discovered when I invited a Sichuanese friend for a buffet supper in one of the hotels: she had never before used a knife and fork and had no idea how to hold them.

Some Chinese hotels I visited tried to please their few foreign tourists by serving 'Western breakfasts'. I remember the odd looks on waitresses' faces as they gave us little plates with eggs on them, fried on both sides, a few deep-fried potato chips on a saucer, some plain steamed buns, and glasses of milk. They offered these things to us as they might have fed live mice to a snake – placing the strange, disturbing, and inedible victuals in front of a possibly dangerous creature, just to see what it did. Would we hiss as we licked them, or just swallow them whole, like a boa constrictor? One elderly Chinese man I met recalled his horror at having been served with a soft-boiled egg for breakfast during a visit to Hong Kong: 'It was still raw inside!' he said, still incredulous after about fifteen years. 'I hardly dared touch it!'

At the tail-end of my time in Chengdu, American fast-food companies began to open their first outlets there, but they didn't do much to rehabilitate local opinions about the cuisines of the West. One young chef I met remarked casually that he 'didn't like Western food'. 'Oh really?' I asked, surprised that he'd even tasted any. 'What have you tried?'

'I had Kentucky Fried Chicken once and it was disgusting,' he replied. This one experience, shocking, unhappy and vividly remembered, had soured his view of the culinary achievements of the entire Western world. I wanted to regale him with mouth-watering tales of sautéed foie gras, shepherd's pie, crême brulée, roasted lamb with garlic and anchovies, Neapolitan pizza, baked oysters with beurre blanc, and everything else I had tasted and adored in the West, but I didn't know how to begin. So I said nothing, but merely gazed at him in stupefaction.

It always seemed to me comically ironic that while most of my compatriots saw the Chinese as barely civilised and promiscuous eaters of snakes, dogs and penises, the Chinese repaid the insult in spades. They saw what we ate as crudely simple, uncivilised in its rawness, and barely edible.

There was nothing new about this attitude to foreign food. In Chinese antiquity, barbarians were grouped into the 'raw' (*sheng*) and the 'cooked' (*shu*). The cooked barbarians were the kind of aliens with whom you could, at a pinch, do business. The raw barbarians (uncooked, un-Chinese, uncivilised), were beyond the pale. Even in modern China, strangers are known sometimes as *sheng ren* ('raw people'), while people you know are 'cooked' (*shu ren*). Such disdain reflects the fact that Chinese people traditionally avoid raw food. There are exceptions, like the marinated shellfish and crustaceans eaten in Chaozhou and the east. Long ago, too, the elite of China's most cosmopolitan dynasty, the Tang, who hobnobbed with bearded foreigners riding in by camel from the western deserts, dined sometimes on raw fish slices, perhaps the ancestor of modern Japanese sashimi. Broadly speaking, however, the Chinese have always liked their food to be not only cut into pieces, but also cooked. Cooking is seen as the root of civilisation: only barbarians remain at the evolutionary stage of 'eating fur, feathers and drinking blood'.

Ancient prejudices about foreign food are encapsulated in the language of modern cookery. Ingredients that were brought in from the West along the desert routes of the old Silk Road still bear a linguistic stigma. Regular pepper is known as 'barbarian pepper' (*hu jiao*); the carrot is a 'barbarian radish' (*hu luo bu*). The character *hu* refers to the old Mongol, Tartar and Turkic tribes of the northwest, but it also means 'recklessly, foolishly, blindly or outrageously'. '*Hu hua*' (hu talk) describes the ravings of a madman; *hu gao* means to mess things up; and other *hu* compounds refer to all kinds of mischievous, fraudulent, wild, careless, irritating and deranged behaviours. In the distant past, people who ate things like *salad* were clearly insane.

Cheese, of course, was almost inconceivable. Dairy products have been largely absent from the Chinese diet. Perhaps in the past they were too strongly associated with the rough dining habits of the northern and western barbarians, cheese- and yoghurt-eating nomads who periodically invaded China. And the Chinese, too, lacked pastureland amid their tight patchworks of rice fields. Although in the late twentieth century Chinese parents started feeding milk to their children, cheese is still widely regarded as disgusting: it was memorably described by one informant of the American anthropologist E.N. Anderson as 'the mucous discharge of some old cow's guts, allowed to putrefy'. Some Chinese friends of mine claim, with a grimace, to be able to smell milk in the sweat of Westerners.

In the glory days of Chinese empire, the Chinese disdain for foreigners and the food they ate must have appeared to have had a certain legitimacy. Chinese cities, with their fine restaurants, bustling markets and glittering aura of civilisation, were the envy of the world. The hairy, round-eyed barbarians who wandered in occasionally from the desert were overawed: they had little to compare with this in their own, distant lands. But by the nineteenth century, the solid Chinese sense of cultural superiority was being eroded by the 'gunboat diplomacy' of the Western powers. The Chinese had been the inventors of gunpowder, paper, printing and the magnetic compass, but they hadn't used them to conquer the world. And the barbarians, with their red hair, staring eyes, filthy beards and uncivilised ways, turned out to be rather smart after all.

Even in the 1990s, history often cast a shadow over the life of a foreigner in China. I found myself accused, often, over the opium wars, when the United Kingdom had bludgeoned China into accepting a deleterious trade of drugs for silver. Was I, personally, expected to apologise for these crimes of my ancestors, I wondered? I was certainly often treated as the personal representative of Her Majesty's Government, and expected to mind that Britain had to give Hong Kong back to the Chinese in 1997.

Many of the Chinese people I met viewed me and my foreign student friends through a bifocal lens of disdain and envy. On the one hand, weren't we in some sense barbarians? We were large; plump and overfed. We were a little bit smelly (all that dairy food). We were loose-living, decadent and immoral: one Chinese student told me the 'Panda Building' was known as a hotbed of sexual promiscuity (it probably was, by the Chinese standards of 1994). On the other hand, we were rich, and we were free. The mere fact that we were able to lark around for a year in China, dining out in restaurants and backpacking all over the country, was a sign of wealth and liberty.

But if the Chinese were confused and ambiguous in their attitudes towards us, one thing was certain, and that was that our food was unbearable. In the beginning, I had a sense of missionary zeal when it came to introducing my Chinese friends to Western delicacies. They were showing me the delights of Chinese food, and I wanted to return the favour, feeling that cultural exchange should not be a one-way traffic. So, undaunted by that catastrophic supper for Teacher Yu and her friends, I went on trying to persuade the people I knew that 'Western food' wasn't as dreadful as they imagined. After all, if I could learn to love rabbit-heads, couldn't they learn to love cheese?

Every time a foreign delicacy found its way into the Panda Building with the arrival of visitors from abroad, I would offer little titbits to my closest friends: Tuscan truffle pastes, fine olive oil, dark chocolate, parmesan cheese. From time to time, I cooked for them. But my efforts always backfired. I crashed into unexpected taboos, bored my dinner guests, revolted them or simply left them unsatisfied.

Once, I made a beautiful Italian risotto, with arborio rice, dried porcini and parmesan. I was convinced that risotto would please my friends: after all, it was rice, with dried mushrooms not entirely unlike their own. I made my own rich stock, I added a dash of white wine, I spent forty minutes adding the liquid, spoonful by spoonful, until the rice was unctuous and creamy, fragrant with mushrooms. They all ate some, but they weren't impressed: no one could fathom why I had spent so long making a simple *tang fan* (soupy rice).

Even on the rare occasions when my friends enjoyed what I made, they always managed to sabotage my plan to give them a real taste of the West. When I took a home-made apple tart to a dinner party at the home of my old friends Zhou Yu and Tao Ping, for example, they cut it up into chopstickable pieces and served it alongside stewed pig's ear, tea-smoked duck and spicy sea-weed salad. I reflected that, although I had certainly given them some 'Western food', in their manner of eating it they had turned it into something entirely Chinese.

Since I first lived in Chengdu, 'Western food' has made enormous inroads into China. Aside from the country's colonisation by McDonalds and KFC, there are coffee bars and pizzerias, and the new supermarkets offer a range of imported products. But what Chinese people eat as 'Western food' is often far removed from what any European or American would consider normal. The UBC restaurant in Suzhou, for example, offers twenty-two kinds of coffee, but can't make a decent espresso. Its menu includes such 'Western' delicacies as 'boiled lemon cola with ginger', waffles with meat floss, fruit pizza, and 'duck chin with maggi sauce' (whatever that is). And when my Chinese friends share a bottle of the newly fashionable dry red wine (*gan hong*) over dinner, they drink it in a wholly Chinese manner, toasting each other with a thimble-ful of wine at a time. (Chinese leaders, invited to state banquets in the West, have been known to dilute fine vintage wines with fizzy lemonade.)

In Shanghai in 2006 I bought a glossy cookery book entitled *British Cuisine* – or, in Chinese, *ying shi xi can* (English-style Western food). Reading it, I laughed till I cried. Highlights of the typically British recipes it offered included a salad of arctic clams covered in a latticework of squirted mayonnaise; macaroni with shrimps; stuffed squid in black pepper and minced apple sauce; and braised cauliflower with quail eggs. The presentation of the photographed dishes was like some nightmare out of the seventies.

Still, these days people try to show a little cross-cultural sophistication. On a visit to Chengdu in January 2007, I was invited by a hotel owner to be guest of honour at a Western-style dinner party. We sat around the only grand oblong dinner table I've ever seen in China. It was laid with brass candelabras, knives, forks and sideplates, with two wine glasses per person. The chefs in the hotel kitchen had been trained in 'Western cuisine', and they served up a menu of cold beef in mustard dressing, baked oysters in hollandaise sauce, cream of sweetcorn soup, deep-fried rabbit leg with french fries, beef steak with onion rings, and some kind of pudding. (There was no cheese course, obviously.) The other guests, chefs and food-writers mainly, ignored the chopsticks that were offered as a back-up, and tucked into this exotic feast, grappling nobly with the unfamiliar knives and forks. But I noticed people stealing glances at me to see what to do with their bread and their sideplates, and I didn't have the impression that anyone particularly enjoyed the food. 'Welcome Fuchsia!' said my host, raising her glass to me with its thimbleful of red wine at the end of the meal, 'We welcome you to Chengdu from the land of Shakespeare, David Copperfield and Anna Karenina!'

If, in my first year in Chengdu, I failed miserably in my efforts to enhance the standing of 'Western food', I continued to throw myself into Sichuanese culinary culture. After that memorable cooking lesson with Feng Rui, my informal food studies gathered pace and my notebooks filled up with recipes. But I still wanted more. And so it was that my German friend Volker and I came up with a plan. Like me, Volker was a keen cook, and he was a veteran of Californian farmers' markets. Inevitably, we fell into the habit of eating out together and comparing recipes. One afternoon, he suggested that we might try to take some formal cooking classes. So we asked around, found the address of the famous local cooking school, the Sichuan Institute of Higher Cuisine, and set off on our bicycles to find it.

It was a nondescript concrete building on a backstreet in the north-west of the city, but we heard the sound of chopping from an open window and knew we'd arrived. Upstairs, in a plain white room, dozens of apprentice cooks in white overalls were engrossed in learning the arts of sauces. They were pulverising chillies with pairs of cleavers on tree-trunk chopping boards, grinding Sichuan peppercorns to a fine brown powder, and scurrying around mixing oils and spices, fine-tuning the flavours of the rich dark liquids in their crucibles. The air hummed with a gentle, rhythmic pounding, and the sound of china spoons in china bowls. On long parallel tables sat bowls of ingredients; pools of soy sauce and chilli oil, piles of sugar and salt. Notebooks scribbled with Chinese characters lay around on the tables amid the blood-red chillies and scattered peppercorns. The light streamed in from open windows. Rushing into the room, eager and excited, we caused the usual commotion among the students by our alien presence alone.

The principal of the school was a stout, jovial man with a crimson face, dressed in a Mao jacket in military khaki. We couldn't really understand his broad Sichuan dialect, so he summoned the school's English teacher, Professor Feng Quanxin, to interpret. A few other teachers gathered around. They all seemed amused, and perhaps flattered, by our unusual plea for tuition, coming out of the blue. The only foreign students the school had previously taught were an American couple who took private classes there in the late eighties. Such a request was not only odd because we were foreigners. The idea that university students like us would rather be in a kitchen than a library was extraordinary.

In that strange, transitional period in Chinese history, there were no administrative procedures for dealing with our request. Was it even legal for foreigners to study, ad hoc, at a school that was part of the provincial bureaucracy? Probably not. But Sichuan is a place where the reins are a little loose, the lines a little blurred, and the people inclined to bend and yield. We settled down to a long afternoon of discussions and good-natured haggling. Cigarette packets were emptied, ashtrays filled. Tea mugs were replenished with hot water and drained countless times. Passing teachers and students dropped in to stare at us, and soon the large office was crowded. As dusk fell we came to a deal. We would take twice-weekly private classes at the cooking school on Tuesdays and Thursdays. They would provide a cooking teacher and an interpreter as well as all the raw ingredients, and we would pay them a reasonable but hard-bargained fee in renminbi.

Volker and I cycled home, elated at our success. Our route took us across the span of the city, from the cooking school in the north-west to the south-eastern university campus. We passed through the old Manchu quarter, with its rows of higgledy-piggledy cottages, black and white with their dark timber frames and whitewashed walls. There were no street lights in the old lanes anyway, and that night there was a power cut, so candles lit the shops, houses and little restaurants that we passed. An old couple sat at a table outside their cottage on bamboo chairs, sharing a few simple dishes with rice. Shopkeepers stood over their packets of cigarettes and tealeaves, their faces illuminated by the glow of candles stuck in puddles of wax on glass-topped counters. Tempting aromas emanated from open-fronted restaurants. The deep, savoury smells of stews simmering away in tall clay pots on a row of gas burners; the whiff of beef in rice meal, small portions steaming away in a tower of little bamboo baskets; potato slivers sizzling in a wok with chilli and Sichuan pepper.

Over the following month, Volker and I learnt how to make sixteen classic Sichuanese dishes. Our teacher, Gan Guojian, was a moody, sardonic man of around forty, with a James Dean look about him and a cigarette permanently hanging out of his mouth. In each lesson, we would first watch Teacher Gan as he prepared the dishes of the day, and then we'd try to re-create them ourselves. We learnt how to hold our cleavers and cut our raw ingredients, how to mix seasonings and how to control the heat of the wok.

Learning another cuisine is like learning a language. In the beginning, you know nothing about its most basic rules of grammar. You experience it as a flood of words, or dishes, without system or structure. When I first went to China, I was already fluent in the language of basic French cookery. I could make a roux, mayonnaise, hollandaise, vinaigrette, pâtes sucrée or choux. I knew how to sauté ingredients at the start of a stew to make them more delicious, and I could often identify the seasonings and techniques that had been used in a finished dish. And so, in a sense, following a new French recipe was easy, it was just a matter of assembling it from the basic building blocks, the rudimentary culinary processes. The elements themselves were rarely new, however unfamiliar their combination. Even without a recipe, I could look at an ingredient and think of several ways of cooking it. But with Chinese cookery I hadn't a clue.

In those private classes with Teacher Gan, I began to learn the basic grammar not only of Sichuanese, but also of Chinese cuisine. An understanding of its structures and processes started to coalesce through the repetition of steps that at first seemed random. As the weeks passed, I found I could watch Chinese friends cooking at home and understand some of what was going on in the wok. And it was thrilling to be able to reproduce a few of the sumptuous dishes I was guzzling every night in the Bamboo Bar and the 'Italian' restaurant. Very quickly, I was hooked.

After each class Volker and I cycled back to the university with tin lunchboxes filled with the fruits of our culinary endeavours, which we submitted to a devouring crowd of fellow foreign students for tasting and assessment. The classes became the highlight of my week. I was in my element.

But time was running out. The cookery classes came to an end, and so did my scholarship. I decided to delay going home, and spent a long summer travelling around Tibet and Gansu Province with my Italian friends Francesca, Davide and Graci. We headed north from Chengdu into the forbidden areas of eastern Tibet, where we were arrested in every county town and had to sweet-talk our way out of fines in countless police stations. We hitchhiked on the back of rattling timber trucks, clinging to piles of unsteady tree trunks with a motley assortment of Tibetan monks and Chinese peasants. (After one particularly perilous ride, along the edge of a crumbling precipice, we discovered that our driver had only one eye.)

It was a magical, unforgettable trip. We crossed wild open countryside to visit remote monasteries, meeting farmers, smugglers, nuns and secret policemen. And every so often, out of the brilliant blue emptiness of the sky around us would echo the sound of horse hooves, and a few Tibetans, dressed like medieval princes in red woollen cloaks edged in gilding and fur, tied around their waists and slung roguishly off one shoulder, would gallop past, their horses' hooves kicking up a cloud of yellow dust. We travelled in a state of awe and wonder.

But if our senses were overwhelmed by the sights and sounds of Tibet, we nearly went crazy with boredom at the food. Sometimes we ate the Tibetan staple, *tsampa*, with monks in their hilltop monasteries, rolling the ground barley flour and yak butter tea with our fingers into balls which we popped into our mouths. Otherwise, day after day, meal after meal, we ate in Hui Muslim restaurants that served almost nothing but pasta in different shapes, flavoured with gristly goat or mutton, green onions and chilli. Most ubiquitous were square sheets of pasta called 'pasta slices' (*mian pian*), which were delicious the first fifteen or twenty times, but which we eventually hated so much we called them 'business cards' (*ming pian*).

One day, after a couple of weeks on the road, we fetched up in a one-horse village on the grasslands, where the usual Hui-run restaurant catered to passing pilgrims, nomads and traders. Tired, hungry and emotionally drained after another terrifying truck ride, we entered the shabby dining room, and were amazed to see an elaborate French menu chalked up on a blackboard near the kitchen. It read:

• MENU •

Foie gras

~

Consommé celestin

~

L'homard grillé

~

Sorbet

(The rest had been rubbed off.)

It was like an hallucination, a shimmering mirage in the dusty eyes of desert wanderers. It was also one of the most exquisitely painful jokes I have ever encountered, and I have often wondered what genius of dry wit was its author (if you are reading this book, please get in touch!). We read, we yearned, we moaned, and then we sat down to our bowlfuls of business cards with gristly mutton, green onion and chilli.

After two months of being richly fed with the beauty and spirituality of eastern Tibet, but starved in a more literal sense, I made my way back towards Chengdu alone, on the slow road that winds south over the grasslands from Lanzhou (the Italians had gone back to Venice to resume their university studies). Sometime in early September I fetched up in Zoigê, which had the wild feel of a frontier town. Tibetans in flamboyant cloaks and hats, edged in rare furs, daggers at their waists, hung around one-storey wooden shops. Horses were tethered along the street. And as I left the long-distance bus station and hauled my backpack towards the only guesthouse at which foreigners were admitted, my nostrils were assailed by the umistakeable scents of sizzling Sichuanese chilli bean paste and Sichuan pepper. My heart leapt: I knew I was on my way home. I ate that night in a small Sichuanese restaurant, which didn't serve namecards with mutton and onion, but fish-fragrant aubergines and twice-cooked pork.

Arriving back in Chengdu, I didn't really have a plan. I had agreed to take over a flat in a workers' district from a British friend, for the princely sum of about £40 a month, with a vague notion of learning more about Sichuanese cookery. Through devious means I had managed to extend my green residence card for six months, although I was no longer at the university. It was unusual, then, for foreigners to live independently in China, and, strictly speaking, illegal. A few years before, it would not have been possible. But now the local police simply registered me and didn't seem to want to know the details.

Soon after my return, I cycled over to the cooking school to say hello to my teachers. I wanted to ask them if I might drop in from time to time to watch a few cooking demonstrations. But the principal welcomed me as an old friend, and told me that a three-month professional chef's training course had just begun. 'Why don't you join?' he asked me. It was a remarkable invitation. No foreigner had ever been accepted as a regular student before, and I suspect this, too, was technically illegal. But China was changing, the borders of possibility were expanding fast, and I had the impression that my teachers had been rather touched by this foreigner's inexplicable passion for their local cuisine. I agreed on the spot. Out of sheer kindness, the school allowed me to pay the same modest fees as my Chinese classmates, which amounted to around £100, all inclusive, for a three-month, full-time course. I enrolled and was promptly issued with a cleaver, a set of chef's whites printed with the name of the school, and two textbooks in Chinese, one on culinary theory, and one a collection of Sichuanese recipes.

And so my real apprenticeship began.

English cooking, Chinese-style: Stuffed squid in black pepper and minced apple sauce

黑椒蘋果鮮魷

1 fresh squid
3.5 oz (100 g) minced pork
0.2 oz (5 g) finely chopped shallot
0.2 oz (5 g) finely chopped celery
0.2 oz (5 g) finely chopped carrot
Salt and ground black pepper
1 tbsp olive oil
Beef stock
2 bay leaves
0.7 oz (20 g) tomato
2 pickled gherkins
0.4 oz (10 g) cooked diced carrot
1 tbsp (0.5 oz/15 g) butter
1.4 oz (40 g) finely chopped apple
1 tsp red wine

1. Clean the squid.

2. Mix the pork with the shallot, celery and carrot and salt and pepper to taste, and use it to stuff the squid. Close the squid around the stuffing and fix with small bamboo skewers.

3. Fry the squid in olive oil on both sides, and then add the stock with some more shallot, the bay leaves and seasoning to taste. Bring to the boil, and then simmer until cooked through.

4. Place the squid on a serving dish. Garnish with the tomato, gherkins and cooked carrot.

5. Pour over a sauce made from butter, beef stock, apple, black pepper and red wine.

CHAPTER 5

The Cutting Edge

It is just before 9 a.m. in a classroom at the cooking school, and Teacher Long is explaining how to make *huo bao yao hua*, 'fire-exploded kidney flowers'. She draws a long flow chart on the blackboard in powdery chalk as she takes us through the various procedures of the recipe, scrawling down the technical terms in Chinese characters. It's all very systematic. The cooking method is *huo bao*, 'fire-exploding', a variation of basic stir-frying that involves cooking finely cut ingredients very fast over a high flame. The flavour profile is *han xian wei*, salty-savoury flavour. And because pig's kidneys, the main ingredient, have a distinctive 'off-taste' (*yi wei*), or more specifically a 'uriney taste' (*sao wei*) in their raw state, it is essential to marinate them in Shaoxing wine to refine and elevate their flavour.

This is all rather a lot to be taking in so early in the morning, especially when you are the only non-native speaker of Chinese in a class of nearly fifty students, and possibly the first Westerner ever to have attempted to train as a chef in China. Most of my classmates are young Sichuanese men in their late teens or early twenties; only two of them are women. I am not just the only foreigner in the class, but the only foreigner most of my classmates have ever met. I sit at a wooden desk somewhere in the middle of the room, my notebook and pen at the ready. The desk has been carved with graffiti by previous generations of students, their names gouged into the wood with the sharp vegetable-carving knives they sell in the school shop. Several of my classmates are puffing away at cigarettes, and sit enveloped in clouds of smoke. The young bloke next to me has a lump of dough in his hand, with which he dreamily forms and reforms the same frilly dumpling as he half-listens to the teacher.

Teacher Long outlines the *te dian* or 'special characteristics' of the dish: 'You must make sure,' she says, 'that the kidneys are cut attractively (*yao hua xing mei guan*), that they are both tender and crisp in the mouth (*zhi nen cui*), and that the taste is savoury and delicious (*wei xian mei*).' The *te dian* are one of the most important parts of the lesson. We never use weighing scales or measuring spoons at the cooking school except in pastry class; we have to learn how to judge with our senses when a dish looks, smells, tastes and feels right at every stage of its preparation. And despite the lingering pretence that China is a socialist country, every dish we learn at the school is firmly fixed in a class hierarchy. Some recipes might be suitable for serving among the hot dishes at an 'ordinary feast'; others to be the grand 'head dish' of a top-class banquet. 'Fire-exploded kidney flowers', however, is a relatively humble affair: 'convenient food for the masses,' says Teacher Long.

After their initial amazement at being expected to study alongside a foreigner, or *lao wai*, most of my classmates have become used to me, although many of them still find the idea of actually talking to me impossibly daunting. They skirt around me as if I am some kind of freak, snigger amongst themselves when I address them, and avoid looking me in the eye. It takes weeks of good-humoured lobbying on my part before I can persuade some of them to stop calling me *lao wai* to my face, and to use instead my Chinese name, *fu xia*, or at least the more friendly term *tong xue*: 'classmate'.

Of course there are exceptions, like Wang Fang, one of the two other women in the class, who has become a particular ally. Her husband has won a scholarship to go to America for his PhD, and she wants to learn to cook so that she can pick up part-time work in restaurants when she goes over there to join him. Perhaps because of this prospect of travelling abroad, she is outward-looking and delighted to have the chance to associate with a foreigner. Right from the beginning, she treats me as a person rather than a circus animal or a Martian. But she is the only student from a relatively 'cultured' background. Our other female classmate is from a peasant household and is overcome with smiling bashfulness whenever she comes face to face with me.

Most of the boys are from working-class or peasant homes. I make friends with one or two of them, including a rosy-faced and exuberant seventeen-year-old called Zeng Bo who breaks the ice by inviting me to his grandmother's birthday party. He is a naively devoted communist who believes the party line that the students who demonstrated in Tiananmen Square in 1989 were manipulated by 'a small handful of political renegades'. But although he is devoted to the Party and dreams of becoming a member like his father and grandfather, he is even more devoted to food. His full, round face lights up as he describes his favourite dishes; his plump, red lips murmur their praises. I find in him a kindred spirit.

While I said that enrolling at the cooking school marked the start of my apprenticeship, that's actually an anachronism, because the system of apprenticeship – officially, at least – is long dead. In the old days, all professional culinary wisdom was passed on orally from master to apprentice; written cookery books barely existed. When a master chef, or *shi fu*, needed some help in his kitchen, he took on as apprentices, or *tu di*, boys in their early teens, who would serve him for years in return for bed and board and a culinary education. They had to rise early to begin making doughs and chopping vegetables; stay up late into the night washing dishes. If their master was cruel, it could be a form of slavery: many apprentices were beaten and abused. Luckier ones found themselves welcomed into the bosom of their masters' families, and treated as adopted sons. Whole networks of professional kinship spread out from masters' kitchens: for the rest of their lives, chefs would speak of those who had trained with the same master as *shi xiong* (older brother under the same teacher) and *shi di* (younger brother under the same teacher).

The master cooks often feared that their apprentices, growing in skills and experience, would steal their secrets and become professional rivals. And so arose the tradition of *liu yi shou*, 'holding back a trick or two'. Talented chefs would deliberately mislead their apprentices, handing down incomplete recipes, giving erroneous instructions, or adding vital ingredients to their soups in secret. And so, according to legend, many of the greatest recipes in Chinese culinary history died out with the masters who made them. Contemporary chefs and gourmets groan when they imagine what has been lost over the centuries, and accuse the jealous old masters of dereliction in their duty to Chinese cuisine.

The master-apprentice system declined during the Cultural Revolution, when haute cuisine was blacklisted and even small-time street traders were banned as capitalists. Senior chefs were persecuted, and the new doctrine of equality smashed the bond of subservience between apprentice and master. Some masters, humiliated by their students after a lifetime of respect, gave up hope in their profession, and refused to continue teaching, even when the madness of the political campaigns subsided.

In the late seventies and early eighties, when the post-Mao government started trying to pick up the pieces after the 'Decade of Chaos', there was a movement to codify and modernise Chinese cuisine. The Culinary Association of China was established, with branches all over the country, to research and promote food culture, and regional cookery books rolled off the presses. The Sichuan Institute of Higher Cuisine was founded in Chengdu in 1985: its mission to teach systematically and professionally, without the feudalistic practices of 'holding back tricks' and institutionalised slavery. Students would learn the techniques that enabled them to create their own dishes, rather than a set repertoire of recipes from a single master. My own teachers there, who themselves had been among the first graduates of the school, promised me and my fellow students that they would teach us everything they knew.

The creation of professional cooking academies was a valiant attempt to modernise attitudes, but echoes of the old apprentice system linger. Restaurant chefs continue to speak of their *shi fus* and fellow apprentices, and many people regard the old ways as superior. 'The difference between the old apprentices and modern students is like the difference between free-range and battery eggs,' one elderly gourmet told me. 'In a cooking school you can produce more chefs, more quickly, but they don't taste as good!'

Mandarin, or Standard Chinese, was officially the language of the classroom all over China, but in practice Teacher Long, like the other teachers at the cooking school, conducted her classes in broad Sichuan dialect. After all, that's what everyone spoke in Chengdu, apart from a few people like me, and as they say in far-flung provinces like Sichuan, 'Heaven is high and the Emperor is far away'. The constant barrage of dialect was a gruelling initiation for me. Although I'd already lived in Chengdu for a year and picked up a few of its words and phrases, most Chinese people switched to Mandarin when they talked to me, so this was my first experience of total immersion. As Teacher Long scribbled in chalk on the blackboard, I struggled to keep up with the flood of unfamiliar words. She didn't write very clearly either, so the characters on the board were usually what the Chinese call 'grassy' (*cao*): fluid and scrawly. I had to beg my classmates to help me out, rewriting the characters in clear strokes in my notebook so I could look them up later in a dictionary. On occasion Wang Fang lent me her notes, which I would photocopy and use to catch up in my own time.

Sichuanese dialect is like Mandarin put through a mangle. So the Mandarin 'sh' becomes 's', vowels are stretched out like warm toffee, there are pirate-like rolling 'r' sounds at the end of sentences, and no one can tell the difference between 'n' and 'l' or 'f' and 'h' (the province of Hunan, for example, is known in Sichuan, helpfully, as 'Fulan'). Furthermore, learning the tones of Mandarin Chinese is difficult enough to begin with: you must distinguish between the flat first tone (*mā*), the rising second tone (*má*), the dipping third tone (*mǎ*), and the fast-falling fourth tone (*mà*), not to mention the unobstrusive neutral tone (*ma*). If you have no sense of tones when speaking Mandarin, people won't understand you, and you may find yourself making mistakes like asking for a kiss (*qǐng wěn*) when you all you wanted was an answer to a question (*qǐng wèn*). But in Sichuanese even the standard tones are all over the place.

And then there are the pure dialect words, which are charming when you get to know them but initially incomprehensible: '*me dei*' instead of '*mei you*', meaning 'have not'; '*sa zi*' instead of '*shen me*' for 'what?', '*bu shao di*' instead of '*wo bu zhi dao*' for 'I don't know'; not to mention a whole gamut of fruity slang and swear words. Luckily, my burning curiosity about Sichuanese cookery spurred me on to retune my ears and tongue, and I learnt, fast. It didn't take long before my pure Chinese-lesson Mandarin was on the skids, and before people I met from Beijing and Shanghai were asking me why on earth I was talking with a Sichuanese accent.

I was also flung headlong into a maelstrom of specialised culinary vocabulary. Professional Chinese cookery is serious, complex and sophisticated. Like the French, with their great canon of sauces, all richly differentiated, and their structured approach to the kitchen and the culinary arts, the Chinese make minute distinctions between different shapes into which ingredients may be cut, different combinations of tastes, and different kinds of braising and stir-frying. The basic word *chao*, for example, means 'stir-fry', but if you want to be really precise, you should specify whether you mean *hua chao* ('slippery stir-fry'), *bao chao* ('explode stir-fry'), *xiao chao* ('small, simple stir-fry'), *sheng chao* ('raw stir-fry'), *shu chao* ('cooked stir-fry'), *chao xiang* ('stir-fry until fragrant'), *yan chao* ('salt stir-fry'), or *sha chao* ('sand stir-fry'). And those are just the ones that I can remember off the top of my head.

One Sichuanese culinary encyclopaedia lists fifty-six different cooking methods currently used in Sichuan. If you go to Beijing, Guangzhou or Shanghai, you'll find countless others, some of them very local and specific. Even as far back as the second century BC, when my own Iron Age ancestors were living in thatched huts on a primitive diet of bread, meat and porridge, a burial inventory found in a Chinese aristocrat's tomb in Hunan listed more than ten different cooking and food-preserving methods, not to mention a whole variety of different cuts of meat, types of stew and seasonings. The Chinese knew how to eat well, even then.

Some of the characters that Teacher Long and her colleagues wrote on the board were so specialised and obscure that they were not listed in mainstream dictionaries. Even my clever, academic Chinese friends at the university couldn't help me when I was stuck with my cooking school textbook, because they didn't know the characters for 'slow-braising with a gently simmering sauce that makes a sound like *gu du gu du gu du*', or 'muttony odour'. I took a voracious pleasure in collecting these arcane terms, learning them like a sutra. (As a result, after my long apprenticeship in Chinese cookery, I have the most bizarre vocabulary of any foreign student of Chinese. I can write out the name of an obscure fungus or an ancient term for pork, and recognise the words for the 'silver ingot' shape of certain dumplings or the bouncy texture of a squid ball – to the astonishment of Chinese culinary professionals – but I couldn't tell you how to write some perfectly ordinary words like 'bank account', 'shy' or 'tennis'.)

After the morning break, we all reassemble in the demonstration room, where curved benches rise steeply in rows above the cooking station. It's like an amphitheatre where some magnificent sporting feat is about to take place. Which, in a way, it is. There's always a scramble for seats at the front, because we know by now that if you sit there you'll get the first chance at the tasting, before your greedy classmates have scraped the platter clean. The air is hot with anticipation. Teacher Long is already preparing the *fu liao*, the accompanying ingredients: ginger, garlic, spring onions, long scarlet pickled chillies, and *wo sun*, the crisp, jade-green stem of a local variety of lettuce.

When we have all quietened down, she begins to give us a detailed explanation of how to cut them. The ginger and garlic, peeled, must be cut into *zhi jia pian*, 'thumbnail slices', she says. Teacher Long wields the broad blade of her cleaver as delicately as a scalpel, reducing the tiny garlic cloves and peeled ginger root to a pile of thin, even slices. She cuts the onions and chillies into long diagonal slices called *ma er duo*, or 'horse's ears', and the lettuce stem into *kuai zi tiao*, 'chopstick strips'. The real technical nightmare of this dish, however, lies not in using a large cleaver to chop garlic cloves without also chopping off your fingers, but in cutting the kidneys themselves. 'Kidney flowers', the rather poetic phrase in the name of the dish, refers to the delicate way in which the kidneys are cut, so that when they are cooked in the fiery-hot oil, they curl up into delightfully frilly little morsels, and don't look like kidneys at all.

Teacher Long peels off the thin, silken membranes of the kidneys, lays them on the chopping board and then slices them in half, her razor-sharp cleaver parallel to the board. She shaves off the pale delta of white drainage tubes, leaving clean the dark, metal-pink flesh. And then it all gets very complicated. She holds the blade at a slanting angle, and covers each kidney with surgical incisions, each one a few millimetres apart from the last, cutting about two-thirds of the way into the flesh but not all the way through, until the whole surface is covered with perfectly precise slashes. Then she turns each kidney so the cuts she has already made are at right angles to the knife, and makes more rows of cuts, close together. And here it gets even more fiddly: each perpendicular cut goes all the way through to the board for *part* of its length, except for every third cut, which goes all the way through for its *whole* length… so she ends up with trios of jagged frills of kidney, joined together at one end. 'These are called "phoenix tails" (*feng wei*),' she tells us. 'Of course, you can also cut them into *eyebrows*,' she continues, giving further, even more complicated, instructions.

Cutting is one of the fundamental skills of the Chinese kitchen, as central to it as the application of fire and flavour. In ancient China, cooking itself was known as *ge peng*, 'to cut and to cook'; and every lesson for a trainee Chinese chef still involves precise instructions for exactly *how* everything should be chopped. This is partly because of the prevalence of fast stir-frying as a cooking method. For a stir-fry, all the ingredients must be cut into small pieces that need little more than a lick of heat to be cooked. If the pieces are too big, they will remain raw inside while their outsides become dry and 'old' (*lao*). If they are cut unevenly, they will all be cooked at different times, so the final result will be rough and unsatisfactory. And with really fast stir-frying methods such as *bao*, which literally means 'burst' or 'explode', the fine, even chopping of ingredients is even more essential. Careful cutting is not a cosmetic matter: it is integral to the success of the final dish.

Chopsticks, used in China for two, maybe even three thousand years, make their own demands. Knives are almost never seen on the Chinese dinner table, so food must be tender enough to be torn gently apart with chopsticks, or otherwise cut into bite-sized pieces. At grand feasts, you may find whole ducks, chickens or pork knuckles, braised so lovingly that they melt away at the touch of a chopstick, but for everyday meals, almost everything is finely sliced or slivered.

But these are simply the practicalities of cutting. What are even more fascinating are its aesthetic aspects. Skilful cutting adds an extra dimension to the enjoyment of a dish. Think only of a stir-fry of eel and vegetables where all the ingredients, different though they may be in colour, taste and texture, are cut into similar snaking strands; or the delicacy of intention that cuts chicken and spring-onion whites into tiny cubes to echo the small, solid shape of the peanuts in Gong Bao Chicken. Delicate cutting is part of a refined and civilised culinary culture that has existed in China for thousands of years. In the fifth century BC, Confucius himself allegedly refused to eat food that wasn't properly cut. 'Knife skills' (*dao gong*) are still the starting point for any aspiring chef.

The meticulous Chinese approach to cutting has spawned a highly elaborate vocabulary. Chefs speak of at least three basic ways of cutting, including vertical slicing (*qie*), horizontal slicing (*pian*) and chopping (*zhan or kan*).

When the angle of the knife and the direction of cutting are taken into account, these multiply into at least fifteen variations, each with a different name. Another dozen or so terms refer to further knife techniques, including pounding (*chui*), scraping (*gua*) and gouging (*wan*).

There is also an extensive vocabulary, some of it quite poetic, to describe the shapes into which cooking ingredients can be cut. There are simple slices (*pian*), strips (*tiao*), chunks (*kuai*), small cubes (*ding*) and slivers (*si*). Each of these has many variations, depending on their precise shapes and dimensions: a slice, for example, might be a small 'thumbnail slice', a rectangular 'domino slice' or a large, ultra-thin 'ox-tongue slice'. Spring onions can be cut into 'flowers', 'fish eyes' or 'silken threads'. All this contributes greatly to the thrilling diversity of Chinese cuisine. Even an everyday ingredient such as pork can reveal so many different selves, depending on whether it is cut into sinuous slivers, tender cubes, juicy mince or gentle slices.

Given the complexity of the art of cutting, you might expect the Chinese chef to have a whole armoury of fancy knives at his disposal. Nothing, however, could be further from the truth. The instrument of almost all this artistry is the simple cleaver, a hammered blade of carbon steel with a wooden handle and a well-honed edge.

At breaktimes, the corridors of the cooking school were filled with young men bearing lethally sharp cleavers, dangling from their hands in the most nonchalant manner. For me, this took some getting used to. In the beginning, I retained my European view of the cleaver as a bloody, murderous knife, the kind of thing a psychopath or a triad hitman might use on a drunken rampage. It was only later that I began to appreciate it as the subtle, versatile instrument that it really is. Soon I, too, had a cleaver by my side at all times. During breaks, I sharpened it on the giant whetstone in the school yard like my classmates, keeping it keen.

The Chinese kitchen cleaver is not a butcher's knife. There are, it's true, heavy cleavers for chopping through pork ribs or the carcasses of fowl. But the everyday cleaver, the *cai dao* or 'vegetable knife', is unexpectedly light and dextrous, as suitable for slicing a small shallot as a great hunk of meat, and used by everyone from the most macho chef to the frailest old lady. A single cleaver can be used to perform almost every task, from chopping a lotus root to peeling a tiny piece of ginger, and it's often the only knife in a Chinese kitchen.

The cleaver is not just for cutting. Invert it and its blunt spine can be used to pound meat to a paste for meatballs: a time-consuming method, but the purée it produces is perfectly smooth and voluptuous. The nub of the handle can stand in for a pestle, to crush a few peppercorns in a pot. The flat of the blade, slammed down on the board, can be used to smash unpeeled ginger, so that its juices permeate a soup or marinade. Best of all, the flat blade can be used to scoop up whatever is on your chopping board, and transfer it to the pot or wok.

My parents gave me a set of fully-forged Sabatier kitchen knives for my twenty-first birthday, but these days, back home in London, I rarely use them. My hand-made Sichuanese knife has become my indispensable cooking tool; it's like a talisman. I bought it in a street market in Chengdu, for the equivalent of a couple of pounds, and I've been using it for years. I know its breadth and its heaviness, the exact shape of its handle, the pewter tones of its carbon-steel blade. I like to hold it in my hand, to feel its lightness and its weight, to place my palm on the flat of its blade, to hold it close to my chest. It makes me feel capable, it's a craftman's tool, dazzling in its multiplicity of uses. And it needs looking after, this knife of mine, honing on the whetstone, oiling to keep it from rust.

When I'm doing cooking demonstrations or making dinner at other people's homes I like to take it with me, wrapped in a cloth and stashed in my handbag. Many times I've travelled on the London Underground with my cleaver, or walked through a dangerous part of the city, late at night. As I wait on deserted station platforms, or make my way through a maze of tunnels, it gives me a sweet, secret pleasure to imagine what might happen if someone were fool enough to try to mug me. 'Shall we start with ox-tongue slices, or dominoes?' I might ask my assailant, blade gleaming in the half-light.

Cleavers, of course, are not only dangerous to those who try to cross a well-trained chef, but to the chef herself. Sharpened, they demand your full attention. If you don't cut mindfully, you may mutilate your hands. I once met a young chef who had lost the top joint of his index finger: he was working with a recently bandaged stump. In my first months in Chengdu I came close to this myself, as I was cutting a pile of candied fruits for a Christmas pudding. The knife was sticking, and dragging in the syrupy fruits. Tired, I became careless. I lost my concentration, and shaved a thick slice off the top of my finger, nail and all. It was a shocking accident, and I still bear the scar. But it reminded me to treat my cleaver with respect. Now, I understand that cutting can be a meditation, and why the great Taoist sage Zhuangzi used the tale of a chef and his knife as a metaphor for the art of living:

Cook Ting was butchering an ox for Lord Wen Hui. Every movement of his hand, every shrug of his shoulder, every step of his feet, every thrust of his knee, every sound of the sundering flesh and the swoosh of the descending knife, were all in perfect accord...

'Ah, how excellent!' said Lord Wen Hui. 'How has your skill become so superb?'

Cook Ting put down his knife and said, 'What your servant loves best is the Tao, which is better than any art. When I started to cut up oxen, what I saw was just a complete ox. After three years, I had learnt not to see the ox as a whole. Now I practise with my mind, not with my eyes. I ignore my sense and follow my spirit. I see the natural lines and my knife slides through the great hollows, follows the great cavities, using that which is already there to my advantage. Thus, I miss the great sinews and even more so, the great bones. A good cook changes his knife annually because he slices. An ordinary cook has to change his knife every month because he hacks. Now this knife of mine I have been using for nineteen years, and it has cut thousands of oxen. However, its blade is as sharp as if it had just been sharpened. Between the joints there are spaces, and the blade of a knife has no real thickness. If you put what has no thickness into spaces such as these, there is plenty of room, certainly enough for the knife to work through. However, when I come to a difficult part and can see that it will be difficult, I take care and pay due regard. I look carefully and I move with caution. Then, very gently, I move the knife until there is a parting and the flesh falls apart like a lump of earth falling to the ground. I stand with the knife in my hand looking around and then, with an air of satisfaction, I wipe the knife and put it away.'

'Splendid!' said Lord Wen Hui. 'I have heard what Cook Ting has to say and from his words I have learned how to live life fully.'

I was often reminded of Cook Ting when I watched our teachers give their demonstrations in that small amphitheatre. Teacher Long, showing us how to remove the bones and innards from a duck, which she would later fill with an 'eight-treasure stuffing', tying the duck around the waist with a cord so that its flesh swelled out on either side like a calabash gourd. She would make a small incision through the neck and spine with her cleaver and then proceed to undress the raw bird, casually removing its entire skin and flesh in one piece from the carcass as she chatted, coaxing out the leg- and wing-bones, caressing its ribcage with the huge shining blade. Or, on another day, Teacher Long's husband, Teacher Lu, cutting pork slivers with an expression of discreet pleasure on his face, his arms and shoulders soft and supple, his composure complete amid the chaos of the classroom.

Over time, Chinese cutting became part of my make-up, too. It began to influence the way in which I viewed the ingredients in my fridge, or assembled a European salad or a stew. Now, it is instinctive to me. I find I get confused when I'm helping a Western friend to prepare a meal. 'Can you just chop up some carrots?' they might say. 'But how do you want them cut?' I ask. 'Oh, just chop them,' they say. But in my mind there are now a thousand possibilities, there is no such thing as 'just chopping'. If I was cooking with a Chinese chef, it would be easy: he'd just say, 'Elephant-tusk strips, please', or, 'No. 2 thickness slivers,' and I'd know exactly what he meant.

Many of my classmates lived in dormitories upstairs at the cooking school, and sometimes the bolder among them would invite me up at lunchtime for a cup of tea and a game of cards or Mah Jong. Their rooms were crammed with bunk-beds, and hung with laundry. Sometimes they were used for nefarious activities, as I gathered one morning during a stern lecture by the school's principal. He admonished the students for gambling away their living allowances, and for smuggling their girlfriends in for the night. 'If you fritter away all your money at Mah Jong, you won't have anything left to eat,' he told us. And he gave his homily a Confucian slant: 'A good cook must lead a good life. Take Master Liu, a chef I know who is now eighty years old. He has never drunk or smoked, and he has always led a virtuous life. His cooking is incomparable.'

Living at the opposite end of town, near the university, I never witnessed any of these alcohol-fuelled orgies or reckless gambling sessions. After lunch, in the sleepy siesta hour, the atmosphere was rather more subdued. One afternoon, I sipped jasmine-blossom tea with a classmate as he gave me a tour of his miniature garden of carved vegetables. As his roommates snoozed or read cookery books, he showed me a painted landscape decorated with ornate pagodas made from pumpkin flesh; graceful swans fashioned out of pieces of white radish held together by toothpicks; carrot-flowers and purple-radish roses.

Chinese vegetable *carving* takes the art of cutting into another league. Here, the results are meant not to be eaten, but to be admired. The truly proficient Chinese chef is not merely a cook, but also a sculptor, like the French pâtissier, with his spun-silk caramel and sugar flowers. Food sculpture is the light-hearted, light-headed froth that floats at the top of the grandest culinary cultures. It is as ostentatious and utterly frivolous as the sugar-paste cathedrals designed by the nineteenth-century French master chef, Antonin Carême, who maintained that confectionary was the principal branch of architecture, itself one of the five fine arts. Vegetable carving can only exist in a society with a surplus of underpaid and underworked youths, who can be persuaded to spend hours engraving the outside of a watermelon with minutely realised scenes from a classic novel, or transforming an orange gourd into a vase carved with frilly-tailed goldfish playing at the base of a fragile water lily. Sometimes I find it fussy and ridiculous. But there is something enchanting about it, all the same.

At cooking competitions in modern China, young chefs may be expected to enter a 'craft dish' alongside the dishes that display their wok techniques and pastry-making skills. 'Craft dishes' include complicated, edible tableaux that have little to do with the practical requirements of either cooking or eating. At one contest I attended, each competitor had produced an ornamental cold platter, or *pin pan*, in which tiny slices of multicoloured ingredients were assembled into grandiloquent collages. One of the entries depicted a pair of swallows, their wings made of sliced thousand-year-old eggs, their bodies and long forked tails composed of hundreds of slices of cucumber skin. They were flying over a variegated landscape of sliced cold meats, including purplish liver, rosy ham and pale-pink prawns.

These food tableaux have a venerable history in China. Their originator is said to have been a tenth-century Buddhist nun, Fan Zheng, who recreated a series of twenty-one paintings and poems by the eighth-century artist Wang Wei in the form of twenty-one cold dishes. Using finely cut pieces of vegetables, gourds, meats and fermented fish, she offered an edible homage to the works that had inspired her, to the wonderment of her dinner guests.

When my classmates weren't carving their names into their desks, they were often toying with a carrot or an odd piece of radish, practising their sculpting techniques. They knew that, in their future careers, they might, on occasion, be required to produce a pumpkin dragon or an edible collage of the Great Wall of China. In the course of our regular culinary training, we had to learn about forty basic shapes into which raw ingredients could be cut, including nine different ways of cutting a spring onion alone. But this was child's play compared to the more esoteric art of vegetable carving.

So in the grand scale of things, cutting pig's kidneys into 'phoenix tails' or 'eyebrows' is fairly pedestrian. In the lecture theatre at the Sichuan Institute of Higher Cuisine, our demonstration is drawing to a close. Later, after lunch and a siesta, we will be let loose on our own sets of kidneys, which we will tear and mangle and cut into uneven pieces, before we acquire the knack of making phoenix tails. But now, after all her careful preparations, Teacher Long whips up the fire-exploded kidney flowers in a matter of seconds. The aromas of ginger, garlic and chilli rise steeply around the room. The kidney pieces curl up in the wok, and, then, for a few short seconds, I am able to admire them on the serving dish, marvelling at the way in which this clumsy offal has been transformed into the most tempting of delicacies. But then Teacher Long hands the plate over to the ravening masses. Students spill over the benches, jostle for position, thrust forward their chopsticks. There are a few whoops and slurps. And the kidneys are gone.

A FEW SHAPES FOR YOUR FOOD

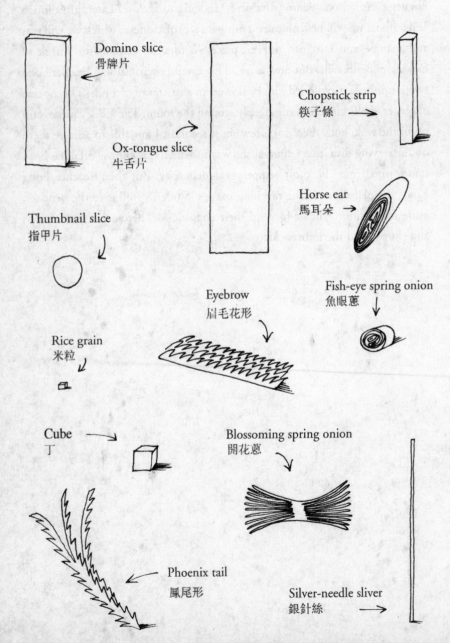

Domino slice
骨牌片

Chopstick strip
筷子條 →

Ox-tongue slice
牛舌片

Horse ear
馬耳朵 →

Thumbnail slice
指甲片

Eyebrow
眉毛花形

Fish-eye spring onion
魚眼蔥

Rice grain
米粒

Cube
丁

Blossoming spring onion
開花蔥

Phoenix tail
鳳尾形

Silver-needle sliver
銀針絲 →

CHAPTER 6

The Root of Tastes

It is my turn at the wok. My classmates leer over me, ready for a laugh. Every afternoon, we cook in the same teams of ten, gathered round a table, with two gas burners, a couple of woks, a chopping board and a few bowls and plates at our disposal. None of my particular friends are in my team, so I am obliged to work with nine young men who make strenuous efforts to avoid talking to me, and who are openly sceptical about the idea of a foreign *woman* becoming a Sichuanese chef. It is tedious, really. I have to fight to participate when we divide up the tasks, or else I find they all scarper to the store cupboards and the sinks without me. And I have to draw on all my reserves of bossy older sisterliness to engage them in the most trivial conversation. But, as always, the cooking itself makes me so sweetly happy that I don't really care about these inconveniences.

I flick on the gas tap and light the burner, ladle some oil into the blackened wok. My teammates smirk, and someone makes a witty remark under his breath in Sichuanese dialect which I don't understand. I just ignore him, and concentrate on the cooking. I have prepped my ingredients already: the snaking strands of pork, marinated in salt, soy sauce, Shaoxing wine and wet pea-starch; the ribbons of cloud-ear fungus; the pale-green slivers of lettuce stem; the pickled chilli paste; the garlic, spring onion and ginger. These are the ingredients of fish-fragrant pork, one of the most famous of all Sichuanese dishes.

When the oil is hot, I tip in the pork and stir-fry briskly as the slivers separate and whiten. Then I tilt the wok, so the oil pools at the side, directly over the flame, and add the pickled chilli paste, which stains the oil a deep, rich orange. I scatter in the ginger and garlic, stirring as they release their punchy fragrances, add the vegetables, mix everything together. Finally, I pour in the sauce, a mixture of sugar, soy sauce and vinegar, with a little starch to make it thicken and cling. Seconds later, the dish is finished, and I ladle it neatly onto a small oval plate. It has turned out rather well. The lazy strands of pork are tender and glossy, entwined with the dark fungus and the green lettuce. The red oil pools prettily around the edges of the dish, and it smells extraordinarily good. My classmates are disappointed by my success, and I feel extremely smug. Ha!

We all take turns to cook amid the jostling, subversive crowd. The boys are merciless in their criticism of each other, and of me. If anything goes wrong, they jeer and giggle. Every failure is jubilantly ridiculed. 'Too much oil!' 'It's all dried out!' 'The sauce has gone all sticky!' 'You stupid melon! (*sha gua*)' As each of us finishes, we troop off to the side of the room, where Teacher Lu is ready to assess our efforts. He sits there with his usual benign smile, but is precise in his criticisms. He ticks us off for careless or irregular cutting: '*Bu hao kan*! (unattractive!) You've got thin slivers, thick slivers and chopstick strips, all mixed up together!' He can tell from the smell of the dish and the texture of the pork if the oil temperature was too hot or too cool, and he will taste to see how skilfully we have balanced the flavours. Today, he approves of my fish-fragrant pork. '*Bu cuo bu cuo* (not bad, not bad),' he says.

Unfortunately we are not allowed to eat what we cook, though we may taste it. The finished dishes are bagged up and sold from a table at the school gates to people in the neighbourhood. They are brave, these guinea pigs, because it's such a lottery: one day they might end up with an appetising supper, another day some ghastly, oversalted, stodgy mess. Reluctantly, I hand over my dish in its haze of delicious aromas, and go back to watch my classmates run the gauntlet of their peers.

Everything we made at the Sichuan Institute of Higher Cuisine was cooked from scratch. We had only rudimentary equipment: there were no mincing machines or food processors to save us time. If we were making pork balls, we had to pound the meat to a paste with the backs of our cleavers, teasing out with our fingertips every wisp of sinew. Eggwhites were whisked on a plate, with a pair of chopsticks. If we were using walnuts, we had to crack them open, soak them and then, laboriously, peel off their skins. ('Sichuanese cookery is so *ma fan*, so much trouble,' moaned one of my classmates, coaxing reluctant shreds of skin from a walnut kernel, dismayed at the prospect of a lifetime performing such tasks.) Some of the ingredients were still alive when we got them. We scrambled competitively to be first to collect our team's allocation of, say, thirty glinting crucian carp, which we had to clean in the sinks on the balcony, ripping their gills out and slitting their bellies as they jumped and twitched in our hands.

As a child, my dream was to live in a cottage in the country, doing everything by hand. I wanted to grow my own vegetables, rear chickens, bake bread, make jam. Growing up, I was moved by the beauty of raw things, the silvery gleam of a fish in my hands, pink juices flowing from a cut beetroot. I enjoyed the kind of basic kitchen jobs that might seem boring to anybody else, like picking over a trayful of rice for stones, or topping and tailing green beans. Teenaged, I learned how to pluck and clean pheasants, and I made my own pastry and mayonnaise by hand. My family mocked me. 'When you grow up, you'll have machines to do everything. It's just a fantasy.' (I think I have the last laugh: years later, I still live without a television, a dishwasher or a microwave, and I still pluck pheasants and make pastry and mayonnaise by hand.)

Life in Chengdu in the mid-nineties appealed to this old longing of mine for the fundamentals of cookery. There were no shortcuts. Centuries-old methods of food preservation were used in most households. On sunny days, the backstreets were hung with cabbage leaves, which had to be half-dried before they could be rubbed with salt and spices and packed into jars to ferment. There were coils of drying tangerine peel on everyone's windowsills. And as the Chinese New Year approached, people started to smoke bacon and make sausages, hanging them out to wind-dry under the eaves.

At the cooking school, the pickles we used in our recipes were made in the traditional manner. There was a storeroom where waist-high clay jars lurked in a constant twilight. We lifted the inverted bowls that covered their mouths, and reached into the glowing scarlet of pickled chillies in brine, plucking them out with our chopsticks. When we wanted to lend a rich brown colour to a stew, we caramelised our own sugar in oil. There were no ready-made sauces, except for the slowly fermented chilli bean paste; we mixed them ourselves from the essential seasonings: sugar, vinegar, soy sauce and sesame paste in various combinations. I loved the alchemy of it, conjuring such basic elements into gold, my only tools a knife, a ladle, a board and a wok.

There was only one thing that jarred for me in this prelapsarian world of cooking, and that was the use of monosodium glutamate, or MSG. Like most Westerners, I saw MSG as a nasty artificial additive, used only in junk food and trashy takeaways. In England, you never find MSG in a domestic kitchen, and it would be a public scandal if it was discovered in the store cupboard of a serious restaurant. Yet in China, every kitchen has its jar of MSG, tucked away amid the soy sauces and vinegars. Top chefs use it in their most acclaimed dishes, and it is treated as a normal seasoning at the Sichuan Institute of Higher Cuisine, the nation's top school for chefs. The Chinese even call this white powder *wei jing*, 'the essence of taste', and translate it into English as 'gourmet powder' (*jing* itself means not only 'essence', but also, among other things, 'refined, perfect, meticulous, clever, skilled, energy, spirit and sperm', which gives you some idea of what a wonderful word it is). There is no shame, in China, in using MSG.

MSG is not a traditional ingredient in Chinese cookery. It was discovered in 1908 by the Japanese scientist, Kikunae Ikeda, who was intrigued by the intensely delicious taste of the broth made from kombu seaweed. In his laboratory, he managed to isolate its source, glutamates in the seaweed, and to their wonderful taste he gave the name *umami*, derived from the Japanese word for 'delicious'. His findings led directly to the industrial manufacture in Japan, and then worldwide, of MSG.

In the beginning, MSG was thought by scientists to be just a 'flavour enhancer', a substance with little taste of its own, but able to react with various savoury flavours to produce a pleasant sensory kick. Recently, however, biologists have found that human tongues have specialised receptors that pick up on the taste of MSG and a wider family of *umami* compounds, and that some of our brain cells respond specifically to the *umami* taste. This has led to growing acceptance that *umami* is not merely a flavour-enhancer, but a discrete 'fifth taste' in its own right, alongside the traditional quartet of sweet, sour, salty and bitter.

Although *umami* is associated with manufactured MSG, the taste is found naturally in many animal and vegetable foods, such as tomatoes, shiitake mushrooms and tuna. Their *umami* flavours come from the building blocks of proteins, amino acids and nucleotides, which include not only glutamates, but also inosinates and guanylates. These delicious molecules appear when animal and vegetable proteins break down, which is why processes such as cooking, ripening and fermentation intensify *umami* tastes. Many of the flavours adored by Europeans and Americans, like those of Parma ham and Parmesan cheese, owe their intensity to these *umami* compounds.

The Chinese have been using *umami*-rich products such as black fermented soybeans and related sauces for more than two millennia. Intensely flavoured broths enhanced by cured ham and dried seafood are among the staple flavourings of traditional Chinese cuisine. Cheesy fermented beancurd and the preserved duck eggs that so appalled me on my first visit to Hong Kong are both prized for their strong and complex *umami* tastes. In a sense, MSG is simply a continuation of this tradition.

But why did the Chinese take to the use of manufactured MSG with such joy when the West rejected it? I suspect it's partly because the Chinese generally have a positive view of science and technology. The kind of Europeans who love to cook and eat often regard science as the enemy: epicurianism tends to go hand in hand with a kind of back-to-nature fundamentalism. People like me think that advances in food technology are forced on humanity by corrupt scientists in the pay of greedy multinational companies. We *expect* that genetic modification will lead to ecological disaster; we are *certain* that pesticides will give us cancer. MSG, as a relatively recent, and artificial, seasoning, is inherently dubious.

In China, it's different. People *like* science. In a country where famine and hunger are recent memories, and drought and floods a constant threat to agriculture, it's not surprising that people are more open to the possibilities of genetic modification. Advances in food technology and the availability of new household gadgets like washing machines have only just begun to liberate women from the treadmill of domestic labour: it's too early for nostalgia about 'doing everything by hand'. And there are also historical reasons for a widespread trust in the benefits of science and technology.

In the late nineteenth and early twentieth centuries, the evident supremacy of the Western powers triggered a crisis in Chinese identity. Some thinkers and political activists came to see traditional Chinese culture as *luo hou* (backward), as a millstone round the neck of the nation: they despised it. The future, they thought, lay in Western science and rationality. The philosophical turmoil of the educated class was one of the triggers of revolution. A century later, these anxieties about the Chinese past, and green-eyed envy of the West, are as strong as ever. Ironically, just as the Western middle classes are losing their faith in science, and getting soggy with emotion over the holistic traditions of the East, the Chinese seem to be on the brink of ditching what's left of their own philosophical and technological heritage.

When I first lived in China, traditional cookery, Tai Chi and Traditional Chinese Medicine were the norm, at least for the older generation. Now I meet young people who tell me they prefer sports to martial arts, pills to Chinese herbal medicine, and hamburgers to Chinese food, because they are 'modern'. In chefs' circles, the hot topic of discussion in recent years has been 'Western nutrition', which is seen as 'very scientific'. I wear myself out reminding advocates of Western nutrition that Westerners are totally confused about what they eat, and increasingly fat, cancerous and diabetic. We are drowning in scientific studies, I tell them! One month we are told that a glass of red wine a day will protect our hearts, the next month that it will give us heart attacks. Yesterday we were told to eat only protein and no carbohydrates, today we are told this will give us bad breath and kidney failure. Our food products are plastered with complicated information about salt and sugar content, calories, glycaemic indices – but does anyone actually know how to eat? Many people just go home and shove some rubbish in the microwave.

Contrast this with the traditional Chinese approach to food which is simple, holistic and, as far as I can see, remarkably beneficial. The older generation may not have figures and facts at their disposal, but they are masters in the art of balance in food. They know what to eat when they suffer from different kinds of illness and indisposition. They vary their diets according to the seasons, and their age. It's one of the things that impressed me most about China, this pervasive knowledge of how to eat well and healthily. 'Your traditional culture of food and medicine is one of the glories of Chinese civilisation! You should be teaching it to *us*!' I tell Chinese friends. They look at me, surprised and nonplussed, as if such a thought had never occurred to them.

MSG, of course, is very modern and scientific, which is clearly part of its appeal. But it must also have taken such a hold because of when it started to become widely available: the seventies. This was a period of great hardship in China, when meat was scarce and even grain was rationed. Suddenly, MSG offered the possibility of emulating the rich, savoury tastes of traditional stocks without using meat. It must have seemed like a miracle. Add a spoonful of MSG to a bowl of hot water, scatter in a few sliced spring onions, and you have a soup of sorts. Sprinkle some into a vegetable stir-fry and it will be fantastically delicious, as if you had added luxury ingredients like chicken oil or Yunnan ham.

My friend Zhou Yu grew up in Chongqing in the seventies. During the Cultural Revolution, he remembers hearing the sound of gunfire as rival Red Guard factions battled for supremacy on the streets. As a teenager, when he was showing signs of the rare talent at the *er hu* or two-stringed Chinese violin that would make his career, he yearned for the delicious savoury powder that added a speckle of stardust to the humblest broth. He vowed that, when he had his own income, he would eat it every day. And so, when he finally enrolled in the Sichuan Conservatory of Music, he celebrated by buying *four kilos* of MSG.

At the cooking school, my classmates and I learned how to add MSG in small quantities to dishes at the final stage of cooking, to enhance their *xian wei,* as the Chinese refer to *umami*. We were taught to mix it into dressings for cold meats and vegetables, and to use it as a dip for appetisers. We were told to add MSG to almost everything. It was and is the same in restaurant kitchens, where MSG is used almost as widely as salt. Superior chefs might be scornful of those who use it as a *substitute* for decent stocks and fine ingredients – I've heard them refer to such amateurs snidely as 'MSG chefs (*wei jing chu shi*)' – but they all use it as a flavour-enhancer.

The ubiquity of MSG in Chinese cookery puts me in a difficult position. Instinctively I loathe it, and I never use it when I cook at home. It's *fake*, it goes against all my principles. And I suspect that the excessive use of MSG in Chinese kitchens corrupts people's palates, deadening them to the pleasures of natural flavours. (Chinese chefs tell me they now have to use MSG, because their customers find everything tastes boring without it.) But is it any worse than refined salt or sugar, both of which are psychologically addictive and damaging in excess? There seems to be no conclusive proof that MSG is harmful to health: the existence of 'Chinese restaurant syndrome' has been widely discredited. Some scientists argue that MSG is a 'neuro-toxin' that overstimulates the pancreas and the nervous system, triggering diseases like autism, asthma, diabetes and obesity: but I'm not in a position to assess their findings myself, and I've seen little reflection of such theories in the wider MSG debate. Furthermore, all my great Chinese culinary heroes use MSG, and their food tastes delicious.

Frankly, I'm still confused about MSG, but I made the choice long ago not to use it in my own cooking. I don't find it necessary, since I buy good ingredients and make my own stocks. I'm also tired of being bombarded with MSG-laden food in Chinese restaurants which makes me thirsty and exhausts my palate. I prefer flavours that are gentler and more natural. For me, MSG is the cook's cocaine, a white powder that offers a turbo-charged intensity of gastronomic pleasure. But isn't life beautiful enough, without taking drugs?

I'm also conscious that, whether or not MSG really is a bad thing, Western prejudice about it has done untold damage to the international reputation of Chinese cuisine. And in my work as a sort of 'ambassador' for Chinese cookery, I realise that including it in recipes written for a Western readership would be shooting myself in the foot. So I stick to the traditional road, rejecting MSG just as I reject unnecessary kitchen gadgets and cable TV. Perhaps I'm still trying to prove something to my family.

Fortunately, my avoidance of MSG made absolutely no difference to my training as Sichuanese chef. No dish *relies* on MSG, and no special techniques apply to it. It is simply added to the wok with other seasonings. So I just omitted it, end of story. And given the overwhelming intensity of the natural flavours of Sichuanese cookery, I didn't miss it at all. My classmates regarded this as eccentric, but then they regarded *everything* I did as eccentric. Not using MSG was just the kind of thing you'd expect from a green-eyed alien like me.

MSG aside, the consideration of flavour was a crucial part of my Sichuanese culinary education. It was a thread that ran through the theory lessons that began each school day, the demonstrations given by Teachers Long and Lu after the mid-morning break, and the practical classes that occupied the afternoons.

Our teachers introduced us to the unsavoury aspects of the natural flavours of meat, poultry, fish and seafood, known collectively as *yi wei*, 'off-tastes', and more specifically as *xing* (fishy), *shan* (muttony), and *sao* (foul, uriney) tastes or odours. As chefs, my classmates and I had to learn how to refine or dispel these unpleasant tastes, and to bring out the delicious *xian wei* (*umami* flavours) that lay behind them. So we blanched our ingredients in boiling water, or treated them with salt, Shaoxing wine, crushed spring onion and ginger; and we discarded the bloody juices that leaked from meat and poultry. With foodstuffs where the *yi wei* were particularly heavy, like beef and mutton, eels and offal, we would add the wine and seasonings with a generous hand, and freshen up the final dishes with garnishes of coriander. Such techniques have been used in China for thousands of years: the chef Yi Yin, who lived in the sixteenth century BC, warned of the fishy, foul and muttony flavours of some ingredients, but said they could become delicious if treated properly.

But these fundamentals are common to all Chinese regional cuisines. It's the *tiao wei*, the *mixing* of flavours, that is the fundamental skill of the Sichuanese chef and the most fun to learn. Outsiders, Chinese and foreign, tend to stereotype Sichuanese cuisine as being simply 'hot and spicy'. It's a gross oversimplification. What really distinguishes Sichuanese cookery is its mastery of the arts of flavour. Sichuanese chefs delight in combining a variety of basic tastes to create dazzling *fu he wei* (complex flavours). A well-orchestrated Sichuanese banquet will titillate your palate in every conceivable way: it will awaken your tastebuds through the judicious use of chilli oil, stimulate your tongue and lips with tingly Sichuan pepper, caress your palate with a spicy sweetness, electrify you with dry fried chillies, soothe you with sweet-and-sour, calm your spirits with a tonic soup. It's a thrilling rollercoaster ride. So many and varied are the *fu he wei* of the Sichuanese kitchen that one might twist the words of Samuel Johnson and say 'If a man is tired of Sichuanese food, he is tired of life.'

As trainee chefs, my classmates and I studied a canon of some twenty-three 'official' complex flavours – the equivalent, perhaps, of studying the composition of the 'official' French sauces. It wasn't a matter of exact measurements or precise ingredients, but of developing a sense of the character of each *fu he wei*, its balance of flavours, its strength and intensity. Take the fish-fragrant flavour (*yu xiang wei*) of our pork sliver recipe, for example, which derives its curious name from the fact that it uses the seasonings of traditional Sichuanese fish cookery (there is no actual fish in 'fish-fragrant' recipes).

'Fish-fragrant' is based on the mellow heat of pickled chillies, sometimes on their own, sometimes in combination with fermented broad beans in the famous Sichuanese chilli-bean paste, but always alongside the intense flavours of ginger, garlic and spring onion. Furthermore, it involves an element of sweet and sour. It's a classic *fu he wei*, engaging the palate simultaneously on several levels, and it's one of the most irresistible combinations of tastes you can imagine. Once you understand the mechanics of the 'fish-fragrant flavour' as a cook, you can apply it to all kinds of ingredients: cold chicken, slivered pork (the most famous 'fish-fragrant' dish), aubergines (that old favourite of mine), deep-fried chicken or seafood.

In contrast, there is the notorious *ma la wei* (numbing-and-hot flavour), which combines chilli heat with the tongue-numbing effects of Sichuan pepper. It can be quite overwhelming if you are not used to it, but it's not meant to be like slamming your tongue with a sledgehammer – more like *rousing* the palate and awakening it to the other flavours of the meal. There are other permutations of the chilli-and-Sichuan-pepper mix, like *hu la wei* ('scorched chilli flavour'). Here, the two spices are sizzled in oil until the chillies are darkening, but not yet burnt and bitter: a marvellous taste. Throw in a bit of sweet and sour, and you have *gong bao wei*, the sweet-sour-scorched chilli combination found in the famous Gong Bao (or Kung Po) chicken. And so on.

This emphasis on flavour makes Sichuanese a robust and confident cuisine. It doesn't rely too much on specialised local ingredients, like the cuisines of the eastern Chinese with their delicate water vegetables and acquatic creatures. You can't make a hairy-crab beancurd without a hairy crab, but you can make a 'fish-fragrant' dish or a 'numbing-and-hot' dish with *anything*. Perhaps this is why Sichuanese people are so open-minded and open-hearted compared with people in other parts of China: they don't have to worry that contact with the outside world will deprive them of their own identity. Just cover the outside world in a fish-fragrant sauce, and you will make it Sichuanese.

When we took our dishes to Teacher Lu for assessment, he would tell us if we had the balance of sweet and sour tastes right for the *li zhi wei* ('lychee flavour') needed for crispy rice crust with pork slices, or if we had made it so sweet that it spilled over into the territory of a regular sweet-and-sour. Had we managed to create the right degree of harmonised chaos for *guai wei* ('strange flavour'), where sesame paste, sesame oil, soy sauce, sugar, vinegar, chilli and Sichuan pepper were mixed together into a sauce for cold chicken? If one seasoning was out of proportion, the flavour would jangle. So we sat there like chemists, scraping our little china spoons in our bowls, mixing and tasting, trying to come up with the perfect formula.

As the one outsider in the class, I found myself not only learning the theory and practice of cooking, but also absorbing some Chinese ways of imagining flavour. On damp winter days, I knew I should eat more heating food than usual, so I spooned extra chilli oil on to my breakfast dumplings, and I discovered that sourness was refreshing in the sultry heat of summer. I learned how to say that someone who felt jealous in love was 'eating vinegar' (*chi cu*). And of course, I realised that 'eating bitterness' (*chi ku*) was the only way to describe the sorrows and hardships of existence. To learn the language of cookery in China was, in part, to learn the language of life. And as I went deeper into my culinary studies, I found that I was not only cooking, but also in some ways thinking, like a Chinese person.

I remember days when the dishes my classmates and I made turned out completely differently, although we were all supposedly following the same recipe. With fish-fragrant pork, the colour of our oil varied from clear to deep orange-red, the fragrance of the ginger-garlic-onion trinity in some of our efforts was light and raw, in others so profoundly mellow it made you sigh. The pork slivers were supple as custard, or slightly chewy and shrivelled. I gazed at the array of dishes laid out on the workbench in front of Teacher Lu. 'Why do they all look so different?' I asked him.

'*Huo hou,*' he replied, smiling at my puzzlement.

Huo hou literally means something like 'fire-time', and it refers to the control of the degree and duration of cooking heat. The third pillar of the Chinese culinary arts, after the arts of cutting and of mixing flavours, *huo hou* is probably the most difficult to master. It cannot be taught in a clinical way, it is grasped only through experience, by trial and error. It's not surprising, therefore, that *huo hou* can also be used to describe the attainment of great skill and sensitivity in other arts, like calligraphy. Taoists traditionally used it, too, to refer to their practice of making pills of immortality.

At the cooking school, we were taught about the different types of flame: the intense heat and dazzling light of the high flame (*wang huo*); the vigour of the strong or 'martial' flame (*wu huo* – the character *wu* is the same as that in *wu shu*, the martial arts); the gentle swaying of the 'civil' flame (*wen huo* - the character *wen* carries connotations of culture and literature); and the pale-blue glow of the tiny flame (*wei huo*). We didn't use thermometers, but we had to become familiar with the Sichuanese scale of oil temperatures, which ran from one to eight *cheng*.

Ultimately, though, *huo hou* was about a general sensitivity to the behaviours of hot oil and water, and to the ways in which they reacted with your ingredients. In the mid-nineties, most Sichuanese chefs didn't even have gas cookers, let alone thermometers. They were working with the ferocious heat of a coal-burning stove, of a design that hadn't changed much in two thousand years. There was no way of simply turning the heat up or down. Everything depended on the ability of their eyes and noses to function like military radar, picking up on every change in the micro-environment of the cooking pot.

So, my classmates and I had to learn to recognise when the oil was hot enough to coax out the deep-red colour of the chilli-bean paste in our fish-fragrant pork, but not so hot that it would scorch it; when it was hot enough to set the velvety starch-and-water gloss on slivers of pork, but not so hot that the slivers would be dry and chewy. Garlic had to be sizzled to unlock its richness of flavour, but not for so long that it became bitter. As soon as we could see bubbles like 'fish-eyes' rising in our syrups, we had to remove the pan from the heat. *Huo hou* is the key to *se xiang wei xing* (colour, fragrance, flavour and form); it is the key to everything important in the Chinese kitchen.

The beauty of *huo hou*, and its relationship with *tiao wei*, are best expressed by the legendary chef Yi Yin, again, lecturing his king on the art of cookery in the sixteenth century BC:

> *Among the five tastes and three materials, the nine boilings and nine transformations, fire is the modulator. At times fierce, at times gentle, it eliminates fishiness, removes foulness and dispels muttoniness. Thus the control of fire is fundamental to nurturing the inherent qualities of all ingredients. Harmonious blending depends on the sweet, the sour, the bitter, the pungent and the salty. But as to when each is added and in what quantity, this is a matter of extremely subtle balancing, for each has its own effect. The transformations that occur in the ding [cooking pot or cauldron] are so supremely wonderful and delicate that the mouth cannot express them in words, nor the mind comprehend them. They are like the fine-tuned skills of the archer and the charioteer, the fluctuations of yin and yang, the passing of the seasons.*

The culinary expositions of Yi Yin were recorded by a merchant called Lu Buwei in an essay entitled 'The Root of Tastes' (*ben wei pian*), written in the third century BC. It is perhaps the world's oldest extant gastronomic treatise. Yet much of what it says, astonishingly, is still relevant in the twenty-first century Chinese kitchen.

During the months I spent at the cooking school, my life in Chengdu settled into a delicious routine. I would rise early in my worker's flat near the university, and cycle across the city, picking up a bowlful of rice porridge or dumplings in chilli sauce for breakfast on the way. Familiar shopkeepers and street vendors would greet me as I passed. '*Chu shi, ni hao*! Chef! Hello!' some of them would say (used, by now, to my sniffing and tasting, my incessant culinary questions). At school, I put on my chef's whites, tied back my hair, unwrapped my cleaver, and spent the day in a kind of kitchen bliss.

Late afternoons, I cycled back to the university district, more slowly this time, savouring the pleasures of the backstreets. Often I would be distracted by a chance conversation, and stay out until late. Sometimes I dropped into the foreign students' building, where I still had a few friends, and we would go out for dinner or drinks in the 'Old House', a revolutionary new bar that had opened in one of the timber-framed cottages just outside the university. In my second year in Chengdu, we no longer had to drink watery beer or Great Wall wine: the bar owners had acquired a stock of imported spirits, so even cocktails were possible.

By now I enjoyed dipping into expatriate life. In my first year in Chengdu I had wanted life to be as Sichuanese as possible. But now that I was spending each day immersed in China, my ears ringing with Sichuanese dialect and twenty-five different expressions for 'fry', nothing was more sweetly relaxing than sipping a gin and tonic with a bunch of other foreign students in one of the Westernised drinking places that had begun to spring up here and there.

Sometimes I threw dinner parties in my flat, testing my latest recipes on Bamboo Bar veterans like Davide and Pasha, or making gnocchi with the Italians. By Western standards, my flat was a grotty place to live. It was drafty and damp in winter; hot and infested with mosquitoes in summer. Laundry, hung out on the balcony for more than a few hours, became grey with fallout from the polluted sky. My mattress and bedding never seemed to be entirely dry. Strange creatures lived in the bamboo furniture; I could hear them munching quietly at night. Fat cockroaches patrolled the kitchen: every evening I went hunting with my spatula, splatting them against the tiles. Occasionally a rat paid a visit, too, and I found myself devising a trap made from a bra, a tape cassette, a plastic basin and a heavy dictionary (amazingly, it worked). But after more than a year in China, I was so besotted by the country that such minor deprivations didn't bother me at all.

Six days a week at the cooking school were not enough for me. In my free time I sought out restaurants and snack shops I hadn't visited before, and begged them to let me study in their kitchens. Sometimes I had to prove my mettle before they agreed.

'So, you're a trainee chef, huh?' said the owner of a beancurd restaurant in Leshan, a city near Chengdu known for its giant Buddha statue. 'Go on then, make us a dish.'

So I rolled up my sleeves, borrowed some chef's whites and a cleaver, rummaged around in the kitchen for the ingredients of Pock-Marked Mother Chen's Beancurd (*ma po dou fu*), and then cooked it, surrounded by twenty young chefs, who had all abandoned their work stations to gawp. When they had seen that I could make a reasonably decent *ma po dou fu*, the boss gave me immediate permission to hang around in the kitchen for as long as I pleased.

The manager of the famous Long Chao Shou snack restaurant in Chengdu, peering at me over his glasses, agreed to take me on as an ad hoc student. 'You are very lucky,' he said, 'I have a daughter who is studying in Canada, so I am sympathetic to your desire to understand another culture.' It was typical of the spontaneous generosity of so many people I met in China. The manager summoned his head pastry chef, Fan Shixian, and asked him to give me a free rein in the kitchens.

Master Fan turned out to be one of the most delightful chefs I'd ever met, and a treasure trove of information on Chengdu street snacks. I spent days in the restaurant, not only during my time at the cooking school, but also when I returned to Chengdu in the following years. There I learned the arts of the 'white board' (*bai'an*), as they call pastry-making in China (the other branch of cookery is known as the 'red board', *hong'an*). I sat for hours with the gossipy wrappers of the famous Long ('dragon') wontons, many of whom had been there for decades, as they turned out hundreds and thousands of dumplings. I learnt how to stuff glutinous riceballs with black sesame paste and to wrap 'cockscomb dumplings'. I made a mess as I tried and failed to master the knack of making *bao zi*, the little steamed buns with twirly tops, but no one seemed to mind. They just looked at the tangled rags of dough and minced meat I produced with good-natured smiles. Master Fan told me stories, made me laugh, and taught me how to make delicate *zheng zheng gao* (literally 'steamed steamed cakes' – it sounds lovely in Chinese – made from ricemeal and candied lotus seeds) and other rarely seen, old-fashioned snacks. The staff at Long Chao Shou took to calling me, teasingly, Master Fan's 'foreign apprentice'.

My kitchen notebooks from that time are smudged and stained, splattered with cooking oil and batter. The words strewn haphazardly over their pages are written in a mixture of English and Chinese characters. It was often easier to write in English, but I had to use Chinese when I wanted to be precise about the name of an unusual vegetable, or to record one of the countless untranslatable cooking terms. There are also sketches and diagrams, reminding me how to wrap a new kind of dumpling, garnish a dish, or cut up a soaked dried squid. In some places there are herbs or flowers flattened between the pages, restaurant namecards, tickets for a Taoist temple or a train.

Sometimes you can see that my notebook has been taken over by someone else: an old woman listing remembered delicacies from her childhood, a chef writing out the names of some obscure ingredients, a noodle-shop acquaintance directing me to a favourite restaurant. (The work always feels like a collaboration, not mine alone.) Some notebooks cover a period of a month or two. Others, written feverishly during a period of intense learning, are filled in a matter of days. And it's not all about food, either. When I'm in China, these notebooks are my life. They contain train times and shopping lists, records of anxieties and inspirations, dreams and memories; descriptions of the view from a train or the swishing sound of bamboo in the wind.

Most importantly, my notebooks are filled with recipes. Daily, I stood at the wok or pastry board, watching, writing swiftly in a mixture of Chinese and

English, whichever was fastest at any particular moment. I became astute at judging quantities by eye. A tablespoon, a rice-bowlful, a handful: I knew my own measures by then.

Chengdu, meanwhile, was changing at surreal speed. One week I would be cycling through a district of old wooden houses on my way to school; the next, it was a plain of rubble, with a billboard depiction of some idealised apartment blocks overhead. Narrow crossroads metamorphosed suddenly into vast open junctions. Familiar landmarks just disappeared. It was like a dream, in which familiar places appeared to me, unmistakeable in their identities and yet strangely unknown. Luckily, I have inherited from my father an internal Global Positioning System that is very reliable, so I always knew where I was going, even if I couldn't *physically* recognise my location.

When I first knew Chengdu, there were only two high-rises in the city – the Minshan Hotel and the People's Department Store – and even they weren't very high. Now, new buildings were sprouting up like bamboo shoots after rain. All too often, I found myself sitting in a peaceful teahouse in a leafy alley, sipping tea and nibbling watermelon seeds, lost in the mellow atmosphere of cards and conversation, only to glance up and find that there was an immense skyscraper looming up over the wooden rooftops. 'Where did that come from?' I asked myself. A whole new city, futuristic in its gleaming ambition, was rising up around me, as if by stealth.

One of my favourite streets, Upper Heavenly Peace Street, which lined the southern bank of the Brocade River, was eaten away, day by day, by the demolition crews with their sledgehammers. First, the Chinese character *chai*, 'demolish', was chalked up like a sign of hopeless disease on the walls and doors. The teahouses and small shops closed. The old houses were reduced to skeletons, and then just stacks of timber on the ground. Household by household, people were shunted out to apartment blocks in the suburbs. When the last house was about to fall, I stole as a souvenir the sign which bore the name of the street (it now hangs in my flat in London).

On the one hand, all this destruction was a tragedy. It felt like a personal tragedy for me, to fall in love with a place that was vanishing so quickly. My culinary researches began as an attempt to document a living city; later, it became clear to me that, in many ways, I was writing an epitaph. It also felt like a tragedy for the people of Chengdu, although they didn't yet recognise it. To start with a city so charming and distinctive, and to replace it with one that might be anywhere in China – what a waste.

On the other hand, there was something so vital and optimistic about China in the nineties. Gone was the utilitarianism, the sexlessness, the uniformity and the stultifying *boredom* of the tail-end of Chinese communism. The whole country was mobilised for action, moving forward by the collective will of 1.2 billion people. In England we agonised over the demolition of every old shack; in Sichuan, they just went ahead and flattened whole cities! You had to admire the brazen confidence of it, the conviction that the future would be better than the past.

So though my heart ached as I cycled through the ruined streets, I was simultaneously buoyed up by this dynamic optimism. I was in a state of flux too, my life was changing. I was rediscovering my creativity, forging fantastic friendships, shedding skins like a snake.

A small taste of the 'complex flavours' of Sichuan

Home-style flavour

家常味

Typical of the hearty tastes of domestic cookery, home-style flavour is salty, savoury and a little hot. Seasonings used include chilli bean paste, salt and soy sauce, perhaps with the addition of pickled red chillies, fermented black beans and sweet fermented paste.
Example: Twice-Cooked Pork

Fish-fragrant flavour

魚香味

Another celebrated Sichuanese invention, "fish-fragrant flavour", is based on the seasonings used in traditional fish cookery; it combines salty, sweet, sour and spicy notes, with the rich fragrance of garlic, ginger and spring onions. The core seasoning is pickled red chillies.
Examples: Fish-Fragrant Pork Slivers, Fish-Fragrant Aubergines

Strange-flavour

怪味

This flavour relies on the harmonious mixing of salty, sweet, numbing, hot, sour, *umami* and fragrant notes. No individual flavour should clamour for the attention at the expense of any other.
Example: Strange-Flavour Chicken

Hot-and-numbing flavour

麻辣味

Sichuanese cuisine owes its notoriety to this powerful combination of chillies and Sichuan pepper. The level of fieriness varies widely from place to place.
Examples: Pock-Marked Mother Chen's Beancurd (ma po dou fu), Sichuan Hotpot

Red-oil flavour

紅油味

This describes a delicious mixture of ruby-red chilli oil, soy sauce and sugar, perhaps with a little sesame oil for extra fragrance. Used in cold dishes.
Example: Chicken Chunks in Red-Oil Sauce

Garlic-paste flavour

蒜泥味

A scrumptious combination of mashed garlic, chilli oil and sesame oil with a special soy sauce that is simmered with brown sugar and spices until it is dense and fragrant. Used in cold dishes.
Example: Cold Pork in Hot-and-Garlicky Sauce

Scorched chilli flavour

糊辣味

Derived from frying dried chillies in a wok until they are just turning colour; other ingredients are then added and tossed in the fragrant oil. Sichuan pepper is typically used in conjunction with the chillies.
Example: Spicy Cucumber Salad

CHAPTER 7

The Hungry Dead

I don't think it ever occurred to me that enrolling as the first and only Western student in a Chinese chef's school was a difficult or a strange thing to do. It was an impulsive decision, like going to China in the first place. I wanted to learn more about Sichuanese food, and I didn't even consider as an obstacle the fact that I would have to study in Sichuanese dialect, in a big rowdy class of boys who weren't necessarily going to accept me.

Of course I had been used to sharing my family home in Oxford with foreigners, and to negotiating cultural difference on a daily basis. It had been no surprise to come down to breakfast and find a Sicilian engineer or a Turkish porcelain tycoon drinking coffee with my parents. Family camping holidays around the British Isles or Europe were never very organised. My father plotted our routes, choosing roads on the basis that they appeared as wiggly lines on the map and were therefore likely to be scenic. We rarely had a firm idea about where we would stay, and often had to pitch camp spontaneously by the side of the road.

In China, my travelling was similarly open-ended. I would just have the thought of going to a particular place, and then go there, without paying any attention to logistics. This was probably the only way to deal with China in the mid-nineties, because if you did stop for a moment to consider the horrifically dangerous roads, the joltingly uncomfortable buses, the hassle from the police and the long hours it took to get anywhere, you would be unlikely to venture out at all.

The same applied to living in China in general. The country was still in the stranglehold of the decaying communist system. Stuffy bureaucrats made key decisions in every state-run institution and state-owned restaurant. If you obeyed the rules and tried to make arrangements through official channels, whether they were for a cooking lesson or a trip to a forbidden part of the country, you would be thwarted at every turn. Everything would be impossible: the system, it seemed, was designed to say 'no'. Yet in other ways, China was positively anarchic: anything was possible. You just had to improvise.

I spent most of my holidays in China travelling into *fei kai fang di qu* ('areas that are not open'). I had to use subterfuge to buy bus tickets, to travel before dawn, and to disguise myself, on several occasions, as a Chinese peasant. Upon arrival in a forbidden area, it became a matter of persuading minor officials and policemen to do things that were against their better judgement. Mostly, they were flummoxed at being faced with a friendly twenty-something Englishwoman chatting merrily to them in Chinese. They would offer me tea and cigarettes, listen to my charm offensive, and eventually agree to waive the fine, let me stay for a little longer, or allow me to take photographs of the local monastery. I was always aided in my outrageous negotiations by the fact that communications in remote areas were lousy: the doubtful policeman would invariably try to telephone his superiors in the nearest town for advice on how to handle the crisis, but the lines were *always* down. It was just him versus me.

In my twenties I relished the challenge of this cloak-and-dagger travel. It was fantastically exciting for a start, wandering off into Tibetan counties that had barely seen any foreigners since the early twentieth-century missionaries. Strange though it may sound, I also adored the sport of my skirmishes with the Chinese police. I was not a Tibetan, who might be sent to a prison camp on trumped-up political charges, or a peasant at the mercy of the vagaries of some local official. I knew enough about Chinese political sensitivities to avoid doing anything stupid. So there was nothing at stake: the worst that might happen was that I might be fined and packed off back to Chengdu.

So I became brazen in my attitude to China. I just went ahead and asked, fully expecting everything to fall into place as I wished, somehow ('La Principessa', my Italian friend Francesca called me). And as often as not, the initial 'no' became 'yes'. It was hard and time-consuming work to make things happen, but then I had the time, and the youthful energy, not to care.

Studying at the Sichuan cooking school, battling against the chauvanism of my classmates and struggling with the language of professional Chinese cookery, was just another of the bizarre adventures I was encountering so often that they had come to seem an entirely normal part of life. By then it didn't require any particular courage or determination. I just got on with it. Far more difficult, in a way, was the time I spent with my friend Liu Yaochun and his family, passing the Chinese New Year in their remote village in the north of China.

Liu Yaochun and I first met when we were fixed up together as conversation partners by the history faculty at Sichuan University. Most of my foreign student friends were introduced by their teachers to dull language partners, with whom they had a few strained conversations about cultural differences before deciding to abandon the experiment. But Liu Yaochun was different. The elder son of two illiterate peasants from one of China's poorest regions, he had managed to win a place at Sichuan University by sheer brainpower. By the time I met him, he was already embarking on the postgraduate history degree that would lead him into a career in academia. (To me, he always seemed like a human advertisement for the social mobility created by Chinese communism.) He turned out to be fantastic company: original, funny, and full of ideas. We spent many hours talking to each other in a wild mix of English and Chinese, about history, culture, politics, philosophy, morality and religion. It is to him that I owe most of my Chinese language skills, and he says the same about me with reference to his English.

Liu Yaochun was a Cultural Revolution baby, born in 1970. When he was small, he lived with his parents, and, later, his brother and sister, in a single-roomed village house built of mud bricks, with an earthen floor. The land his parents farmed was dry and dusty, the northern winters harsh. His primary school was another mud hut, and there was little to eat most of the time besides dried sweet-potato chips that were sent as famine relief by the authorities. But Liu Yaochun was clever and hard-working, and he swotted away in his mud hut, learning his Chinese characters and doing his sums. His parents, knowing that a good education was his only chance to escape a life of peasant drudgery, sent him to high school in the nearby county town, where he lodged with an aunt and uncle. Six years later, at the age of eighteen, he passed the national university examinations and matriculated at Sichuan University, one of the best in China.

My first visit to the village where Liu Yaochun had grown up was a culture shock, despite my growing familiarity with China. I had leapt at the invitation to spend the Lunar New Year with his family, and made my way there on a series of trains and long-distance buses. The village lay in a distant corner of northwestern Gansu Province, not far from Inner Mongolia and the northern fringes of the Chinese empire. It was midwinter, and freezing cold. The white, wintry sun hung over a bleached landscape, eerily bland, devoid of feature and colour. Monotonous, pale, dusty hills rose to the north; the pale dusty fields were bare; and the houses were built out of the same pale earth as the land on which they stood. Even the poplar trees, leafless in winter, were covered in dust, and the sky was so feeble a blue that it looked scarcely different from the land. It made me feel desolate, this monochrome emptiness.

Liu Yaochun's parents no longer lived in a mud hut, but they were still illiterate. Some years before, they had built themselves a traditional home from pine and poplar trunks, bricks and earth: five rooms and a grain store opening on to a walled courtyard. Outside the walls, there was a small orchard, and a shed for the ass. The main room was bright and high-ceilinged, with exposed beams. One end of it was taken up by the *kang*, the raised earthen platform that is the social centre of rural houses in northern China, beneath which smouldered a fire of animal dung, keeping it constantly warm. We sat on the *kang* during the day, brewing tea on a wood-fired stove whose tin chimney lurched crazily upwards to a hole in the roof; at night I slept there with Liu Yaochun's mother and sister, each of us wrapped in quilts. The men, Liu Yaochun and his father and brother, slept on another *kang*, in a room across the yard.

Although his parents were still in their forties, they looked older, worn out by a life of gruelling agricultural labour. They had lived through the tumult of land reform, famine and the Cultural Revolution. (Liu Yaochun's father, with an embarrassed grin, recalled his fatuous political activities during those years – like dancing the 'loyalty dance' to Chairman Mao, which involved skipping around the outline of the Chinese character for 'loyalty' on the ground.) Because they couldn't read, and spoke a thick local dialect, travelling was difficult for them. The furthest they had been from the village was to the provincial capital, Lanzhou – and even that was adventurous by the standards of most of their neighbours.

At that time of year there was little farm work to do, so the men of the village whiled away their days in conversation, drinking sweet black tea and eating watermelon seeds. Since I was the first foreigner to have visited the village within living memory, I was treated as a *gui bing*, an honoured guest. Everyone wanted to meet me. A village 'intellectual' composed a poem in my honour; the women presented me with pairs of carefully embroidered cotton insoles.

No one in the village possessed a camera, so news of my arrival with an old Olympus SLR slung around my neck had spread like wildfire. Overwhelmed by the villagers' kindness and hospitality, I found myself agreeing to photograph them all.

In a neighbour's courtyard, an old woman sat down in a wooden chair, taking her place at the centre of my picture. Her eldest grandson stood behind her right shoulder; her second grandson behind her left. The last and youngest grandson, a naughty little boy of five, squirmed with impatience as his parents positioned him between his grandmother's knees. Then there was silence, a moment of seriousness, and I clicked the shutter.

I started taking my pictures casually, but quickly realised that I was documenting a moment in the history of the village, its social hierarchies and tight family units. The old woman's grandsons were known, according to Chinese tradition, as *lao da, lao'er* and *lao san* – oldest, second oldest and third oldest. She had several granddaughters too, but, being female, they didn't count in the family hierarchy. They huddled together on the periphery of the courtyard as their brothers posed, excluded from the photograph just as they were excluded from the family lineage.

The grandmother sat regally at the centre of the photograph. Behind her, and beyond the curtain that hung over the main door of the house, a black-and-white image of her deceased husband presided over the family shrine, a constant reminder of the social supremacy of the older generation. The old lady's sons and grandsons were expected to kowtow before this image when they entered the room, and to burn incense and ghost money for their ancestors at every festival. When the old woman died, her photograph would be placed there too.

With Liu Yaochun at my side, I wandered from house to house, courtyard to courtyard, taking the official family photographs: a young woman and the fiancé chosen by her parents; baby sons with penises proudly displayed through the gaps in open trousers; old people posing solemnly for my portraits, perhaps their last. These photographs, the most serious, would be the ones that would grace the family shrines, to be revered by future generations. The old people preferred to be photographed in black and white, feeling it, perhaps, to be a more ancestral medium.

And then there were the people I didn't photograph. The madman who had lost his mind when his wife died and his 'cradle-to-grave' state job was taken from him. He crouched by the side of the road, rocking gently on his heels, lost in reverie. The illegitimate child whose mother had run away to the city because of social ostracism. And, of course, the baby girls.

I felt awkward as a female visitor. Liu Yaochun's mother and sister did all the household work. While the men and I lazed around on the *kang*, smoking cigarettes and chatting, they swept away the fag ends and the watermelon husks we had cast to the floor. In the kitchen, they kneaded flour into dough for steamed buns; they mixed flour with water, rolled it and cut it into noodles, or pulled it into *ma hua* twists. They chopped wood and stoked the fires in the stove and beneath the *kangs*. At mealtimes, they waited on us, and ate their own food afterwards, in the kitchen. Then they washed the dishes. My most strenuous efforts to help were resisted, so I yielded, guiltily, accepting my odd status as an honorary man.

The meals we ate were simple and monotonous; this was not the rich gastronomic landscape of Sichuan, but the arid north, and winter too, when there was little to eat besides wheat, pork, chilli and garlic. Rice was an occasional luxury. Sometimes the staple grain on the table was millet, an ancient Chinese cereal that city dwellers regard as lowly peasant food, but even that was unusual. As my Sichuanese university teacher once said to me disparagingly: 'In the north all they eat is *mian* (flour-foods).' We sat at the square wooden table in the main room, slurping our noodles or chomping on plain buns, adding crushed garlic or chillies in oil to enliven their blandness. There was little difference between breakfast, lunch and dinner. We ate scarcely any meat, and the only fresh foods were home-grown onions, celery, garlic and apples. After a few days my bowels had turned to concrete.

You have only to visit places like Liu Yaochun's village to realise that the concept of a single 'Chinese cuisine' is rather flimsy. For a start, China is divided, north-south, between the wheat-eaters and the rice-eaters. The inhabitants of Gansu belong to the former, their province part of a great swathe of pasta- and bread-eating territory that extends west from the eastern coast and Beijing to the borders of Central Asia, and even further. Certain northern Chinese pasta forms are strikingly similar to those found in Italy: like the 'cats' ears' eaten in Xi'an, which are identical in shape and manufacture to *orecchiette*. The Italian folk explanation is that Marco Polo introduced the Chinese to spaghetti and its ilk during his travels in the late thirteenth century, while the Chinese like to think that pasta was a gift *they* gave to the world. In 2005, Chinese archaeologists claimed to have clinched the argument by discovering a four-thousand-year-old bowlful of millet noodles in a site they excavated along the Yellow River. Many experts, however, believe that the true origins of pasta-type foods lie further west, in Persia.

In the days leading up to the New Year, I watched Liu Yaochun's family make their preparations for the feast. Liu Yaochun was in charge of the Spring Festival couplets: with a calligraphy brush he inked auspicious phrases on to strips of red paper that would be pasted up around every doorway in the house (sometimes it's useful to have a literate son in the family). The fattened pig had already been slaughtered and brined, but his father took the cockerel outside and dispatched it with a cleaver, letting its blood drain out into the dusty earth. In the main street that ran through the village, local lads practised their drumming, and the children made beautiful lanterns out of wooden struts and multi-coloured paper. The girls were dressed brightly in scarlet, fuchsia pink, or red-and-pink, as if to defy the bleached monotony of the landscape.

The elderly are revered in China partly because they are ancestors-in-waiting. After they die, their descendants will (they hope) place their images on the shrine table in the main room of the house, and honour their spirits with offerings. Some of the grander old families in Liu Yaochun's village still possessed ancestral scrolls, family trees illustrated with pictures of the deceased, generation by generation, which traditionally hang over the shrine. Pictures of Mao Zedong may have taken the place of these images and scrolls during the Cultural Revolution, but now they were creeping back, alongside Mao. The Chinese family consists not only of the living, but also of generations of the dead.

Sharing food, in China, binds the living family together, and it is also the ritual that connects those on both sides of the grave. On New Year's Eve, Liu Yaochun's extended family, from the grandparents down to the smallest child, processed to the orchard to invite their ancestors to join in the feast. They knelt on the ground, burning paper money and incense, kowtowing repeatedly, pouring libations of strong grain liquor into the earth. The uncles lit strings of firecrackers that shattered the air. Then everybody trooped over to the house of the eldest son, Liu Yaochun's uncle, where the men kowtowed before the main family shrine. The women had laid out a New Year's Eve dinner for the dead: little dishes of meat and vegetables, a bowl of noodles with chopsticks, cups of tea and wine.

One of the peculiarities of the Chinese world of spirits and ancestors, for a foreigner, is its close resemblance to the earthly world. Chinese gods hold bureaucratic sway in their heavenly offices, considering petitions from mortal beings and accepting gifts and bribes much as communist officials do down below (and as imperial officials did before them). Dead people need material things just as the living do: clothing, money, and, these days, even mobile telephones. At funerals, relatives of the deceased burn paper effigies of all these objects, sending them heavenwards in a cloud of smoke. Special shops for mourning goods sell cars, washing machines, watches, and mobile phones, all made out of cardboard and coloured paper.

The tombs of the wealthy were, in the past, well equipped for life beyond the grave. Most famously, the great, brutal unifying first emperor of China, Qin Shi Huangdi, was laid to rest with an entire terracotta army to protect him. My favourite Chinese tomb site, however, is at Mawangdui, near the Hunanese capital, Changsha, where a marquess was buried with his wife and son in the second century BC. The tombs were unearthed in the seventies, their contents in a state of almost miraculous preservation. This noble family was interred with scores of wooden figurines: servants to wait on them and musicians to entertain them. There were wooden models of chessboards and make-up boxes, musical instruments and luxurious gowns, and sophisticated medical and philosophical manuscripts painted on silk. There was also plenty of food, because, above all, the dead need to eat.

The Marquess' wife was buried with a whole last supper of real food, laid out on a painted lacquer tray. Five cooked dishes had been prepared to whet her appetite, along with skewers of barbecued meat, a bowl of grain, cups of soup and wine, and a pair of chopsticks. There were painted lacquer wine cups inscribed with the phrase 'Gentlemen, please drink', and extravagant serving dishes. There was also a store of raw ingredients: many different grains, beasts and fowl, fruits, eggs, millet cakes and medicinal herbs that included cassia bark and Sichuan pepper. A burial inventory inscribed on bamboo strips recorded flavourings such as malt sugar, salt, vinegar, pickles, fermented sauce and honey, various dishes and soups and some ten different cooking methods, among them barbecuing, boiling, frying, steaming, salt-curing and pickling.

Across the Chinese empire, people took care to satisfy the appetites of the dead. In the Astana Tombs of Turpan, on the edge of the Taklamakan desert, archaeologists have unearthed *jiao zi* dumplings in Tang Dynasty graves: a little dry and brittle, perhaps, but in all other respects exactly what you might have for lunch in the same region today, 1200 years later. The early twentieth century European explorer Aurel Stein returned from the same region with not only the priceless Dunhuang manuscripts, but also some 'jam tarts' and other pastries from the Astana tombs, which still lie in a vault in the British Museum. In Shaanxi Province in the Ming period, people were buried with miniature ceramic tables, laden with dishes of food modelled in clay: sheep's heads, whole chickens and fish, persimmons, peaches and pomegranates.

People in contemporary China often feed their recently dead relatives in a way that seems to emphasise their closeness to the living. They might lay little dishes of cooked food by their graves, home-smoked bacon, green beans and rice, whatever the rest of the family is eating, so the deceased seems to take part in a shared household meal. For long-dead ancestors, the food offerings on the shrine may be more abstract: a whole smoked pig's head, perhaps, or an unpeeled pomelo, neither of them immediately edible. In China, the worst thing you can do to a corpse is dismember it. Ghosts need their legs for walking, and their eyes for seeing. And their stomachs must be filled.

On New Year's Day, Liu Yaochun and I continued with our exhausting round of visits, paying our respects in every house in the village, from dawn to dusk. The food we were offered was lavish by comparison with everyday fare, but varied little from home to home. We nibbled watermelon seeds and walnuts, dried persimmons, peanuts, tangerines, and sweets wrapped in cellophane. Then there were the main dishes: slices of pig's liver and pig's-ear terrine; braised pork ribs; pork slivers stir-fried with celery or green onion; pretty slices of a pork-and-egg roll; steamed porkballs studded with ricegrains; and whole river fish (an obligatory New Year's treat because 'having fish' – *you yu* – is a pun that also means 'having plenty'). The staple foods were sweet-potato noodles, wheat noodles, and little steamed buns, served with pickles, chilli and garlic. Each table was laid with nine bowls, arranged in a square.

If a family elder entered the room, in whichever house we were visiting, Liu Yaochun and the other boys and men leapt to their feet and kowtowed before the family shrine. Liu Yaochun's knees were dusty with all these prostrations. One bearded grandfather we met wore a huge, rough sheepskin over his Mao suit and carried a wooden staff. He told Liu Yaochun he had discovered a miracle medicine. 'It is made with the charcoal from under the *kang*,' he said, 'and it can cure many diseases, including AIDS.' He handed Liu Yaochun some lumps of coal wrapped in paper. 'Since you are a research student at a university, perhaps you could investigate its scientific properties?' As Liu Yaochun pointed out to me later, 'this project has nothing to do with my major, which is medieval European history.' But in this place of reverence for the elderly, he listened carefully to the old man, nodding solemnly at his every word.

Over the days, I met almost everyone in the village. There were the descendants of the former landlord, whose fortunes had been dramatically reversed in the land reforms of the fifties, but who were now clawing back their relative wealth with a successful minibus business. We exchanged pleasantries with the local communist party secretary, and with an old lady who hobbled around on tiny bound feet, encased in miniature black cotton shoes (the Nationalist government outlawed footbinding in 1911, but it persisted for years afterwards in out-of-the-way places like this).

We also called on a family with six daughters and a baby son. It was illegal, of course, to have so many children, but they had a relative in the local government who had forged a sterilisation document for the mother as a special favour. With so many mouths to feed, the parents were desperately poor: they had even been compelled to give away daughter Number Five for adoption. But they needed a son, badly. Daughters, in the traditional Chinese scheme of things, married out into other villages, so they were useless as pension schemes and future feeders of ancestors. ('My brother and I will have to support my parents in their old age,' Liu Yaochun told me, 'Because in the end, my sister doesn't really belong to the family.') Now, finally, after all these unlucky girls, they had a little emperor, plump and beautiful in his tasselled silk hat. The relief of everyone in the family was palpable.

Perhaps they had visited the only village temple to which women were admitted, to implore the local gods to bring them sons. The side walls of this curious shrine were lavishly decorated with a landscape scene in relief, covered in green-painted hills and grottoes. All over it were colourful little plaster figures of boys in any number of poses, each brandishing a tiny clay penis through a gap in his painted trousers. When Liu Yaochun and I paid a visit, the old man who watched over the temple gave us a tour. 'The women, they break off the penises and eat them,' he said, 'And then I give them a piece of red thread to tie around their necks. It's very effective.'

On the evening of the third day, we ate oversized *jiao zi* pork dumplings for supper, according to local custom, dipping them in soy sauce and vinegar. After nightfall, loud drumbeats drew us out into the street, and we spied the tail end of the New Year procession, wending its way up a nearby hill. It was an old tradition that had recently been revived - such 'feudal' customs were banned under Mao. We ran to catch up. The air was electric with the clash of gongs and cymbals, and the frenetic beating of the drums. Homemade paper lanterns, lit by candles and held aloft on sticks, cast a flickering light over the shadowy crowd of figures and the jerky undulations of a dancing lion. The atmosphere was raw and wild.

The procession reached its climax outside the main temple of the village, at the top of a hill. Lights blazed beyond the open doors of the shrine. Firecrackers exploded in a blitzkrieg of light, illuminating the crowd like a photographic flash. Everyone was burning incense and paper money. The drumbeats became louder and more insistent. Boys lit fireworks that rocketed off in unpredictable directions, whooshing into crowds of small children – one exploded next to my ear, and almost deafened me.

Then the drumbeats took a slower pace and a young girl, the village beauty, stepped out, wearing a ceremonial 'ship' made from brightly coloured paper, decked in rosettes. An 'old man' in a battered straw hat and a false beard made of horse hair (actually one of the village lads) led the 'ship' in a gentle dance, to uproarious laughter. Then the lantern-bearing boys joined in, and their coloured lights wheeled around in the smoke and incense. People yelled and whooped in the mayhem. We were all muffled up against the searing cold.

Later the procession left the temple and called on every house in the village, pouring into each courtyard in a rush of light and colour. Firecrackers rent the air, driving away evil spirits. Family members burned offerings at their ancestral shrines, and rewarded the dancers and the drummers with gifts of fruit and nuts. A sick woman knelt on the ground as the lion danced around her, and flaming ghost money was passed over her head. A paper lantern caught fire and withered in a blaze of light. Overhead, the new moon was a sliver of light amidst a glittering canopy of stars.

Day after day, I was paraded around the village like a zoo animal or a celebrity, a real flesh-and-blood foreigner, just like those the locals had seen on their crackly black-and-white TVs. ('I just had a conversation with a Foreign Devil!' whispered one man to Liu Yaochun, after meeting me.) I was forced to eat vast quantities of noodles, dumplings and pig's-ear jelly, and I talked myself hoarse in polite conversation.

One evening we piled on to a tractor cart, swaddled in sheepskins, and went to a richer neighbouring village to see their New Year celebrations, which were famously lavish. Young men in silken robes and heavy make-up performed elaborate dances; there was an open-air staging of local opera. Sick of being the centre of attention, I wore dark glasses and swathed my head in a woollen scarf. But at the end of the evening, when I climbed back on to the trailer with Liu Yaochun and his uncles, I removed my disguise. Suddenly, a crowd materialised around us, and actually chased us out of town. Someone shouted after the tractor: 'Please! We live in the countryside! We never see any foreigners! Please bring her back!'

Shortly before I left the village, we were invited to attend a wedding, where a large, buxom young woman was entering into an arranged marriage with a slender young man whom she hardly knew. We watched them light the wedding incense, and make their bows to the gods, their parents, their ancestors and, finally, to each other.

After the ceremony I was roped into what I can only describe as a kind of press conference. I was invited to sit on the *kang* in a side room, and the wedding guests crowded in to look at me. There were people trying to push in from the courtyard, craning their heads around the door, peering in at the window. The air was hazy with cigarette smoke.

Someone took it upon himself to be the master of ceremonies, inviting members of the audience to quiz me. 'How can England be a democracy when it has a Queen?' asked someone. 'In your opinion is it *better* to have straight or curly hair?' demanded another. The eyes of one man widened in concern and amazement when I told him that Winston Churchill was dead. I felt a heavy sense of responsibility. To many of them, apparently, I was the outside world. I was the diplomatic representative not only of her majesty Queen Elizabeth, but of the nations of Europe, the United States of America, everywhere that wasn't China. So I tried not to laugh at the more ridiculous questions, I tried my best to answer seriously.

My reward for this exhausting Q&A session was a seat of honour at the wedding feast: a lavish spread of chicken with ginger, slow-braised belly pork, eggs and tomatoes, fried pork with spring onions, potato chips in honey sauce and whole fried fish. It was an incredible menu for rural Gansu in midwinter. The bride and groom made their rounds, toasting everyone with strong grain liquor. Enamel dishes of cigarettes lay on every table and the men smoked furiously, tucking extra cigarettes wherever they could – in jacket pockets, behind their ears.

By the end of the day I was succumbing to a rotten cold. Walking home with Liu Yaochun, I burst into tears. I couldn't help it: I was ill, I was tired, I was lonely. I had exhausted all my reserves of patience. I was sick of being a foreign diplomat, of having people nodding sagely at my every trivial utterance as if I was expressing the wisdom of Confucius. And I was desperate for privacy. All those nights on the *kang*, sleeping alongside the women of the family and occasional female visitors. The visitors watching, fascinated, as I poured hot water into the basin on the washstand in the morning, washed myself, dressed and undressed. Even when I went to the loo, on a designated patch of earth next to the orchard, I had to perform under the gentle scrutiny of the family's ass.

Liu Yaochun was furious with me for weeping. 'Someone might see you!' he said, 'And then they will think that my family are mistreating you! We'll lose face in the village.' I was furious with him for caring so little about my feelings. It was the only serious altercation we had ever had.

Perhaps I was also feeling the weight of tradition on my shoulders. After two weeks in the village I was being sucked into its patriarchal vision, and it was one in which people like me didn't exist. Although only in my mid-twenties, I was already antique by local standards. The only other unwed woman my age I met, Hong Xia, was being married off in a few months to a man she barely knew, who lived in an even more impoverished village. She was dreading her wedding, but knew that if she waited any longer she wouldn't be able to find a husband, and the old village gossips would start to wonder if there was some sinister reason for her solitude.

And then there was the disturbing matter of the Hungry Ghosts. In China, the worst thing you can do is to leave no descendants to honour your memory. The spirits of the childless, neglected and unfed, are malignant. They wander the earth looking for mischief, venomous in their hunger. During the seventh lunar month, the Ghost Month, the gates of the underworld open and the spirits of the dead pour forth. It's an inauspicious month, a bad time to move house or marry. It's a time when people make renewed offerings to their ancestors, serving them dinner and burning effigies of all the things that they might need in the coming year. But they take care not to forget the marauding Hungry Ghosts, who must be appeased by rice thrown into the sacrificial fire.

People in China normally greet a young woman by asking her, first, if she is married, and then how old she is. If the answer to the first question is no, and to the second is more than about twenty-three (in a village like this), the response is a sharp intake of breath, and an expression of incredulity. Day after day, in this remote community, I was reminded that my whole life was invalid unless I married quickly, and reproduced. The Hungry Ghosts hovered in the background, menacing. Would I end up as one of them, I asked myself, roaming the streets of Oxford, yearning for sustenance, hoping that my nieces and nephews would remember to feed me?

Perhaps it was all this that made me so glad to return to Sichuan after the Chinese New Year. My stay in Liu Yaochun's village had been fascinating, but I certainly didn't want to live there. Chengdu, with its spirited women, gentle climate and marvellous food, felt much more like home. Liu Yaochun and I travelled back there together at the end of the holiday, on the long, slow train from Lanzhou, winding our way through the mountains as we philosophised endlessly and sipped from our mugs of green tea.

Towards the end of my time at the Sichuan Institute of Higher Cuisine, I began to think seriously about writing a Sichuanese cookery book. And I knew that if I wanted to do it, I had to go back to England, at least for a while. I was also running out of money, and needed to decide whether or not to return to my old job at the BBC. So, when my cooking course ended, I said farewell to my teachers and my fellow chefs, not knowing when I would see them again. I packed up my possessions, and sent home many boxes of things that seemed terribly important at the time but turned out to be useless in England, like Chinese army plimsolls, bamboo ornaments and thermal underwear. And then I left Chengdu, with an aching heart.

But the end of my course at the Sichuan cooking school turned out to be just the beginning of a project that would take over my life. Back in London, I left the BBC and spent a year at the School of Oriental and African Studies, reading for a masters degree in Chinese studies and writing my final dissertation on Sichuanese food. My first proposal for a Sichuanese cookbook was rejected by six publishers, and after my course had ended I returned to work at the BBC, this time in radio. Living in London, I cooked my favourite Sichuanese dishes for various English friends, and the reception was often ecstatic. No one had ever tasted Chinese food like it before, so spicy and exciting. I was astonished by the absence of authentic Sichuanese restaurants in a city as diverse as London, and the near-total lack of Sichuanese recipe books in the English language.

After a year, I thought I would give the book one last try, so I wrote a much better proposal, and to my delight was offered a publishing contract. Thanks to the support of various BBC managers, I spent many months in Chengdu over the following three years, continuing my research. And whenever I stepped off a plane or a train into the damp Sichuan air, smelt the chillies and Sichuan pepper, and heard again the languid tones of Sichuan dialect, I had the same glad feeling of returning home.

Over time, I met an increasing number of Sichuanese chefs and food writers, and was welcomed into culinary circles. People began to invite me out for the kinds of banquets I'd only heard about as a scholarship student and a trainee chef. I attended a food history conference where we barely had time to give our papers before we were ferried off, at the end of each session, to another fabulous restaurant.

Liu Yaochun and I, of course, continued to spend whole afternoons and evenings talking in teahouses. But he never shared my culinary passions. Liu Yaochun has always been a puritan when it comes to food. He grew up in the hard north, after all, on a diet of sweet potatoes, steamed buns and noodles, and he tut-tuts at the dietary promiscuity of the southern Chinese: 'They eat so many weird things. It's revolting. I really think there should be limits.' The amusing thing about our friendship is that, through me, he has found himself invited, over the years, to endless banquets in the finest restaurants in Chengdu. He acts as interpreter for foreign journalists on gastronomic tours, and is on friendly terms with some of the best chefs and cooking teachers in the city. 'I'd really be just as happy with a bowl of noodles,' he says with a self-deprecating grin, sitting down to another stupendous feast.

Gansu New Year Dumplings

Serves 6–8

60–80 circular flour-and-water dumpling wrappers
For the filling:
10.6 oz (300 g) Asian green or white radish
8.8 oz (250 g) minced pork
One egg
Salt and pepper to taste
To serve:
Soy sauce
Chinese black vinegar
Chilli oil
Crushed garlic

1. Peel the radish. Cut into very thin slices, and then into very fine slivers. Blanch the slivers in boiling water, and then drain well. When they are cool enough to handle, squeeze as much water out of them as you can.

2. Mix the radish slivers with the minced pork, the egg, and salt and pepper to taste.

3. Place a dumpling skin flat on your hand, and place a good teaspoonful of filling in its centre. Fold one side of the skin over the meat, make one or two tucks in it, and then press it tightly to meet the other side to make a little, half-moon-shaped dumpling. You can seal the dumpling with a series of little pinches if you wish. Make sure you pinch the skins together tightly so the filling can't ooze out. Lay the dumplings, separately, on a lightly floured tray, plate or work surface.

4. Place the soy sauce, vinegar, chilli oil and crushed garlic on the dining table in separate containers. Give each guest a small dipping dish and encourage them to make their own dipping sauce from the seasonings.

5. Heat a generous panful of water to a vigorous boil over a high flame. Stir the water briskly, and throw in a couple of handfuls of dumplings. Stir once to prevent them from sticking to the bottom of the pan. When the water has returned to the boil, throw in a coffee-cupful of cold water. Allow the water to return to the boil again, and throw in another coffee-cupful of cold water. When the water has returned to the boil for the third time, the dumpling skins will be glossy and puckered and the meat should have cooked through – cut one dumpling in half to make sure. Remove from the pan with a slotted spoon, drain well, and serve steaming hot. Dip into the seasonings to eat.

6. *Xin nian kuai le!* Happy New Year!

CHAPTER 8

The Rubber Factor

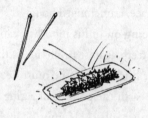

It is Saturday night in a restaurant in downtown Chengdu, and it feels as though I have never been away. A hotpot simmers in the centre of the table, steam rising from the sea of chillies on the surface of its broth. We all have red faces. My old friends Zhou Yu and Tao Ping are roaring with laughter, as usual, at my feeble jokes. The whole restaurant is buzzing with lively social energy (in Chinese, it is '*re nao*' – as hot and noisy as a marketplace). Five years or so after I first lived in Chengdu, I am back yet again, this time for three months to continue work on my Sichuanese cookbook. I have returned to my grubby worker's flat, which a few European student friends and I have kept on, paying the peppercorn rent between us, taking it in turns to live there. And I have slipped effortlessly back into my usual routine of studying in the kitchens of restaurants, reading cookery books in teahouses, and dining out with friends. So, of course, now that my father has come to visit Chengdu for the second time, this time with my mother in tow, I have done the Sichuanese thing and invited them out for a hotpot supper.

Encouraged by Zhou Yu and Tao Ping, I have ticked the boxes on the order form myself, and our waitress has already stacked my chosen raw ingredients around the pot. There are rabbits' ears and goose intestines, bony little catfish, shivering sheets of ox tripe and throat cartilage, slices of luncheon meat, mushrooms of various kinds, and water spinach. I explain to my parents how to cook pieces of raw food in the broth and then dip them into the seasonings, and soon we are all tucking in. I am an assiduous host, and make sure that I give my mother and father lots of interesting things to eat.

It is only when I notice my father struggling with a rubbery goose intestine that I realise something is not quite right. He sits opposite me, a polite expression fixed on his face, crunching. Though the restaurant is noisy, I know perfectly well what is going on in his mouth. I can hear it in my mind's ear: the skid and squeak of teeth against rubberiness, the graunch of it, the sheer unpleasantness of it, for him. I realise he must be wondering, as I did half a decade before, what on earth the point is of eating these tasteless bits of rubbish, these old bicycle inner tubes. He must be wishing his horrible daughter had ordered something actually edible.

It will be the same with the tripe, the rabbits' ears and the ox throat cartilage. The rabbit kidneys and bony little fish won't be much better. Glancing at my mother, my heart sinks further, because I'm quite sure she isn't enjoying them either, though she too is chewing nobly. Couldn't I at least have ordered some lean beef fillet or slices of chicken for my poor parents? What induced me to inflict such a meal on them? The answer is painfully clear: goose intestines, and the whole rubbery array of Sichuanese offal delicacies have become utterly normal to me. Or not merely normal, actually. On this occasion, as on many others, I ordered the goose intestines because I positively wanted to eat them, and I remarked earlier to Zhou Yu (something of a goose-intestine expert) how lovely and crisp they were. Oh blimey.

It's all very well learning to cook in China, but it's equally important to learn how to eat. You can't just waltz into a Chinese restaurant and attempt to judge the food as you might a Michelin-starred restaurant in Paris. If you do, you'll find much of it rather disgusting. Chinese gastronomy is unlike European gastronomy: it has very different criteria for the appreciation of food. I think it took me years to fully understand this. In the beginning, although I ate with great gusto, I was able only to appreciate Chinese food that resonated, at least distantly, with my own experience. Though I prided myself on my early love of the spiciness of Sichuanese cuisine, for example, and even took to the local breakfast of rice porridge served with peanuts and spicy pickled vegetables, this kind of food was hardly a challenge for someone whose mother had always cooked regional Indian for the family, and slathered her food in harissa.

Yet in some senses, during those first two years in Chengdu, I was still eating as a European, because whole swathes of Chinese gastronomy remained inaccessible to me. I spent evenings politely munching my way through goose intestines and grappling with chicken's feet, but I can't say I really enjoyed them. The rubberiness, the bones and the crunchy cartilage seemed to me to be obstacles to pleasure, not the cause of it. I greeted the discovery of a clawed turtle's foot in my mouth or a bit of tripe in my rice bowl with resignation rather than relish. I ate them, of course, but it was as a favour to my friends and as a dare to myself; I would never have ordered them from a menu. Eating everything was, for me, a public declaration of intent to leave behind the treaty ports of the palate in which so many Westerners in China still lived, and venture into the gastronomic hinterland. But in my stomach of stomachs, I remained an observer, an anthropologist taking part in bizarre tribal rituals in order to learn rather than to belong.

The main problem was texture. Texture is the last frontier for Westerners learning to appreciate Chinese food. Cross it, and you're really inside. But the way there is a wild journey that will bring you face to face with your own worst prejudices, your childhood fears, perhaps even some Freudian paranoias. It will disgust you, disconcert you, and make your compatriots view you, at times, with a scarcely disguised revulsion. Think, for a moment, of the words we use to describe some of the textures most adored by Chinese gourmets: gristly, slithery, slimy, squelchy, crunchy, gloopy. For Westerners they evoke disturbing thoughts of bodily emissions, used handkerchiefs, abattoirs, squashed amphibians, wet feet in wellington boots, or the flinching shock of fingering a slug when you are picking lettuce. Did you shudder slightly while reading this paragraph? Be honest.

Watching a Chinese person eat, say, a chicken's foot for the first time can be a nauseating experience. See that old woman, on a park bench, taking a spiced chicken's foot out of a paper bag. It looks like a human hand, almost, with its thin wrist and bony knuckles, but it has tight, scaly skin and long pointed toenails. The old woman puts it, feet first, into her mouth, and begins to gnaw. Her teeth, like a rodent's, strip off the skin. There is a slightly wet crunch as she bites through the cartilage of the knuckles. You can see her jaw moving as she chews them, making more little crunching noises. And then, after a while, she very delicately spits out the tiny bones and the toenails, which are perfectly clean.

My father classifies foods according to what he calls their 'grapple factor'. Whenever my mother cooks something that is complicated to eat, like quails, or sprats, he complains, to her exasperation, about the 'high grapple factor'. Although not everyone would be so fussy about quails, most Westerners are only willing to grapple with something if it is particularly delicious. Anyone in their right mind, surely, would agree that lobsters are worth a bit of a grapple, but shell-on prawns? It's a matter of opinion.

Aside from a few rather messy, tricky foods, like pork ribs and chicken wings, that have been enshrined as favourites by supermarkets and fast-food chains, the vast majority of Britons and Americans tend to prefer breasts and fillets that can be cut into neat pieces with a knife and fork. Fiddling around with a bony fowl's neck for the sake of a few wisps of silky meat, as the Chinese do, or working your way through a pile of small, husky melon seeds, seems like a crazy waste of time and effort.

Westerners with a particular interest in food have a much higher threshold for grapple than most people. You might find them scooping the luscious marrow out of ox bones at the St John restaurant in London's Smithfield, shucking oysters for dinner, or sucking the brains out of a langoustine's head. A willingness to tackle the more intricate ingredients has become a badge of honour, signifying the rejection of infantilised fast-food culture, with its dumbed-down eating rituals, bland tastes and pulpy textures. Such people have no difficulties with the middle ground of Chinese eating, and may enjoy, as the Chinese do, the struggles to extract and separate. Yet it takes several years of quite dedicated Chinese eating, in my experience, to begin to appreciate texture *for itself.* And that is what you must do if you wish to become a Chinese gourmet, because many of the grandest Chinese delicacies, not to mention many of the most exquisite pleasures of everyday Chinese eating, are essentially about texture.

Take the sea cucumber, also known as *bêche de mer* or trepang. These warty, sluglike creatures spend their lives cruising the sea floor, hoovering up decaying organic material. When frightened or irritated, they shoot out sticky threads from their anuses to entangle would-be predators, or zap them with bits of digestive apparatus, which they can use as a missile and then regrow. Dried sea cucumbers are one of a pantheon of exotic dried foods that form the very pinnacle of Chinese banquet culture. In their raw state, they are dark-grey, wizened and hard, and look rather like fossilised turds. Preparing them is a laborious process. You have to salt-roast them in a wok until they are swollen and puckered, or char them black in a naked gas flame. Then you soak them in hot water until they are soft enough to be scraped clean, and slit them open along the belly to remove their viscera. What do you have after all this? Gristly, rubbery, sluggy things with a faintly unpleasant fishy taste. So you have to simmer them in stock with a little Chinese leek to remove the fishiness, and if you are a really good chef, you end up with… gristly, rubbery, sluggy things with no taste at all!

Of course, by the time you actually serve them, you will have added some extravagant seasonings. In Beijing I have eaten one of the most legendary northern delicacies, sea cucumber braised with Chinese leeks. It is made with spiny sea cucumber, which looks even less appetising than the smooth kind to a European eye. Each sea cucumber costs about 200 *yuan*: a tidy sum with which you could easily buy dinner for a family of four. It lies on your plate in a slick of dark sauce, glistening, inescapably phallic in appearance and covered in rows of playful little spikes. The accompanying sauce is delicious, of course, but the sea cucumber itself only makes sense in textural terms, with its squelchy rubberiness, that surprising hint of crispness in the bite.

Chinese chefs and gourmets talk often about *kou gan*, or 'mouthfeel'. Certain textures are especially prized. *Cui*, for example, denotes a particular quality of crispness that is found in fresh crunchy vegetables, blanched pig's kidneys, and goose intestines, not to mention sea cucumbers that have been properly cooked. *Cui* crispness offers resistance to the teeth, but finally yields, cleanly, with a pleasant snappy feeling. It is distinct from *su*, which is the dry, fragile, fall-apart crispness of deep-fried duck skin or taro dumplings. Some foods, like the skin of a barbecued suckling pig, can be described as *su cui* because they offer both types of crispness, simultaneously.

If you want to express the springy elasticity of a squid ball, you might refer to its *tan xing*, which also describes the bouncy aspect of that sea cucumber texture. (In Taiwan they call the same mouthfeel 'Q', or even, of foods that are *very* bouncy, 'QQ', in an unusual and inexplicable borrowing from the roman alphabet.) *Nen* is the tenderness of just-cooked fish or meat, or the fresh suppleness of very young pea shoots; *hua* the smooth slipperiness of 'velveted' slices of chicken. Another lovely texture word is *shuang*, which evokes a refreshing, bright, slippery, cool sensation in the mouth: one might use it for certain starch jellies soused in vinegar and chilli oil. Mouthfeel terms often stray over any notional border between the experiences of taste and texture: like *ma*, for the lip-tingling numbness of Sichuan pepper, or *wei hou*, 'the flavour is thick', suggesting a lingering, many-layered taste and aftertaste.

In the English language, with all its expressive beauty and startling diversity, it is hard to describe the appeal of a braised sea cucumber. Try as you might, you end up sounding comical, or revolting. A Chinese gourmet will distinguish between the bouncy gelatinous quality of sea cucumbers, the more sticky, slimy gelatinousness of reconstituted dried squid, and the chewy gelatinousness of reconstituted pig's foot tendons. In English, it all sounds like a dog's dinner.

Some people have suggested that it was the experience of famine that drove the Chinese to seek gastronomic pleasure in unlikely places. The poor things, they invite us to think, so famished that they are driven to enjoy duck's tongues, insects and other rubbish! But you only have to watch a Chinese gourmet appreciating a duck's tongue or a caterpillar fungus (having paid through the nose for it in a glamorous restaurant) to understand that such an explanation is risible.

The refined appreciation of food seems to be an eternal trait of Chinese culture. Two and a half millennia ago, Confucius was fussing over whether he was given the correct sauce for his meat. Not long afterwards, the poet Qu Yuan was describing food so good he hoped it would bring back the dead:

O soul, come back! Why should you go far away?
All your household have come to do you honour; all kinds of good food are
ready...
Bitter, salt, sour, hot and sweet: there are dishes of all flavours.
Ribs of the fattened ox cooked tender and succulent;
Sour and bitter blended in the soup of Wu;
Stewed turtle and roast kid, served up with yam sauce;
Geese cooked in sour sauce, casseroled duck, fried flesh of the great crane;
Braised chicken, seethed tortoise, high-seasoned, but not to spoil the taste;
Fried honey-cakes of rice flour and malt-sugar sweetmeats;
Jade-like wine, honey-flavoured, fills the winged cups...

Century after century, men of letters wrote essays and poems on the pleasures of eating, like Shu Xi, of the Jin Dynasty, who penned a rhapsody on pasta; and the Tang Dynasty poet Du Fu, who waxed lyrical about the river fish of Sichuan. These famous epicures were far from unique: a passionate appreciation of food was respectable, even desirable, in the traditional scholar-gentleman. He might exercise his discernment in matters gastronomical as much as in the enjoyment of music, painting, poetry or calligraphy.

Chinese people are generally proud of their sophisticated and sensuous culinary culture. Unparallelled in the world, it is undoubtedly one of the glories of Chinese civilisation. Yet this pride is tinged with a certain sheepishness, because of the sneaking suspicion that Chinese epicureanism and general self-indulgence have been partly responsible for the country's 'backwardness' in relation to the modern West. In the early twentieth century, the exasperation of Chinese intellectuals at the smug self-satisfaction of traditional culture helped to trigger the first revolution against the old imperial order. Later, the Cultural Revolution saw a violent backlash against the 'Four Olds': old ideas, old culture, old customs and old habits. Even today, Chinese people often remark, with a snort, that while their ancestors *invented* gunpowder, they simply made it into firecrackers: it was Europeans who thought of using it in artillery, which they then pointed up the noses of the unsuspecting Chinese. Similarly, as one Xi'an taxi driver moaned to me, while the Chinese realised the power of steam as a force for cookery in the Stone Age, they left it to the British to invent the steam engine.

Would the Chinese have made more advances in biology if they had been content to sit patiently and scrutinise living creatures instead of eating them? Would they have produced more outstanding chemists if they hadn't been so preoccupied with the chemical reactions taking place in the wok? Perhaps it was the abysmal diet of the British, along with cold showers and the stiff upper lip, that enabled them to establish a global empire. And if the Chinese hadn't been so busy eating, maybe they would have got around to industrialising earlier, and colonialised the West before it colonised them.

Such anxieties aside, Chinese people continue to appreciate food with the passion and refinement of their ancestors. And as a European or an American, you can watch a Chinese gourmet negotiate the cartilage, gristle and rubbery flesh of a duck's tongue in two different ways. If you wish, you may stand on your European high horse and pity him for his perverse and desperate pleasures. 'The poor Chinaman! Scraping around on the farmyard floor for something to eat, just because he can't lay his hands on a nice fat steak!' Or you can look at him with a kind of slant-eyed envy: 'He's really enjoying that! And just think, if I could learn also to *enjoy* eating these obscurities, how interesting life might be...'

Believe me, 'mouthfeel' adds an extra dimension to gastronomy. The Chinese know it, and make the most of it. Perhaps it's we in the West who should be pitied, because it's we who are missing out.

After the publication of my Sichuanese cookery book, my life in China changed dramatically. The faith my cooking school teachers and my professional mentors had placed in me was vindicated. For years they had been encouraging me in my work out of sheer kindness. Now I was able to give something back. Journalists were using my book as a way into writing features about Sichuanese cuisine; travellers from countries as far apart as the United States and Korea were arriving in Chengdu and using it as a guide. I was able to travel back to China more frequently myself, to research and write articles for international publications. Best of all, I found that talented Sichuanese chefs were queuing up to show me what they could do.

Early evening in a restaurant in one of Chengdu's last remaining old lanes, and I am doing some 'research', which means sitting down to yet another fabulous banquet. The chef, Yu Bo, sits opposite me, eyeing me in that deliberate, excited way in which you look at someone you are about to astound. I can't believe my luck. During my apprenticeship at the Sichuan cooking school, I *dreamed* of attending real Chinese banquets. I'd read about these forty-course extravaganzas. I knew they were happening around me, here and there. I could almost sniff their traces on the wind – but they were out of the social reach of a young foreign student like me. Now, as a published food-writer, I am being invited out for banquets almost every night, and they don't get much better than they do at Yu Bo's.

Yu Bo is my favourite culinary genius. Now in his late thirties, he's a gruffly spoken and awkward-looking man, but he works miracles in his kitchen. Born into a family of well-to-do workers, the elite class of the Maoist years, he failed a critical exam in his teens and was forced to spend five punishing years working in a factory canteen. Later, he managed to wangle a casual job in the Shufeng Garden, a well-respected Chengdu restaurant, where, by dint of sheer hard work and persistence, he was eventually promoted to the rank of chef. He went on to win gold and silver medals at national culinary contests, opened his own restaurant, and is now regarded as the *enfant terrible* of the Chengdu cooking scene. He has many imitators.

Yu Bo's style is a peculiar mix of the traditional and the radical. On the one hand, he is dedicated to reviving a grand style of banqueting that was lost to the ravages of communism. His restaurant evokes the atmosphere of pre-revolutionary China, when mandarins kept private chefs in their courtyard houses. The place consists just of six private rooms, furnished with traditional Chinese furniture and ceramics, which can seat a total of seventy guests. There is no menu: bespoke banquets are arranged to order. And before you eat, you may take tea in a wooden gazebo in the courtyard, listening to the twitter of caged songbirds and watching goldfish flit in the pond.

Strangely, Yu Bo describes himself as a 'man without culture' in that pejorative Chinese manner, although, in his own way, he is one of the most cultured people I've met in China. Notwithstanding his lack of formal education, he is devoted to the study of the Chinese culinary past. He pores over cookery books and pesters the old master-chefs for their secrets. 'I find it tragic that the Japanese have more respect for traditional Chinese culture than we do,' he says.

Despite this strain of aching nostalgia, other chefs tend to see Yu Bo as an eccentric mould-breaker. They accuse him of being too extreme and esoteric, and say his work is 'beautiful but impractical', out of touch with commercial demands. But Yu Bo doesn't care. He is cooking for the cognoscenti, not for the mass market.

I first met Yu Bo before my book was published, when he was running a catering operation on the ground floor of an indifferent Chengdu hotel; even then, his food was eye-opening. A few years later he fulfilled his ambition to open his own restaurant with his wife and business partner, Dai Shuang. It's called Yu's Family Kitchen, and it's spectacular.

On this particular evening we are offered a characteristic chequerboard of sixteen square porcelain dishes, each one containing a different, vegetarian starter. Together, they are a rainbow of colours and flavours. There are tiny, geometric shapes cut out of potato and dusted with a tickle of Sichuan pepper; preserved quail eggs scattered with chopped green chillies; spiced water bamboo; and delicately tied knots of bitter melon. The absence of meat and fish in such a spread is remarkable, but deliberate: 'Anyone can make a delicacy out of lobster or abalone,' says Yu Bo, 'but I like to show that it can be done with the most common ingredients.'

This glittering kaleidoscope of delights is just the start of the feast, a tasting menu that encompasses twenty-five more dishes. Some are served on grand platters, like the rice-jelly with fresh abalone in a rumbustious chilli-bean sauce, and the tangle of dried squid with opened-out miniature peapods. Others, like the soymilk custard topped with glossy morsels of rabbit, come in tiny individual dishes. Yu Bo's longserving head waitress, Xiao Huang, explains every dish in detail as it is served.

There are no fancy gadgets in Yu Bo's kitchen, no centrifuges, dehydrators or liquid nitrogen. Almost all the work here is done with minimal equipment: Chinese cleavers, wooden blocks, steamers and woks. Yet in its wit and artistry, its delicious flavours and extraordinary presentation, his cooking recalls in many ways the most acclaimed haute cuisines of the West. Take, for example, the *bing fen*, a refined version of a Chongqing street snack. An icy, transparent jelly made from a kind of seed, simultaneously soft and crunchy, it is served in small crackle-glazed bowls and garnished with haw flakes, sultanas and nuts.

As I sit enjoying the rubbery texture of the duck gizzards, which have been smoked over tea and camphorwood in the traditional Sichuanese style, I think of my parents back in Oxford, and reflect on how, after more than five years of studying Chinese gastronomy, I am able to appreciate Yu Bo's food in a way that I would not once have been able to imagine. It violates no taboos for me: I am no more offended by the scaley strips of snake or the spicy snails than I would be by a fried egg. I relish the tenderness of the pig's-brain custard that is offered to me as an off-menu aside. But beyond that, I realise, my hard-won understanding of the cultural background to Yu Bo's cookery adds an extra layer of pleasure to eating in this marvellous restaurant.

In every society, cutting-edge cooking is about much more than taste. Like any art, it is a kind of cultural dialogue, rich in references to its broader context. You cannot appreciate it completely without an understanding of the themes and traditions with which it plays. Take, for example, Heston Blumenthal's Fat Duck restaurant in England. A dish such as his renowned sardines-on-toast ice cream may taste delicious, but its wit and novelty lies in the knowledge that ice cream is *supposed* to be a dessert, and that sardines on toast is a casual supper dish you don't expect to find in a top-class restaurant. His raw oyster with horseradish, passionfruit purée and lavender is exciting partly because of the extraordinary juxtaposition of ingredients. The familiar is shown in a different light.

Yu Bo's cooking is also intended to titillate not only the tastebuds, but the mind. As his banquet takes its course, we are served with an intriguing dish of fresh, ice-cold ox-foot tendons, glossed with a mustardy, sweet-sour sauce and topped with raw salmon roe. It is a stirring textural experience, the sensuous burst of the fish eggs married with the slick chewiness of the tendons. But it is also a clever commentary on Chinese culinary tradition, because ox tendons are usually a dried food, reconstituted and then braised with rich flavourings; and raw salmon roe are a novel, Japanese-influenced ingredient. You need to know this to understand what Yu Bo is doing: the pleasure of the dish lies as much in its inventiveness as in its tastes and textures.

Such subtleties are inevitably lost on the casual foreign visitor. Perhaps this is why the West so rarely gives Chinese cuisine the recognition it deserves. An English-speaking chef like Jereme Leung of the Whampoa Club in Shanghai may be able to explain to Westerners the thinking behind his food, and to promote understanding of the complexity of Chinese haute cuisine. But language difficulties and cultural barriers make it hard for others, like Yu Bo, to do likewise.

Yu Bo also reworks traditional Sichuanese supper dishes, transforming them into banquet foods. A crayfish concoction plays with the flavour themes of everyday twice-cooked pork. The sublime artisan-reared pork with garlic and dried longans, or 'dragon-eye' fruit, cooked for 24 hours until the meat is almost melted, is served with miniature Sichuanese flatbreads (I am reminded of Heston Blumenthal's miniature Lancashire hotpots). It is, in terms of Chinese gastronomy, *fei er bu ni*: richly fat without being greasy. And one of Yu Bo's classic side dishes never fails to thrill me: a blue-and-white china jar filled with what appear to be calligraphy brushes. In fact, the brushes at the ends of the bamboo stems are made from a fine flaky pastry with hair-like folds that conceal a minced beef filling. You dip one into a china inkdish of sauce, and then pop the 'brush' part into your mouth, leaving the bamboo stem on the plate.

The artistry of the finest Chinese cooking, with its subtle command of colour, aroma, taste and mouthfeel, still leaves me speechless with admiration. Those fugues on a single theme – imagine, if you will, an entire banquet based on duck: wings, webbed feet, liver, gizzards, intestines, tongues, hearts, heads, skin and flesh, each part cooked according to its particular character! That combination of intellectual thrill with raw, sexy, sensual pleasure! Those smooth and bouncy and silky and chewy and crunchy and tender textures! Those games with hot and cold! Apply yourself to the study of Chinese gastronomic culture, and most particularly, to the understanding of texture, and whole worlds open up.

The only notable Western chef who gives due credit to Chinese gastronomy seems to be Ferran Adrià, the genius of El Bulli in northern Spain. He told the *Financial Times* journalist Nick Lander that he thought the most important political figure in cooking of the last half-century had been Mao

Zedong: 'Everyone wants to know which country is producing the best food today,' he said. 'Some say Spain, others France, Italy or California. But these places are only competing for the top spot because Mao destroyed the pre-eminence of Chinese cooking by sending China's chefs to work in the fields and factories. If he hadn't done this, all the other countries and all the other chefs, myself included, would still be chasing the Chinese dragon.'

If you are lucky enough to dine at El Bulli, you will find that in many ways Adrià's culinary explorations are proceeding along Chinese lines, with his *cui* seaweeds, his *hua shuang* exploding jelly 'olives', his *su* sesame-and-seaweed crackers, his endless playfulness with form and mouthfeel. Like the great Chinese chefs, he composes fugues on a single ingredient, playing with all the creative possibilities of pumpkin, coconut, or passion fruit. Dinner at El Bulli is a dance of tastes, textures, temperatures; to eat there is to eat with all the senses, as you do at a really fine Chinese banquet.

Mao Zedong may have done his best to annihilate Chinese haute cuisine, but ancient habits die hard. Since the end of the Cultural Revolution, Chinese gastronomy has been recovering something of its old vivacity. And, as chefs like Yu Bo rediscover and recreate their culinary traditions, perhaps we will find ourselves chasing the Chinese dragon, after all.

As for myself, I can't remember any one Eureka moment when I suddenly saw the point of pure texture in food. But by the time I was ready to inflict on my poor parents, quite thoughtlessly, the revolting experience of a goose-intestine hotpot, I must have been long gone. My English values, when it came to what was disgusting and what was not, had simply disappeared: not only had I crossed the boundary into Chinese gastronomic territory, I could barely even remember where it had lain. Now I compared gristly experiences with as much delicate consideration as I might have compared the bouquets of a couple of bottles of vintage Bordeaux.

But if there was no single moment of conversion to the pleasures of rub-beriness, there were several small epiphanies along the way. One was in Hong

Kong, where I did some one-off market research for an abalone farm. Dried abalone is, of course, one of the grandest Chinese banquet ingredients, like shark's fin and sea cucumber. The finest of these sought-after shellfish come from Japan, where they are dried by a secret and mysterious method: a single large, top-class Japanese abalone can fetch the equivalent of more than £500 in a smart Hong Kong restaurant.

My investigations took me, inevitably, to the door of the undisputed 'King of Abalone', Ah Yat, a Cantonese chef who has become an abalone celebrity across Southeast Asia (the concept of an abalone celebrity is not bizarre from a Chinese standpoint). He also has something of a global reputation, as attested by his large collection of international medals and tributes, including a 'Highest Honour Award' from the French parliament in 1997. I was taken to his Forum restaurant in Causeway Bay by a rakish food writer who was an old chum of one of my mentors: let's just call him the Gentleman Gourmet.

The Gentleman Gourmet is dressed in a three-piece suit, he carries a walking cane, and a rapier wit. He speaks in the rah-rah tones of a colonial Englishman, although he is Chinese-born. And he is so early-twentieth-century elegant that I almost expect to see spats if I cast my eyes to his feet.

We sit at our table, and the Abalone King brings me a single abalone, long-stewed in his secret-recipe stock, dark and waxy-looking, with the erotic contours of an oyster or a clam.

'I haven't offered it to you in a sauce, or as a finished dish,' he tells me. 'I want you to have it on its own, so you can appreciate it for itself.'

With bated breath, I take it in my chopsticks, and raise it to my lips...

The abalone is soft and muscular at the same time, yielding and resistant, gently springy, with a subtle stickiness at the end of each bite that is entirely agreeable. When I first lived in China, I would have been underwhelmed by the experience of eating such a thing. It would have been just another encounter with a perplexing Chinese delicacy, and I would have murmured polite approval, while secretly wondering why on earth people would pay so much for something so tough and rubbery. But now, for the first time, I understand the serious, sensual appeal of the abalone, the elusive delights of its strong and tender bite. I feel lightheaded with pleasure.

The Gentleman Gourmet leans over the table towards me with a suggestive grin. 'We are all adults at this table, so I hope you'll forgive me if I speak frankly. It's just so hard to express the loveliness of that sensation. The only true comparison in my opinion' (here he lowers his voice to a whisper) 'is with gently biting your lover's hardened nipple. Something only a masterful lover will truly appreciate.'

Blushing, I take another bite.

MENU
Dinner at Yu's Family Kitchen

~

COLD DISHES
16 vegetarian starters
Five-spiced cold beef
Tea-smoked duck gizzards
Chicken breast and salted egg roll
Pork and lava seaweed roll
Boiled peanuts in their shells
Salted edamame

~

HOT DISHES
Rustic three-colour fruits
Beef and wild mushroom consommé
Tuna fish on fortune-telling sticks
Braised rich jelly with fresh abalone
Rabbit with sweet fermented paste on soya custard
Dried squid with sweet mangetout
Spiced snake
Tibet-raised pork braised with longan fruit
Iced ox-foot tendons
Sichuan-style stir-fried crayfish
Pork and hair fungus meatballs on bed of choy sam
Fragrant-and-hot snails
Sweet glutinous rice paste with ground roasted nuts

~

'SMALL EATS'
Jadeite fresh flower beancurd
Crisp calligraphy brushes
Iced bingfen seed jelly
Steamed hedgehog buns
Chicken-shaped pumpkin dumplings
Golden-silk noodles

CHAPTER 9

Sickness Enters Through the Mouth

It was one particular paragraph in the *China Daily* cover story that caught my eye. 'After four days of examination and investigation, the World Health Organisation team has found that most of the SARS (Severe Acute Respiratory Syndrome) patients in Guangdong, apart from local medical workers, are employed in the province's restaurant and food industries.' Oh shit.

It was February 2003. I'd just arrived in China to start researching my second book, a collection of recipes from Hunan Province, and now I was in the midst of a major health panic. Hordes of frighted migrant workers were fleeing the centre of the growing epidemic in Guangdong Province, and many of them were returning to Hunan, which is precisely where I was planning to spend the next four months. And, of course, most of that time would be spent in the company of chefs, now pinpointed as the main human vectors of the epidemic.

In retrospect, my decision to write the book was altogether naïve. In my many years of travelling in China, I had never visited Hunan, and I knew no one who lived there. Furthermore, I knew virtually nothing about Hunanese cuisine, my attempts at preliminary research having been thwarted by the almost total absence of authentic Hunanese cookery books in either English or Chinese. In a way, that was the point: I wanted to write about an unexplored culinary region, and to discover it for myself. I was attracted, too, by the knowledge that Hunanese cuisine was hot and spicy like Sichuanese, that it was popular in the restaurants of Beijing and Shanghai, and that everybody told me it was delicious. There was also the intriguing fact that Chairman Mao had come from Hunan, and had retained a lifelong affection for its food. For a couple of years, I'd had the notion of writing a book in which recipes were interwoven with stories of China's revolutionary history, and Hunan struck me as being the perfect place to do it.

But as I scanned that newspaper report, I began to think that I might have made a serious mistake. I cast my mind back to the restaurant kitchen where I had spent that very morning – a crowded, oil-blackened room where feeble extractor fans had done little to combat the savage fumes of sizzling chillies, which made us all choke and weep. Every so often, a junior chef had come up the stairs with a few freshly slaughtered chickens from a nearby poultry market, where birds and other creatures lurked in cramped cages, and the air was filled with drifting feathers and the smell of chicken waste. It was an ideal breeding ground for infection. Was this research project a good idea, I wondered?

It was a question that returned to me often over the next few weeks. I thought of it when I travelled on crowded minibuses, surrounded by coughing, spitting people. I thought of it after a banquet at a fashionable restaurant near the Hunanese capital, Changsha, to which I'd been invited by a new acquaintance, a local restaurateur. We sat in a pavilion decked out in Qing Dynasty style as the rain roared down outside. The ladies dominated the party, with their outrageous laughter and witty repartee; the men sipped their tea quietly, or knocked back cupfuls of strong and anaesthetising spirits. Towards the end of the meal, one of the waitresses brought in a clay pot of soup in which pieces of bony flesh mingled with slices of ginger. 'Civet cat!' announced my host, proudly. A few days later, civet cat was highlighted in the media as the possible source of the whole SARS epidemic.

With the benefit of hindsight, and the knowledge that SARS fizzled out after a few months, it is hard to remember how terrifying it was at the time. It really did seem for a while as if the whole of China might sicken, and many, many people die. There were those first, mysterious deaths in Hong Kong, traced back to a secret plague in Guangdong, covered up by the local authorities. Then came the spread of the virus across the country, the rapid explosion of cases in Beijing, the incarceration of the sick in makeshift hospitals.

In the end, of course, I decided to stay. This was partly because I had a limited window of time in which to research my book, on account of my BBC commitments: if I missed this opportunity, I didn't know when I could come back for so long to China. But it was also out of a kind of fatalism. In the course of my Chinese adventures I had been in many risky situations. I had rattled along the brink of plunging chasms in clapped-out lorries, been caught in a blizzard late at night on a Tibetan mountain pass, eaten all kinds of questionable and unhygienic foods. I had spent my twenty-sixth birthday at a sinister party hosted for me by a branch of the Lanzhou mafia, and had narrowly escaped a lynching in the anti-foreigner riots that blew up after NATO bombed China's Belgrade embassy in 1999. More mundanely, I had spent more days than I could remember in restaurant kitchens with slippery floors, dodging chefs who rushed around with sharpened cleavers and unsteady woks filled with boiling oil.

When I first went travelling in China, I was a worrier, rinsing my chopsticks and rice bowls in boiling water before I ate, asking bus drivers if they really needed to drink half a bottle of rice vodka before driving over the Tibetan plateau in pitch darkness. Later, I realised that if you want a real encounter with another culture, you have to abandon your cocoon. It is necessary to dine with the natives in a metaphorical as well as a literal sense, and danger is part of the territory. Over time, I became nonchalant about risk.

I remember one winter in Yunnan Province, taking a bus back to Lijiang after hiking the perilous Tiger Leaping Gorge. Three other English people were on the bus too, and they pointed out that our driver was falling asleep.

It was true: I looked in the windscreen mirror, and his eyelids were drooping, he could barely keep them open. Meanwhile the bus was lurching down a multitude of hairpin bends, the mountainside falling away in a sharp drop to one side. An anxious Englishman urged me to go and speak to the driver in Mandarin. So I asked the driver if he was feeling all right, to which he replied that he was perfectly fine, and would not fall asleep. I shrugged my shoulders and returned to my seat, but the driver's eyelids continued to droop, and the Englishman, far from reassured, went and sat next to him, and spent the next two or three hours *singing* to him, trying to keep him awake. 'What shall we do with the drunken sailor, what shall we do with the drunken sailor…' all the way down the mountain. The driver glanced at him from time to time, as if he were mad. It was a measure of how blasé I had become that I, too, thought the Englishman was overreacting.

But there was another reason for my decision to stay in Hunan: somehow I felt that I had bound myself to China, through thick and thin. It was an emotional as well as a professional commitment. My Chinese friends couldn't leave the country if a little trouble flared up; why should I? It was part of my life, like a marriage.

When I first arrived in Hunan, the slow train to Changsha disgorged me before dawn, at a forbidding Soviet-style station. Although I had no friends in the city, I had in my bag a clutch of phone numbers and letters of introduction from people in Chengdu food circles, including the number of a friend-of-a-friend who had found an apartment for me to rent. But it was not quite five in the morning, and far too early to call him or anyone else. Having nowhere to go, I hauled my luggage into the seedy station café, and sat for hours over a cup of tea, as shifty figures wandered around in the twilight. Later, I called my contact, and he came to pick me up on his scooter.

For the few few days, I was in a state of shock. I had expected Hunan as a neighbouring province to be akin to Sichuan, but in fact it was like another country. The local dialect was totally incomprehensible: for the first weeks I could understand nothing, unless people I met switched to standard Mandarin. The sounds of Hunanese, too, were a world away from the soft melodies of Sichuan dialect: the local tongue had a staccato beat, impatient and in-your-face, faintly aggressive. People in the streets, unused to foreigners, just stared at me blankly, without the warmth and curiosity I'd encountered in Chengdu. I had thought I knew China, but as always I had underestimated its vastness and diversity. In Hunan I realised, to my dismay, that I had to learn the workings of another culture, all over again.

I had no particular plan when I arrived in Changsha. My methodology for researching and writing about Chinese cookery is simple but chaotic. I just go somewhere with interesting food and find out *everything* I can about it. Usually I try to make contact with local chefs, food writers and members of the official culinary association. I comb bookshops and libraries for printed sources. Mainly, though, I just do what comes naturally to me, which is to talk to everyone I meet about food, and then follow them into their kitchens with my notebook. My work is like a treasure hunt, because I never know what each day may bring. I might waste days on a futile expedition, or, conversely, meet someone who in half an hour presses five out-of-print cookery books into my hands.

Talking about food is a particularly good way to make friends in China, because everyone talks about it all the time. As soon as I mention my area of research, the floodgates of conversation open. And I have discovered more about China in general through my food explorations than I ever did when I was interested in explicitly social or political issues. People let their guard down over dinner. Yet, while researching my Sichuanese cookery book was a joy from beginning to end, the Hunan book was a completely different experience, shattering in many ways.

I moved into my apartment, a sub-let in a concrete block that was part of a state work unit. It was grim, like most of Changsha. The Hunanese capital must have been beautiful, once. It has a recorded history of some three thousand years, and has been a cultural centre for more than two millennia. But the city was torched in 1938 as part of a botched response to the Japanese invasion. Temples, courtyard houses and grand old restaurants all went up in smoke and flames. Little survived apart from a small section of the Ming-Dynasty city walls, and the Yuelu Academy, a school of classical learning that was founded in the year 976 and now forms the heart of Hunan University. The 'old' part of town that I found in 2003 consisted of one or two shabby streets by the river, dating back mainly to the post-war years; the only older remains were some ancient flagstone slabs with which one of these streets was paved (even they have since been removed, to make way for a pedestrianised shopping precinct). The rest of the city was a grim miasma of concrete and flyovers, shrouded in a suffocating pall of pollution. And in the spring of 2003, it rained almost every day.

Living in Hunan made me realise how exceptional Sichuan was, and how easy it had been to live there as a foreigner. The Sichuanese are so laid-back and charming; there is always an undertone of sweetness to their manner, as there is to their food. The spiciness of Hunan, by contrast, is bold and uncompromising. People have no patience with sweetness, here. Dishes are seasoned with fresh, dried and pickled chillies, more aggressively hot than they are in Sichuan, combined with the punchy sourness of vinegar and pickled vegetables, the forthright saltiness of fermented black soybeans. The mellow, autumnal red of Sichuan chilli-bean paste plays but a small part in the local cuisine: people in Hunan prefer the striking scarlet of fresh and pickled chillies.

The Hunanese are often similarly brusque in manner. The professional culinary people to whom I had been introduced were largely friendly, but they were busy, and not especially interested in either me or my work. Most of them were sceptical at the idea that an alien might write a book about their cuisine: the Hunanese themselves had barely written anything about the cultural and historical background to their food; how on earth could an outsider attempt it? (I once spent an amusing afternoon in a teahouse with two local journalists who chatted to me in Mandarin, and to each other in Hunanese.

By then I was already becoming acquainted with the local dialect, but they didn't know it. So I listened to one of them explain to his friend that my ludicrous project was doomed to fail. To me, in Mandarin, he offered some patronising words of encouragement.)

Hunan also seemed to me, after ten years of travelling in China, to be provincial and old-fashioned in many ways. It was inward-looking, and way off the map for tourists. No foreigners went to Hunan unless they had to, for business or to adopt a Chinese baby. But to the Hunanese, as I quickly discovered, their province is the centre of the universe, no question. For the last two hundred years, it has produced a disproportionate number of movers and shakers, from the Qing Dynasty General Zuo Zongtang (the General Tso of chicken fame) to Mao Zedong and a whole host of communist luminaries. More recently, Hunanese television has gained a reputation for being the most advanced and creative in the nation.

In the eyes of the Hunanese, their province is the beating heart of the nation, an engine of talent that has powered China forth on its road to modernity since the nineteenth century. They see themselves as clever, capable and straightforward: an ideal blend of northern strength and southern softness, without the slippery cunning of the Sichuanese. Likewise, they think Hunanese cuisine is perfectly balanced, unlike the sickly-sweet fare of the East, and the irritating food of Sichuan, which is so tingly and numbing that you can't taste anything. Often, I had the impression that people in Hunan considered the rest of China, not to mention the rest of the world, to be largely irrelevant.

Some of the people I met in those first weeks were immensely kind to me. One female restaurateur took me under her wing. She gave me free rein in her kitchens, and had a habit of whisking me away in her chauffeur-driven car for day trips that involved lavish banquets, market shopping, and indulgent sessions in foot-washing emporia. The manager of the old Guchengge restaurant let me study in his kitchen, too, and it was there that I learned many of my favourite Hunanese dishes. Otherwise, it was hard going. Changsha felt deeply foreign to me, and I met no one with whom I really clicked. The few overseas teachers I ran into in my first week or so fled the country as the SARS epidemic spread, and I never saw any tourists. Most nights I spent hours on the phone to old friends in Chengdu, Beijing and Shanghai, but my days were long and lonely. Unwilling on principle to sacrifice my personal life for my work, I came to the brink of abandoning my entire Chinese food-writing career. That's when I met Liu Wei and Sansan.

It was another grey, wet, wind-swept day, and I took a minibus out of town to visit the Lei Feng Memorial Hall. I'd always had a soft spot for Lei Feng, the communist model soldier known as the 'rustless screw'. He was born in 1940, into an impoverished household just outside Changsha, and was orphaned at a very young age. Later, he joined the People's Liberation Army, where he distinguished himself by doing good deeds like darning his comrades' socks and making tea for his superiors. In 1963, his diary, a paean to the glories of communism, was 'discovered' by Chairman Mao and propagated as an inspiring set-text for generations of schoolchildren. A cheerful song was written in his honour: 'Learn from Lei Feng! What a good role model! Loyal to the revolution, loyal to the Party!'

Lei Feng himself met a tragic end – he was killed by a falling telegraph pole in 1962 – but his spirit lives on. Even today, Chinese schoolchildren are occasionally obliged to take part in 'Learn from Lei Feng' campaigns, although a certain cynicism has crept in to the public view of him. Lei Feng is not alone as a communist role model: in the nineties the party sought to revive flagging public morals with a campaign based on the heroism of another young soldier named Xu Honggang, who was reportedly stabbed in the stomach by thieves while defending a woman bus passenger. (The official media gave a memorable description of Xu's brave deed: 'Holding his dangling intestines with his sleeveless sweater, he jumped out of the window of the bus to chase the criminals despite acute pain.') But if Lei Feng is not the only star in the firmament of socialist heroes, he has always been my favourite.

The Lei Feng Memorial Hall was disappointing. Lei's childhood home, a mud-brick cottage, had been engulfed by a vast sprawl of pavilions filled with boring communist propaganda, and there were almost no visitors besides me. The children of Changsha, I supposed, were these days glued to the TV or the computer screen, their role models David Beckham and Britney Spears. At the foot of the Lei Feng statue near the entrance to the park, I fell into conversation with a stranger. When he saw the sketches in my notebooks he seemed to feel a certain affinity with me, so he gave me his phone number and told me to call if I felt like it. Two days later, desperately lonely, I did, and Li Rui took me out for dinner. Afterwards, he said he wanted to introduce me to some friends.

That night was a turning-point in my hitherto desolate life in Hunan. Through Li Rui I found myself entering a kind of oasis of friendship, with one couple, Liu Wei and Sansan, at its centre. As soon as Li Rui took me to their apartment, I felt at home. Their little son, Xuzhang, was playing on the floor when we arrived, and the main room was decorated with carved wooden panels and other antiques. They invited us to sit down in the 'tea room', where a carved Guanyin Buddha presided over offerings of fruit and incense, and old tapestries hung on the walls. Liu Wei set the kettle to boil, and started performing the delicate ritual of *gong fu cha*, a Fujianese tea ceremony. Sansan called some other friends, a calligrapher, a designer and an antique-collecting businessman, and we stayed up half the night, drinking fine oolong tea, nibbling nuts and sweetmeats, and talking about everything you can imagine. For the first time in Changsha, I was happy.

Liu Wei and Sansan introduced me to a gentler side of Hunanese culture. They and their friends, mostly writers, artists and other 'intellectuals', were nostalgic for the lost ways of the Chinese literati. They were hardworking and technologically savvy, but they gathered in the evenings to drink tea, practise calligraphy, and listen to classical Chinese music. Somehow they found, and created, places of beauty and tranquillity in the concrete jungle in which they lived; at weekends they went on day trips in search of Buddhist monasteries and ancient villages. They were curious and open-minded, and with them I could be honest about my thoughts and feelings: I didn't have to be a foreign diplomat.

Once we all drove out of the city on a moonlit night. The neon and high-rise buildings of the centre gave way to dusty suburban streets, and then to looming hills and scattered farmhouses. We left the car in a clearing and picked our way up an overgrown path, the darkness around us alive with the raucous chatter of frogs and the hum of cicadas. A low, mud-brick farmhouse lay at the foot of a hill, flanked by old camphor trees and teeming undergrowth. Its inhabitant, a reclusive painter, came out to join us on wooden stools in the yard, and a few minutes later a young musician arrived with his *gu qin*, or ancient zither, wrapped up in a cloth.

We set water from the spring to boil and Sansan made the tea, infusing the leaves of oolong in a small clay pot and pouring the hot liquid into tiny bowls. And as the musician plucked the strings of his *qin*, we sat back and sipped. The music was fluid and beautiful, evoking the strange melodic pulses of wind and water. The musician's hands moved gracefully over the strings. The fragrant tea, the moonlight, and the plaintive rhythms of the *qin* combined to make an evening of quite ethereal loveliness.

I spent most of my days in markets and smoky restaurant kitchens, researching my book. But in my free time, I was always with Liu Wei and Sansan, only going back to my apartment to sleep. They welcomed me without question into their extended family, and paved my way to other parts of the province with introductions to relatives and friends. Sansan and I went on several gastronomic excursions together, most memorably to the wild west of Hunan, where we climbed a Buddhist mountain, swam in a crystal-clear river, and bought wild honey in villages of the Miao and Tujia ethnic groups.

Events outside this golden circle of friends were often infuriating. Once, for example, I went to visit a cooking school in a northern Hunanese city. The deputy principal, Mr Li, welcomed me, and we spent a wonderful afternoon and evening together talking about our common fascination with food and cookery. He introduced me to chefs and food historians who offered to share with me some of their skills and knowledge. But then the principal of the school returned from a trip, and the atmosphere suddenly changed.

The next day Mr Li, shaking with nerves, told me that all my meetings had been cancelled. The chefs and food historians let me know that they'd been warned not to talk to me. The principal, it turned out, had decided that I was intent on 'stealing commercial secrets', and issued a blanket ban on any contact with me. So followed a horrible few days of secret late-night assignations in teahouses, where men in dark coats and hats handed over photocopies of essays on culinary history, and chefs, looking furtively around, answered my questions on cooking technique.

Of course it wasn't the first time I had been taken to be some kind of spy. Some of my English friends have long been convinced that I am a secret agent. To begin with, I studied at an eccentric and notoriously conservative Cambridge college where one of my tutors was said to be a recruiting agent for MI5. Then there was that long spell as a 'sub-editor' at the BBC Monitoring Unit at Caversham, a mysterious organisation that most people confuse with the government spy station, GCHQ. Any early suspicions were more or less confirmed by my decision to study Chinese, and by my prolonged stays in remote and obscure regions of China, 'collecting recipes'.

While in China, too, I have been assumed to be a spy on more occasions than I can recall. I've been shadowed by a plain-clothes policeman through the cornfields of northern Sichuan, and turned back at military checkpoints in the mountains of the far west of China. Most of the time these suspicious officials clearly feared that I was collecting information for human rights groups or news organisations rather than stealing the secrets of red-braised pork. Some Chinese cookery books that fell into my hands over the years were considered classified material: they bore the tell-tale characters *nei bu fa xing*, 'for internal circulation only'. But Hunan was the first place I'd actually been accused of *culinary* espionage.

In my twenties I adored this kind of subterfuge. But by the time I went to live in Hunan, my patience was wearing thin. 'Don't you understand?' I wanted to say to the old-style bureaucrat running the cooking school, 'the outside world has barely even heard of Hunan or Hunanese food! Here I am, exhausting myself in this difficult country, with its impossible script and thousands of incomprehensible dialects, trying to tell people that Chinese cuisine isn't just about junk food and sweet-and-sour pork, and you accuse me of *theft* and *espionage*! You should be *paying* me to take your recipes!' At times like these, I felt like giving up. I would call my friend Rob in Beijing to vent my exasperation with China, and he would say: 'Fuchsia, don't you think it's about time you wrote a *Tuscan* cookbook?'

But however sick I felt of Hunan and China during that difficult spring, I had only to return to the tea room in Liu Wei and Sansan's apartment for my anguish to melt away in love and laughter, and to feel that my struggle to show the world the best of China through its food was worth it. If it hadn't been for them, I doubt very much that my *Revolutionary Chinese Cookbook* would have been written.

Although Liu Wei was a successful designer, with his own business, he looked more like a Buddhist monk, with his shaven head, slight physique, and delicate features. And he exuded an aura of such peace and compassion that people were drawn to him, in search of something. I went to visit him one afternoon when I was in a particularly bleak mood, raw and jagged after another clash with a Chinese bureaucrat. As usual, Liu Wei's presence was balm. 'You don't want to dwell too much on these things,' he told me. 'Try to think of your life as a sketch. The world offers everything, but it's up to you what you include in your drawing. Try to choose the beautiful things, and to leave the ugly things out.' Perhaps it was this attitude that enabled Liu Wei to live a life of such grace in the unpromising surroundings of downtown Changsha.

As a compassionate man with Buddhist tendencies, Liu Wei refrained from eating the flesh of living creatures. His diet was not only vegetarian, but vegan, and he also avoided the pungent vegetables that are frowned on in

Chinese Buddhist monasteries: garlic, onions, chives and their relations. (Eating such smelly foods was traditionally thought to be antisocial for monks who spent hours sitting together in meditation, although some people insist that they must be avoided because they inflame the carnal passions.)

Vegetarianism has a long association with Buddhism in China, but there were no explicit prohibitions on the consumption of meat in the rules of early Buddhism. In ancient India, Buddhist monks were allowed to eat whatever food was put into their begging bowls, including meat, as long as they didn't suspect an animal had been killed for their benefit. When Buddhism began to enter China around two thousand years ago, Buddhist acolytes fell in with mainstream Indian teachings in their acceptance of meat-eating under certain circumstances. It was Emperor Wu Di of the sixth-century Liang Dynasty who did much to promote vegetarianism as the norm for Chinese Buddhist monasteries. He was a Buddhist convert who became a lifelong vegetarian and advocated vegetarianism on compassionate grounds.

These days Chinese Buddhist monks live on a mainly vegan diet, while lay Buddhists can choose the degree to which they maintain a vegetarian regimen. Some renounce meat on certain days of the calendar or while visiting a temple; others are completely vegetarian. Buddhist monasteries all over China keep vegetarian kitchens, and in many of the larger establishments there are restaurants providing food for tourists and pilgrims. Such restaurants offer astonishing banquets, where vegetarian ingredients are used to create dishes that mimic the appearance, taste and texture of fish and meat. So you might have, for example, deep-fried 'beef' slivers made from the stalks of shiitake mushrooms, 'spare ribs' fashioned from pieces of wheat gluten impaled on 'bones' of hard bamboo shoot, and a 'fish' that is really a mass of seasoned mashed potato, wrapped in beanmilk skin, deep-fried and covered in sauce. Such culinary subterfuge enables monasteries to entertain their wealthy patrons in suitably opulent Chinese style, but these grand dishes bear little relation to the everyday diet of the monks themselves, which consists mainly of simple grains, legumes and vegetables.

Through my friendship with Liu Wei, I found myself spending much of my spare time with vegetarians. We paid a visit to a sprightly eighty-one-year-old monk in a Changsha temple, who talked to me about the health benefits of a meat-free diet, and assured me that the flesh of the dog was such an inflaming meat that eating it would drive the most devout friar to break his vow of celibacy. One weekend we went to a hilltop monastery where a renowned Buddhist sage was teaching: there, we lunched simply on rice and vegetables.

At that time I was reaching my own peak of omnivorousness. The Hunanese were almost as extreme as the Cantonese in their wide-ranging eating habits, and in the course of my research, I ate dog hotpot, braised frogs and deep-fried timber grubs without giving it much thought. The carnage of the markets hardly bothered me.

I had realised quite how Chinese I was becoming in my tastes when, shortly before I left for Hunan, I went for a walk in a Kentish village and passed a field of geese. In my pre-China life, I would just have seen them as part of the scenery of the village. This time, before I knew it, I was imagining them braised in a sauce of chilli paste and Sichuan pepper, bubbling away on a gas burner. I caught myself at it, and smiled. It was true what they said about the Chinese: everything that moved, everything that ran across the earth apart from the motor car, everything that flew through the sky apart from the aeroplane, everything that swam in the sea apart from the ship, was a potential ingredient. Once in Hunan, embarrassingly, I assumed that a bagful of live frogs that Liu Wei's nephew had brought on a daytrip with us were for lunch – when in fact he was planning to release them into the wild as part of his Buddhist practice.

Liu Wei never expressed any disapproval at my rapacious eating, but his own simple and compassionate diet made me feel a little guilty. This sentiment laid the seeds of a doubt that would later come back to haunt me.

Meanwhile, the SARS epidemic raged on. People were sick and dying in many parts of the country. Beijing had got it badly, and everyone suspected that Shanghai would be next. Six people in Hunan were ill with the virus, and one had died, although they had reportedly all caught the disease outside the province. Life in Changsha became increasingly difficult. One day I returned home to my flat and was stopped at the entrance gate by security guards. 'Health certificate,' one of them said, holding out his hand. 'But I live here,' I said, 'I've been living here for a month.' 'No, I'm afraid you need a health certificate,' he said. 'We'll let you in for now, but you'd better go to the hospital for a check-up or we won't allow you to return to the compound.'

Any fool could see that the most dangerous place for a healthy person to go at that time was the respiratory diseases clinic of a hospital. But, as usual, I was faced with the simple choice: do I want to be sensible, or do I want to write this book? So I went to the respiratory diseases clinic, where I stood at the centre of a small crowd of spluttering, feverish people, trying not to breathe too much, as a doctor wearing a flimsy gauze mask listened to my chest with a stethoscope. He was apparently satisfied with what he heard, and gave me a certificate covered in official stamps. So I was able to regain access to my apartment compound.

The shadow of SARS began to darken every aspect of life in Hunan. Men and women in white coats would leap at me in the entrances of department stores and hotels, and take my temperature with a gun-like gadget. Posters hung all over the city, as they had done during the Cultural Revolution, this time warning not of 'capitalist roaders' but of the need for vigilance against coughs and fevers. The Guchengge restaurant where I had spent so many days of study closed down, like many others, because most people had stopped going out to eat. When Liu Wei, Sansan and I had lunch in one of the few fashionable restaurants that had remained open, waitresses in green surgical masks came to take our order, their voices muffled by the gauze. One night, a bored millionaire, a client of Liu Wei's design business, took us to a luxurious country club, where he hired a former member of the national tennis team to give us lessons on a floodlit court. Afterwards we showered in the vast, unpeopled changing rooms, and drank tea in a drafty café lounge where ranks of empty tables and chairs extended almost as far as we could see.

Trips out of town became a nightmare. When I pitched up at the bus station, I had my temperature taken by people clad from head to toe in germ-warfare whites; boarding a bus, I had to write down my name, passport number, address, telephone number, and seat number, just in case I or any other passenger fell sick. One day when I drove to Changde with some friends, our car was surrounded by a swarm of masked inspectors who covered it in disinfectant. And despite the fact that SARS had been hatched and incubated in China by a combination of official secrecy, poor hygiene and nasty slaughter practices, people were often wary of a foreigner like me, because they feared I might recently have arrived from the infected south. Sometimes I had my temperature taken four or five times in a single day.

Those were strange, disturbing times, and I felt as though I was moving around in ever-decreasing circles. First, I was unable to travel to other parts of China, later to other parts of Hunan. Then, with most of the restaurants shutting down, I couldn't continue with my kitchen research. The closure of all the Internet cafés was almost a last straw, as it meant I was cut off from easy communication with the outside world. But by then I had settled into my life in Hunan and I didn't want to leave.

The epidemic also threatened to have an effect on table manners. In general in China, shared dishes are placed at the centre of the table, and you serve yourself using your own chopsticks. Before the Cultural Revolution, which encouraged a certain proletarian boorishness, more refined people would avoid touching food on the common dishes with the tips of their own chopsticks. Instead, they would use the handles of their chopsticks to transfer food from the common dishes to their bowls, and then turn the sticks around again to eat. Alternatively, they would use *gong kuai*, 'public chopsticks' that would be placed at the side of each serving dish, and would never enter anyone's mouth.

During the height of SARS paranoia, people in Hunan started talking about *gong kuai* again. At dinner parties, 'public chopsticks' would be laid at the side of each serving dish, so we didn't have to risk contamination by each other's saliva. The host would say something ostentatious about the need for *gong kuai*, and invite everyone to use them, and then we would all talk about how important it was to be hygienic under the circumstances. But no one ever actually used the *gong kuai* in more than a token fashion. It just felt too artificial, and before long they were left forlornly at the side of the plates, and we all carried on helping ourselves and eating as normal.

Like many people I knew, I developed psychosomatic SARS symptoms that were quite alarming, including a nasty, hacking cough. I was fever-free, so felt sure I didn't have the deadly pneumonia, but I knew perfectly well that if anyone saw me coughing in public, I could be carted off to a hospital and kept there under lock and key until they were sure I was clean (or until I caught the fatal bug from another patient). Rumours abounded of people being incarcerated in isolation wards, their mobile phones confiscated. So I concealed my symptoms, trying to avoid breathing as I scuttled past the guards, zoomed across the yard to my staircase, ran up twelve flights of stairs, unlocked my door and threw myself onto my bed, where I could cough and splutter to my heart's content.

According to the official media, there was no local transmission of the SARS virus in Hunan. But it was hard to trust the official media, and the rumour mill was active. Was there a cover-up in Hunan? Well, yes, almost certainly to some extent, as I was to witness at first hand. The wife of a Very Important Person in Changsha had invited me back to her home for a family dinner. It was just the VIP (who was probably near the top of the SARS chain of command), his wife, their housekeeper and me. We talked for a while, and they showed me photographs of the VIP with various national leaders and other celebrities. Then we sat down for dinner.

Our meal was interrupted by a young man with a clipboard and an earpiece who strode into the room with an air of urgency. Because he spoke with my hosts in thick dialect, I couldn't understand every word they said. But I did make out that they were talking about a disturbing development concerning SARS, in which someone who had just returned from Beijing was either sick or showing suspected SARS symptoms. They talked anxiously for a few minutes, and then the young man bustled out again. Naturally, I was worried. Did this mean that the epidemic was now snarling at the ankles of Hunan? I gently asked what had happened.

And to my amazement, because I had thought I was among friends, they carried out a cover-up, right there at the table, in front of me.

'Nothing has happened,' said the wife, with a glassy smile. 'It's nothing to do with SARS. Do have some more peas.'

Like everyone else, she had underestimated my growing comprehension of Hunan dialect. I emerged from that dinner almost hysterical, both with laughter at the brazenness of their evasion and all it said about official attitudes, and with terror that Hunan really was on the brink of a devastating epidemic.

Chinese people reacted to SARS either with nonchalance, or with deranged anxiety. Some continued to go out and about, smoking, spitting and coughing in the streets. Many security guards wore their obligatory facemasks slung low, so they could put cigarettes into their mouths. Meanwhile, other people barricaded themselves in their homes, refusing to receive visitors, sipping vinegar as a supposed prophylactic and using fumigation and disinfectant washes in an attempt to sterilise everything around them. But whatever their personal level of anxiety, almost everyone tried to maximise their chances of survival by eating and drinking rather more carefully than usual.

In China, more than anywhere else, you are what you eat. The right foods will sustain your health; the wrong ones will make you ill. As they say: '*bing cong kou ru* (sickness enters through the mouth).' While the Chinese often find it embarrassing or difficult to discuss emotional matters directly, they use food as a way to address them. At moments when an Italian friend would have thrown her arms around me and encouraged me to talk, a Chinese friend would thrust another bowlful of soup into my hands, urging me sternly to

'Drink, drink!' The idea of food as medicine, medicine as food runs through every aspect of Chinese social intercourse: it is a constant background chatter. My private Chinese teacher at Sichuan University used to give me candied fruits or walnuts to 'build my brain' if she felt that my spirits were flagging. And that day in Gansu Province, when I disgraced Liu Yaochun's family by falling ill and weeping, his relatives demonstrated their concern for me by bringing out a frozen melon that they had kept, stowed away under the eaves, since October. Sometimes this ceaseless fussing over my diet would irritate me, but I came to understand that it was an expression of love.

Food is used to heal and balance the mind and body in many different ways. Chinese folk dietetics have much in common with the humoral systems of the Ancient Greeks, Persians and Indians, all of which classify foodstuffs according to whether they are 'heating' or 'cooling', and, to a lesser extent, 'moistening' or 'drying'. No one is sure exactly where the roots of these traditions lie, but it seems likely that they influenced China in the early part of the first millennium, when Buddhism was entering the country with all kinds of foreign ideas. The humoral system, anyway, must have resonated deeply with the ancient Chinese concepts of *yin* and *yang*.

In the heating–cooling scheme of things, some symptoms, like fevers and rashes, are the expression of an excess of fire; they must be countered with cooling foods like lettuce and cucumber; other symptoms, like diarrhoea, may indicate a surfeit of cold, and must be tackled by a warming diet of meat and ginger. The energetic balance of an individual's body is influenced not only by climate, but also by the seasons: this is why, in Hunan in midwinter, some people like to eat the exceptionally 'hot' meat of the dog. The classification of foods is a matter of both empirical observation and superstition: dog, for example, is a high-calorie food and really does help to raise the body heat of someone malnourished in winter, while the idea that walnuts nourish the brain and cashews the kidneys because they resemble the organs has its roots in sympathetic magic.

In China, there is no strict boundary between ingredients that are considered primarily as foods, and those that are considered to be medicinal herbs. The white radish, a common vegetable, is cooling and can be used in the treatment of ailments of the lung and stomach. Ginseng is an expensive and age-old tonic medicine that you might find in your herbal prescription from a Chinese doctor, but you might equally well be served it in a venison soup. Some foods are taken to rebalance the body; others to enhance its functioning. Women seeking to become pregnant might cook with *gou qi zi* or Chinese wolfberries, because they act as a tonic on the reproductive organs. And if you see a group of businessmen tucking into an ox-penis hotpot - well, you can easily guess what they have in mind.

In Chengdu, there is a famous restaurant, Tong Ren Tang, that specialises in medicinal foods. The place is an offshoot of a long-established herbal pharmacy of the same name. Its menu, which changes with the seasons, lists the tonic properties of every dish. Salt-water chicken with Astragalus or milkvetch root, for example, 'nourishes the kidneys and boosts *yang* energy', while lotus root with carrot 'relieves internal heat and detoxifies'. In general, the most serious Chinese tonic dishes have bland and understated flavours: think, for example, of a broth, unsalted, made with a whole duck and the fabulously expensive Tibetan caterpillar fungus, or an unseasoned black-rice congee with barley, foxnuts, lily bulb, lotus seeds, jujubes and wolfberries. Tong Ren Tang, however, is a fashionable restaurant, where people go to enjoy themselves as well as to restore their health, so everything tastes delicious. Ironically, the last time I dined there, I ate so many dishes intended to rebalance my body that I thought I would simply explode.

Chinese bookshops now have enormous sections devoted to medicinal cookbooks that offer advice on the properties of different foods and the treatment of ailments. They might be modern and glossy, but they have ancient roots. Ritual texts on the staffing of the ancient Zhou Dynasty court referred to the lofty status of the 162 dieticians in charge of the daily menus of the royal family; while the Ming Dynasty *Compendium of Materia Medica* listed the curative properties of many ordinary foodstuffs, and included forty-four recipes for medicinal porridge. In China today, the older generation don't usually need to consult books on dietetics. They just know that you shouldn't eat aubergine with cucumber, and that the dangerously cold flesh of the hairy crab should be counterbalanced with Shaoxing wine and heating ginger. When they fall sick, they will self-medicate through diet long before they consider visiting the doctor. '*Yao bu bu ru shi bu*' is a Chinese saying: 'repairing and nourishing with medicine is not as good as repairing and nourishing with food'.

Over the years, I have found myself deeply influenced by the Chinese approach to treating mind and body through food. If I have an outbreak of spots on my face, I steer clear of heating foods like pork and lychees; I know to drink green tea and eat cucumbers on a hot summer's day. This is partly an irrational response to familiarity with Chinese ways – I've no idea if these food practices actually work. Yet it is also a rational acceptance of the pervasive Chinese notion that I as an individual should take responsibility for my own health, that I can't just gorge myself on inappropriate foods and then expect my doctor to sort me out with a pill. In China, people try to treat their illnesses at their roots, and now that's what I try to do, too. I accept the need for Western medicine in times of acute illness, but I rarely take pills for low-level complaints like headaches. Instead, I interpret such symptoms as a sign that I need to treat myself better, with healthy food, rest and exercise. And occasionally, of course, with a soup of caterpillar fungus.

In the plague days of 2003, the people of Changsha tweaked their diets in an attempt to boost their immunity to SARS. Waitresses in restaurants offered customers cups of anti-SARS herbal teas as an aperitif. People queued up to fill bottles with spring water from the ancient White Sand Well because they were sure it had curative properties.

One day the manager of the Changsha Food and Drink Company, Liu Guochu, invited me to lunch at the historic Huogongdian restaurant with some longstanding members of its staff. The dishes we ate included a whole stuffed duck, wrapped up tightly in lotus leaves and rice straw, stir-fried asparagus with the flesh of crayfish, and sticky-sweet glutinous rice dumplings. We talked at length about the history of the restaurant: its origins as a temple to the Fire God, and its heyday as a place where storytellers, musicians and snack sellers gathered to entertain the crowds of temple pilgrims. The conversation was fascinating and the food delicious, but the spectre of SARS hung over the feast. 'You must drink more of the chicken and papaya soup,' said Manager Liu, 'it'll be good against the pneumonia'.

All spring, we worried about the disease. I listened every night to the BBC World Service for bulletins on the progress of the epidemic, and kept my ears open anxiously for every rumour in Changsha. My cough worsened, and I slept fitfully. But despite the flood of labourers returning to Hunan from infected regions, the public spitting, and the steady march of the disease across parts of northern China, it never really hit Hunan. Most people were convinced that this was because they ate chillies. 'Look at the map,' they would say. 'Do you see any SARS in Sichuan, Hunan, Guizhou, Yunnan: all the places where they like to eat spicy food?'

Chicken and papaya soup,
good for the pneumonia

木瓜燉雞

1 really good chicken, preferably an organically reared boiling bird (about 3½ lb/1.5 kg)
A 0.7 oz (20 g) piece of fresh ginger, unpeeled
2 spring onions
2 tsp Shaoxing wine
2 ripe papayas
Salt and pepper to taste

1. Blanch the chicken in a panful of boiling water, and then rinse.

2. Slightly crush the ginger with the side of a cleaver or a heavy object. Wash and trim the spring onions and break them into a few long sections.

3. Place the chicken in a saucepan or casserole dish with just enough water to cover it (2½–3½ quarts/2.5–3.5 litres). Bring the liquid to the boil over a high flame, and skim off any scum that rises to the surface. Add the ginger, spring onions and wine, then turn the heat down and simmer gently, half-covered, until the chicken is very tender and comes easily away from the bone.

4. Shortly before the chicken is ready, peel and de-seed the papayas, cut them into chunks and add them to the soup.

5. Season with salt and pepper if desired. Serve each guest with some chicken and some papaya, covered in broth.

CHAPTER 10

Revolution Is Not a Dinner Party

A communist party flag fluttered above the glass-topped desk in Mr Chen's office, next to an ornamental hammer-and-sickle.

'You see,' said Mr Chen, 'the *feng shui* of Shaoshan village is among the best in China. That's why it produced a Mao Zedong. Mao is like an emperor to the Hunanese people, a true Son of Heaven! He was a politician, a military man, a writer, a calligrapher, a poet and a thinker – a really outstanding genius!'

Mr Chen used to be a policeman in the northern Hunanese city of Changde, but, so he told me, he admired Mao so much that he decided to come and live here in Mao's home village instead. Now he is a rose-growing entrepreneur. His investment – row after tidy row of rose bushes – flanks the main road into the village.

I thought it strange that an entrepreneur, of all people, should be so devoted to the man who wiped out private business in China, persecuted capitalists and wrecked the national economy for at least two decades. Shouldn't his hero really be Deng Xiaoping, the architect of the reforms of the eighties and nineties that launched the Chinese economic boom?

'Aha!' he replied, undaunted by my counter-arguments. 'But you see, Deng Xiaoping's reform and opening up was only possible because of what happened before, under Mao Zedong!'

As far as I could see, this was like asserting that the dropping of an atom bomb on Hiroshima was useful because it enabled the rebuilding of the city, but I realised there was no point in arguing with him, so I just smiled sweetly and said good night.

I had gone to Shaoshan to research Maoist cookery – or, rather, the spurious offshoot of Hunanese cuisine that canny Shaoshan restaurateurs have named 'Mao's family cuisine' (*mao jia cai*). I was intrigued by the idea that a small culinary school could be named after a brutal dictator, not to mention the contradictions of Chinese people's relationship with Mao, their great national hero and nemesis. And I had long been fascinated by the ways in which Chinese cuisine had been influenced by the political upheavals of the twentieth century. Since I wanted my Hunanese cookery book to be not only about the food of the region, but about its social and political background, Shaoshan was one of the places that I felt I had to visit. It turned out to be a surreal weekend.

After taking the bus from Changsha, I wandered through Mao's village. It was surprisingly pretty, with its surrounding cradle of hills, its green fields and orchards. In the centre there were stalls and shops selling Mao memorabilia: badges and portraits in gilded frames, cigarette lighters that played 'The East is Red'. A number of restaurants advertised their Maoist specialities. After a while I found a tranquil guesthouse that stood on the brink of a little farmland and offered its own menu of 'Mao's family cuisine'. I fell into conversation with the landlady, and we sat for a hour or more on the terrace, chatting over cups of tea as the birds twittered in the trees. She pointed out her vegetable crops and fruit trees, and recalled her childhood glimpse of Mao in 1959, when she was lifted above an adoring crowd, everyone chanting: 'May Chairman Mao live ten thousand years!' Before long, we were in the kitchen, and I was watching her make Mao's favourite dish, red-braised pork.

It turned out that Mrs Liu, or 'New Army' Liu as she had been named by her parents in a fit of revolutionary enthusiasm, was the wife of the Shaoshan

Communist Party Secretary, Mao Yushi. In their main living room, Secretary Mao and his wife had the largest Mao statue I had ever seen in a private residence: a larger-than-life bronze bust on a black marble plinth, standing in pride of place, right next to the television. Unusually, it was even bigger than the TV. That evening, I sat down with the family and the communist rose-growing entrepreneur (who was lodging upstairs) to a dinner of the red-braised pork I had watched Mrs Liu make, along with some others of Mao's favourite dishes, including fire-baked fish with chilli and dried radish with smoked bacon.

'Chairman Mao adored red-braised pork,' said Secretary Mao. 'And he got angry with his doctor for suggesting that he should eat less of it because it is so fatty. Actually, though, it's very healthy – I eat two bowls of it every day, to build my brain. And you should eat it too, because it's good for the female complexion.'

Secretary Mao was not the only person I met in Shaoshan who was himself surnamed Mao. In fact, almost everyone I met there had the same name, because, as in most Chinese villages, almost everyone is distantly related. (Traditionally, women marry out of a village, while men bring their wives in from elsewhere and sire sons to continue the family line.) So when one senses that people in Shaoshan have a kind of family feeling towards their famous namesake, it's not surprising.

The village comes across as a hotbed of communism, and a throwback to a vanished era. Here, people still call each other 'comrade', whereas in the rest of China, the only people who use the term these days are gays and lesbians, for whom it has a subversive, tongue-in-cheek air.

Mao's family home, a mud-brick courtyard house, has been lovingly preserved in every detail; inside, no opportunity for communist propaganda is missed. In the kitchen, racks for smoking meat are suspended over the old wood-burning range, and a blackened kettle hangs on a hook over the open fire. 'It was by the side of the kitchen fire,' says a plaque on the wall, 'that Mao Zedong gathered the whole family together for meetings. He encouraged them to devote themselves to the liberation of the Chinese people.' In a nearby room, we are told 'this is the place where Mao Zedong used to help his mother with her household chores when he was a little boy.' The targets of all this unlikely information, mainly schoolchildren and gullible peasants, troop through the house in large parties, and have their photographs taken outside the front door.

Of course the inhabitants of Shaoshan have Mao to thank for their thriving tourist industry, so they have a financial incentive for marketing him as a national hero. But it's not just about money, and the Shaoshan villagers are not alone in their enduring love for the despot who wreaked havoc on their country. All over Hunan, otherwise intelligent and sensible people continue to view Mao as the last great leader of China, and the man who restored the country's dignity after a century of humiliation. They smile a little sadly when they reflect on his 'mistake', the Cultural Revolution, but they forgive him: after all, doesn't everybody make mistakes?

They won't even blame Mao for his most atrocious crime, the man-made famine of 1958–61 that killed at least thirty million people. 'The weather was bad, the harvests were poor,' people tell me, time after time, and I can't tell if they really believe this, or if they say it because the truth is too painful to admit. The official Communist Party verdict on Mao is, bizarrely, that he was '70 per cent right and 30 per cent wrong'. But in Hunan, as my friend Liu Wei told me once, 'It's more like 90 per cent right and 10 per cent wrong.'

Mao Zedong's nephew, Mao Anping, drew on his cigarette as he recalled meeting his famous uncle at a dinner in Shaoshan in 1959. 'He was great fun. A really witty man. And he always spoke with a Shaoshan accent. And the funny thing was, he didn't smoke the kind of fancy cigarettes you'd expect of someone in his position. He liked the Luojia Mountain brand, made in Wuhan, you know, two *mao* a packet.'

We were having lunch in the Shaoshan Guesthouse. Mao Anping, an official in the local government, was a friend of my landlord's, and he had agreed to talk to me about Maoist cookery. We sat before a table covered in dishes. Inevitably, there was a dishful of red-braised pork, seasoned with star anise, ginger and chilli. We also ate shrimps in their shells with garlic and chilli, deep-fried fish with black beans, and a soup of pig's tripe with medicinal herbs. But most of the food was the simple peasant fare that Mao enjoyed most: spicy beancurd, wild ferns with a little pork, bitter melon with chives and pumpkin soup.

By all accounts, Mao remained a Hunanese peasant in his eating habits to the end of his life. He was addicted to spicy food, and famously told a Soviet envoy that you couldn't be a revolutionary if you didn't eat chillies. He was also said to have retorted to a doctor who advised him, in his old age, to cut down on chillies for the sake of his health: 'If you are scared of the chillies in your bowl, how on earth will you dare to fight your enemies?'

Mao's macho attitude to chillies was echoed by his dislike of the effete style and exotic ingredients of Chinese haute cuisine. While living in Changsha, I met Shi Yinxiang, the master chef who catered for him during his return visits to Hunan. The first time he had to cook for Mao, Master Shi was almost paralysed with nerves, so he questioned everyone close to the Chairman about his tastes, in order to work out a suitable culinary strategy. Fortunately for him, Mao was delighted with the rustic dishes he prepared, the steamed bacon and smoked fish laced with chilli, the beancurd and cabbage, the wild vegetables that were generally disdained as peasant food, and the coarse grains that were normally the last resort of the rural poor. In fact, Mao like them so much that he ordered the other chefs in his retinue to take some lessons from Master Shi.

It is tempting to suppose that Mao's own unsophisticated tastes and his loathing of fancy food played a part in his willingness to oversee the destruction of elite and bourgeois culture. Fine dining had always been one of the foremost trappings of wealth in China. In the dying days of the Qing Dynasty, the great mandarins still kept private chefs in their official residences, and threw lavish dinner parties. The Hunanese capital Changsha was known for its grand and glittering restaurants, ten of which were known as the 'pillars' of the trade. After the overthrow of the emperor in 1911, the Nationalist elite took on the culinary mantle of their imperial predecessors. Tan Yankai, for example, the Hunanese scholar-gentleman who served as premier in the Nationalist government, was obsessed with food. He stood over his personal chef, Cao Jingchen, in the kitchen, issuing minute instructions and detailed criticisms. Between them, the two men developed a style of cookery so extravagantly delicious that people talked about a new culinary school, Zu'an Cuisine, named after Tan Yankai's *nom de plume*.

Meanwhile, the poor in China were starving, and the communist movement was growing. The American writer Graham Peck described seeing a party of Nationalist officials dining lavishly in a restaurant during the hard years of the Japanese invasion, as a family of refugees stood by in silence, gazing at the food 'with narrowed, starving eyes'. For the communists, food was a political issue. In Mao Zedong's own 1927 report on the peasant movement in Hunan, he described how impoverished farmers were taking revenge on the landlords who had oppressed them. Women and children were gate-crashing temple banquets, and the new peasant associations were banning the recreational activities of the rich, including fine dining. In Shaoshan itself, it was decided that 'only three kinds of animal foods, namely chicken, fish and pork' should be served at a banquet.

When the communists took over Mainland China in 1949 at the end of the civil war, the defeated Nationalists fled to the island of Taiwan. With them, they took their household retinues, including some of the country's finest chefs, and for forty years they laid claim to being the custodians of Chinese gastronomic culture. Meanwhile, on the Mainland, the communists implemented their socialist economic reforms. In 1956, they nationalised private businesses, including restaurants, and Chinese cuisine embarked on a long, sad period of decline. But if the levelling policies of the new government had been implemented with the aim of putting food on the tables of the masses, they ended in catastrophe. In 1958 Mao Zedong launched the Great Leap Forward, a mass movement intended to kick-start industrialisation, revolutionise agriculture and enable China to catch up economically with the Western powers. Peasants were organised into communes, and encouraged to build backyard furnaces to make steel. Their cooking pots were melted down to feed the furnaces, private cooking was banned, and they were allowed to eat only in commune canteens. Lunatic agricultural policies took root all over the country.

In an atmosphere of collective self-deception, local officials vied with one another to impress their superiors with outlandish claims of grain and steel production. Convinced that they were living in an age of unprecedented plenty, people gorged themselves, and by the winter of 1958–9 the village granaries were bare. The little food that was available was directed to urban centres, and some of it was even exported. Meanwhile, the rural population starved. Over the following three years, at least thirty million people died. Bodies lay in the fields because no one had the strength to bury them; peasants gnawed at shoe leather and the bark they stripped from trees; and the most desperate of all resorted to cannibalism.

Mao survived the Great Leap, politically. And then in 1966 he launched the Cultural Revolution, in an attempt to discredit his rivals in the Party. This violent attack on bourgeois culture and Chinese tradition affected every aspect of Chinese life, including its food. Famous old restaurants were encouraged to 'serve the revolution' by offering 'cheap and substantial food' for the masses instead of the expensive delicacies for which they were known. Many were given new, revolutionary names. In Changsha, the old Heji noodle restaurant was renamed 'The present is superior to the past', while in the northern Hunanese city of Yueyang the Weiyu Restaurant became 'Love the masses', and its former owners were persecuted as capitalists. Huogongdian, the old fire-temple restaurant in Changsha, was vandalised by a neighbourhood committee, who ripped down its most important wooden tablet and took it away to be used as a tabletop.

China has been trying to recover from Maoism for the last 30 years, and since Deng Xiaoping began his programme of reforms in the eighties, the country has experienced an economic boom. After years of rationing of basic foodstuffs, there is meat on the table for many Chinese households. Perhaps some aspects of Chinese culture were damaged beyond repair by the Cultural Revolution, but in many ways the country is finding its feet once again. And one of the symptoms of this recovery has been the revival of Chinese gastronomy and haute cuisine. As they did half a century ago, the glamorous rich sit down to banquets of exotic delicacies, men (and now women) of letters write essays about food, and talented chefs seek to dazzle their customers with their skills. Mao, that coarse-mannered eater of roast corncobs, farmhouse pork and wild vegetables, must be squirming in his mausoleum in Tiananmen Square. There is no evidence that he ever regretted the mayhem that he caused in China. Indeed, he seemed to relish it. You can't change the world through political debate and polite conversation, Mao believed, violence and struggle are the key. 'Revolution,' as he famously said in his report on the Hunan peasant movement in 1927, 'is not a dinner party.'

When I lived in Hunan, I often caught glimpses of the misery caused by the Great Leap and the Cultural Revolution. I spent one memorable Spring Festival with a lovely couple I had met through my friends in Changsha. Tian Zhengqian was a teacher of art and calligraphy; his wife, Fan Qun, worked in a kindergarten. Fan Qun had grown up in a remote village, but when she left school, had joined the great tide of migrant labour, and headed southwards to Guangzhou to work. Some years later, having broadened her horizons, she went to live in the northern Hunanese city of Yueyang, where her aunt introduced her to Teacher Tian as a possible husband.

That January, the three of us travelled together by bus and boat from Yueyang to the village where Fan Qun's parents still lived. It was a beautiful place, with gentle lakes and waterfalls, and steep hills clad in pine and bamboo. We spent days sitting around in the living room of the farmhouse, playing cards, chatting, and toasting our feet above the glowing embers in the brazier beneath the table. Fan Qun's mother and sister-in-law might be in the kitchen, chopping up food for supper; her father would be pottering around. Every so often, a neighbour would walk in through the unboarded, open front of the house, and linger for a few cigarettes and a cup of tea. Fan Qun's brothers had come back from their casual jobs in Guangzhou, while she and her husband had returned from nearby Yueyang, so the whole family was together, and the mood was festive. Her parents were living in a smart, white-tiled house they had built a few years before, to replace a crumbling old farmhouse with stamped-earth floors. There was plenty to eat: meat at every meal, rice wine, treats the sons had brought back from the south.

Yet underlying this happy family atmosphere was the usual tragic history. Fan Qun's mother was orphaned during the famine, at the age of twelve, when both her parents died of exhaustion and malnutrition. Some of her eleven younger siblings were given away to other families, a couple died of hunger. Fan Qun's father remembered having had to forage for disgusting 'food substitutes': wild leaves and roots that were barely edible. 'Today's animals live better than we did then,' he told me. He himself, a kindly, mild-mannered man who spoke a little English, was the local schoolteacher, which made him a target of persecution during the Cultural Revolution. The illiterate people who tormented him, goaded on by local officials, were his neighbours, and most of them were relatives too. He still lives amongst them, and many are good friends; he has forgiven them all.

But that's not the end of it. Teacher Tian's father was a Nationalist county chief, so his parents were blacklisted after the end of the civil war. They were sent away to reform camps, and his father eventually committed suicide under the shame of persecution. His mother, weakened by hard labour and malnutrition, died of an untreated illness when he was twelve years old, leaving him and his brothers to labour in the fields and look after themselves. Incredibly, he later taught himself to paint, and managed to enrol at art school. Somehow, he doesn't feel bitter, but accepts the past as his inescapable fate. In fact, he is one of the most cheerful people I know. When I stayed with him and Fan Qun in Yueyang, he rose early every morning to practise his calligraphy, and to sing.

To a person like me, whose parents grew up in England in the Swinging Sixties, and who has never been hungry, these wretched life stories are hard to comprehend. But in China, they are normal: scratch beneath the surface, and almost everyone you meet over the age of fifty has similar tales to tell. Yet still, in Fan Qun's parents' house, a Mao Zedong poster hangs in pride of place, over the Mah Jong table. 'We want him to protect us, to bring us peace and safety,' her sister-in-law told me, as she came to join in the New Year's fun.

Lunching with Mao's nephew that day in Shaoshan, I'd had a creepy feeling. It was partly that, from behind and in profile, he bore a striking resemblance to his megalomaniac uncle, with his height, his hairstyle, and certain of his facial features. But it was also because of my own misgivings about cosying up to the nephew of a brutal dictator in an attempt to find out about his favourite recipes. Of course, Mao Anping was in no way implicated in Mao's crimes: he only met him once, after all, at that dinner in Shaoshan in 1959, when he was a young man. But was I contributing in some way to the Mao cult, and making myself complicit in the collective brainwashing of the Chinese people, by my fascination with the Chairman's diet?

I've read the eye-opening account of Mao Zedong's private life by his personal physician, and Jasper Becker's devastating book on the famine; I've read Jung Chang and Jon Halliday's recent, damning biography. I am well aware of the unpleasant truth about Mao. I've spent a lot of time in China trying to argue gently with my Chinese friends, to expose them to historical facts and opinions about Mao that they haven't yet heard. But, in Hunan, people didn't really want to know. They answered me with their heartbreaking platitudes about bad weather and poor harvests, and about how everybody 'makes mistakes'. So I shut up.

When I finally published my *Revolutionary Chinese Cookbook*, my publishers and I decided that the jacket should be a communist red, emblazoned in gold with the five stars of the Chinese flag. A recurring motif on the pages inside is the cover of Mao Zedong's 'Little Red Book', and his smiling face, as depicted on badges from the Cultural Revolution.

A couple of critics lambasted me for it: Bee Wilson in the *Sunday Telegraph* said the references to Mao and the historical context of the book made her lose her appetite; Rose Prince wondered how many people a man had to murder for a dish to be named after him; and Anne Mendelson in the *New York Times* was critical of the pervasive use of Mao's image. Strange though it may sound, their comments took me completely by surprise.

There is no way I would have a statue of Hitler on my mantelpiece. But Mao is there in my flat in London, smiling and waving amid the candlesticks and invitations. I know he was responsible for the deaths of millions. I've seen at first hand some of the consequences of his crazed political campaigns. But at the same time Mao has, in a weird way, become part of my cultural and emotional landscape. His image swings from the windscreen mirrors of buses and taxis in which I ride; it hangs on the sitting-room walls of many of my friends. He is not just a man anymore, he is a symbol of the whole gut-wrenching tragedy of China's twentieth century, from the naïve hopes and reckless optimism of the early communist state to the convulsions of the Cultural Revolution. His presence looms large over the China I know, for better or for worse. I'm used to him now, desensitised.

These thoughts are, for me, a sobering reminder of the fact that immersion in another culture doesn't come for free. It is a risky business that can undermine your own, fundamental sense of self. It was in Hunan that I really lost myself in China. I made the decision to live there like a Chinese person, and so I did. For months, Chinese became my daily language, and I spent all my time with Chinese people. Everyone knew me by my Chinese name, *Fu Xia*, not as Fuchsia. The outside world receded from view. I found myself not only talking like Liu Wei and Sansan and their friends, but in some senses *thinking* like them too. At one point I felt so utterly disconnected from my own home and background that I thought I might never leave. And it was then that I thought: I am too much of the chameleon, I can't even remember my own colours anymore.

Chairman Mao's red-braised pork

毛氏紅燒肉

18 oz (500 g) belly pork (traditionally including skin)
2 tbsp peanut oil
2 tbsp white sugar
1 tbsp Shaoxing wine
0.7 oz (20 g) ginger, skin left on, sliced
1 star anise
2 dried red chillies
A small piece of cinnamon stick or cassia bark
Light soy sauce, salt and sugar to taste
A few lengths of spring onion greens

1. Plunge the belly pork into a panful of boiling water and simmer for 3–4 minutes until partially cooked. Remove and, when cool enough to handle, cut into ³/₄–1¹/₄ inch (2–3 cm chunks).

2. Heat the oil and sugar over a gentle flame until the sugar melts. Then raise the heat and stir until the melted sugar turns a rich caramel brown. Add the pork and splash in the Shaoxing wine.

3. Then add enough water to just cover the pork, and add the ginger, star anise, chillies and cinnamon. Bring to the boil and then turn down the heat and simmer for at least 45 minutes. Towards the end of the cooking time, turn up the heat to reduce the sauce, and season with soy sauce, salt and a little sugar to taste. Add the spring onion greens just before serving.

CHAPTER 11

Chanel and Chickens' Feet

When I finally left Hunan, I stayed for a few days with some English friends in Hong Kong before flying back to London. I felt completely disorientated. I didn't know how to express myself and had forgotten how to behave like a normal English person. My friend Rob, who I have known since we were teenagers, and his wife Leslie helped me to ease myself out of my Chinese life.

In my years of travelling back and forth, I have come to think of Hong Kong as a kind of decompression chamber, a halfway house between home and China. It's been like that for me ever since my first visit, when I stayed with my cousin Sebastian in his apartment in Wanchai, on Hong Kong Island. Then, I was so terrified of my impending trip to China that I wondered if I could go through with it. I woke up every morning and looked through the window towards the Mainland, cold with fear.

Hong Kong helped me to cross the border gently. It was China in some ways, but in others it wasn't. I could meet English friends for a cocktail in the Captain's Bar at the Mandarin Oriental, or I could watch live fish being dismembered in the Wanchai wetmarket; I could windowshop in the glitzy designer boutiques of Central, or lose myself in the feverish backstreets of Kowloon. I remember, on that first trip, entering a Chinese temple, the Man-Mo, in the old Chinese trading district of Sheung Wan. In the red-glowing, gold-gleaming, cavern-like interior, old ladies shook out their fortune-telling sticks and candles flickered. The strange gilded statues and smouldering coils of incense brought me out in goosepimples. But then I was able to take a taxi back into a more familiar world, meeting Sebastian and his girlfriend for dinner and English conversation. By the time I boarded the train that ran to the border with China proper, my fear had abated and I was ready to face the Mainland for the first time.

Three years later, on my way back from Chengdu at the end of my cooking course, I stayed with Sebastian again. Once more, I was in a state of potentially traumatic transition. For eighteen months I had been completely immersed in China, and had had very little contact with anyone at home, even my family. My perfect Oxford English was going to seed, because I had become used to speaking with people for whom English was a second language. In the Sichuan University dormitory, we had coined our own lingua franca, a mixture of English and Chinese with a bit of Italian and French thrown in. So I'd picked up all kinds of English phrases and neologisms that weren't really English, and my syntax was often a little foreign. I was badly dressed too, as I remember, with my army boots and cheap Chinese clothes. I felt like a peasant, completely out of touch with the slick modernity of Hong Kong.

Sebastian sat me down and told me everything that had happened while I'd been away: Oasis, Brit Pop, the National Lottery. And there was this new thing, he said, the Internet, that everyone was talking about. It was going to change the way we did *everything*. Shell-shocked by the sudden assault of news, cars, and Western advertisements, and the frantic pace of life in Hong Kong, I didn't really understand what he was talking about.

My heart was heavy that week: leaving Sichuan had wrenched me. I stood one sunny afternoon in a secluded spot on the shore of the Tai Tam reservoir on Hong Kong Island, practising the *qi gong* movements I'd learned from my elderly teacher in that temple garden in Chengdu, trying to create a sense of continuity between the present, the immediate future and the life I was leaving behind. By the time I finally arrived at my parents' home in Oxford, I was ready to do what felt like stepping on to dry land again, after years at sea.

When I haven't visited the Hong Kong decompression chamber on my way into deepest China, or at least spent some time in the lesser decompression chambers of Shanghai or Beijing, I have been struck with the bends. Flying direct from London to Changsha, for example, pausing only to change planes in Beijing, is a disaster. I feel uprooted and horribly confused every time. My tongue gets lost in a linguistic soup of English, Mandarin and dialect, and I find it hard to function socially for at least a couple of days. Hong Kong gives me the space to brace myself on my way into China, and to collect my thoughts and impressions on the way home.

It works like this because everybody there is on the brink, like the place itself. My Hong Kong friends know what it's like to be juggling cultures on a daily basis. We can all swing either way, East or West, and we eat ambidextrously. In conversation, there is much that doesn't need to be explained, which is a huge relief. And Hong Kong is multicultural and international in a way that China still isn't. Even the taxi drivers speak a mix of Cantonese, Mandarin and English.

Sometimes these days, when I'm in a totally English environment – a Fulham dinner-party scenario, say – I feel like a foreigner, with my altered perspectives and traveller's tales. And in China, of course, I'm all too often still a big-nosed barbarian. But Hong Kong has been a hybrid ever since the British Crown wrested the unlikely island, with its deep and sheltered harbour, from China at the end of the first Opium War in 1842. Hong Kong people will choose, in an evenhanded way, whether to have croissants and Italian coffee or steamed chickens' feet with oolong tea for breakfast. They might go out for a bit of 'soy sauce Western food', or shop in a delicatessen that sells both dried abalone and Spanish membrillo. Everybody dips their deep-fried prawn dim sum in salad cream; their beancurd rolls in Worcestershire sauce. To visiting tourists this seems like a bastardisation; in Hong Kong, it makes perfect sense.

I first met Rose through some old friends who thought we might get along. And although at first it seemed as though we might have little in common – Rose is a slick, international businesswoman after all, while I am a writer living in a dodgy part of East London – we never run out of things to say. Because despite her appearance – as petite and delicate as a fawn, and always impeccably well dressed – Rose is a gourmet extraordinaire and a restaurant sleuth.

Whenever I'm planning to visit Hong Kong, I email Rose, and before the day is out, I'm at the receiving end of the first of a volley of replies, each one outlining suggestions of yet more restaurants and food shops to visit, delicacies to try, and food people to meet. Rose is a social chameleon, like many glamorous and well-heeled Hong Kong Chinese. Raised in Chicago by her Chinese parents, she speaks fluent English, Cantonese and Shanghai dialect, and passable Mandarin. She is equally at home in Chinese or international society, and with Chinese or Western food. One weekend she will be flying to Barcelona for dinner at the world's most exclusive restaurant, El Bulli, the next she will be crammed into a tiny upstairs room in Sheung Wan, eating raw crabs with her fingers and chomping her way through a Chiuchow stewed goose with garlic vinegar.

At home, you might find her tea-smoking her own oysters, sautéeing foie gras, or preserving osmanthus blossoms with salt and sugar. And whenever we meet in London on one of her globe-trotting business trips, she takes out of her elegant designer handbag a stash of Chinese goodies that she has brought especially for me: dried sea-moss and salted bamboo shoots from Shanghai, perhaps, or some special shrimp-and-chilli paste from Hong Kong.

Soon after our first meeting some five years ago, Rose arranged a Sunday lunch for our mutual friends and me at the Ningbo Residents Association restaurant. It was the kind of restaurant I could never have found on my own, tucked away in an office building and officially open only to the association's members. Rose ordered for us all in fluent Shanghai dialect, and the meal was a revelation. There were smoked eggs, their yolks like liquid gold; tiny clams steamed in a delicate, savoury custard; braised meatballs with bamboo shoot and shiitake mushrooms; chopped Indian aster leaves with dry beancurd and sesame oil; a scrumptious mash of broad beans with preserved greens and dried scallops; and, most remarkable of all, cold, raw mud snails steeped in sweet Shaoxing wine, their shells so thinly crisp they could be eaten whole. Afterwards, we filled up on sesame flatbreads and sticky rice-cake stir-fried with bamboo shoot.

It is testament to the diversity of Chinese cuisine that after more than ten years of dedicated research, I encounter new ingredients and new dishes not only every single time I visit the country, but often every single day. Even in Chengdu, which I know better than anywhere else in China, I am constantly surprised, and in Hong Kong, which I dip into every couple of years, the novelties flow thick and fast. Of course, it helps to have friends like Rose, who have their noses to the ground, sniffing out all kinds of delicacies hidden like truffles in the back alleys. By now I associate Hong Kong with these little gastronomic expeditions to basement delicatessens, teeming wet markets, restaurants in unlikely places, and tea shops in the backstreets of Sheung Wan or Central.

One of the places Rose introduced me to was the Lin Heung teahouse on Wellington Street, a rare survivor of the old teahouse culture of Hong Kong. I went there one morning for breakfast and warmed to it immediately. Outside, a woman was laying out the day's newspapers on a stand; inside, at just after 6 a.m., it was already busy, and the air hummed with Cantonese chatter. Most of the customers were elderly or middle-aged working men. Some sat alone, engrossed in the papers as they slurped tea and ate their breakfast; others gossipped with their friends. Bleary-eyed after my early rising, I found a perch at one end of a glass-topped table, and a waiter swiftly brought me my bowl, teacup and spoon, and a pot of musty *pu'er* tea. Soon waitresses were passing by with their trolleys, calling out the names of dumplings and other titbits. One lifted the lids of towers of small bamboo steamers to offer me fluffy buns stuffed with pork, and small dishes containing folds of tripe. Another had sticky rice with chicken, wrapped in fragrant lotus leaves. The tea-waiters rushed around with their kettles, replenishing teapots and bowls. Every few minutes, more customers arrived, and the clamour of conversation grew louder, mixing with the clatter of teacups.

Lin Heung is a rough-and-ready sort of place, with a worn tiled floor, metal spittoons, and ceiling fans whirring away in the corner of your eye. The walls are a clutter of framed calligraphies, and red plastic boards listing the dishes and dumplings on offer. One of my neighbours at the table that day, Mr Wong, fifty years old, had been coming almost daily for four years, to wake himself up before he clocked on for his job as an office cleaner. 'The tea is good, the water is good, and the boss is a smart man, he doesn't cheat us, he knows how to keep everyone happy,' he told me as he prodded the pile of Dragon Well tealeaves in his cup. His friend Mr Lau, eighty-three, said he had been a regular for fifty years. 'I come every day,' he told me, 'and some of the staff have been here for decades, too. Nothing changes, including the quality of the food, that's why I keep on coming.'

Lin Heung, or 'Lotus Fragrance', was founded in the 1920s, although it has moved several times from its original location. The first such teahouses opened in Hong Kong in the 1840s, but they began to flourish only after 1897, when the British authorities abolished their night-time curfew for Chinese people. From the 1920s until the 1940s, they sprang up all over the territory, and they acquired a vital social function in the post-war economic boom. Whole families were then living in cramped accommodation, sharing apartments with limited cooking facilities, or even no kitchen at all. Teahouses were cheap and convenient, as much for family meals as entertaining guests or discussing business. Some became known for particular trades, like the Kam Kong restaurant, frequented by dealers of watches and gemstones; others for their board games or musical entertainments. Visiting a teahouse became so central to Hong Kong life that people began to greet one another by asking, 'Have you had tea yet?' instead of the more traditional, 'Have you eaten?'

While the teahouse ritual is known as *yum cha* ('drink tea'), the dumplings and other 'small eats' that are traditionally served are known collectively as *dim sum*, the Cantonese dialect form of the Mandarin *dian xin*. *Dian xin* is a curious term that defies direct translation into English, but means something like 'touch the heart'. It dates back at least to the Song Dynasty, when historical sources mention it as a name for the snacks customarily served for breakfast. Though *dian xin* are eaten all over China, it is in Hong Kong and the Cantonese south that they are most dazzling and abundant.

The *har gau*, or fresh prawn dumpling, is the best-known of the delicate steamed dumplings, and one of the most perfect when properly made. A *dim sum* cook will tease the white wheatstarch dough into a perfect circle with the flat of a cleaver blade, and then wrap it around whole prawns, lightly seasoned and mixed with a scattering of crunchy bamboo. After a swift steaming, the faint pink of the prawns glows through the pearly translucence of the wrapper, with its neatly pinched edge. The prawns are simultaneously crisp and tender, the wrapper soft and glutinous in the mouth. *Cheung fun*, sheets of slithery rice pasta wrapped around deep-fried doughsticks, barbecued pork or fresh prawn, and served with a drizzling of sweetened soy sauce, are made by pouring a thin riceflour batter on to a sheet of muslin, steaming it, and then wrapping it around the chosen stuffing with a few flips of a spatula blade. Steamed *char siu* buns are soft and fluffy, their white dough breaking open into a smile of barbecued pork in a savoury-sweet sauce.

A *dim sum* breakfast or lunch is a casual and often chaotic affair, but it has a few of its own, particular rituals. You may thank your host for pouring tea into your cup by tapping your index and middle fingers lightly on the table. This practice is said to date back to the late eighteenth century, when the Qianlong Emperor went on one of his fact-finding missions to the south of China. Travelling incognito, as emperors sometimes did in those days in an attempt to understand what was really going on in their realm, he dropped in on a teahouse with his small retinue. When the emperor poured them some tea, his footmen were flustered, because palace etiquette dictated that they should respond by falling to their knees, and yet they knew they should not give away his disguise. So they tapped their two fingers on the table as a miniature form of prostration, laying the foundations of a habit that remains common in Cantonese communities all over the world.

Booming properties prices and competition from restaurants spelled the end of the heyday of the Hong Kong teahouses. ('If it *doesn't* move, build on it', Hong Kong people quip). Their vast, sprawling premises were knocked down and replaced by skyscrapers; some teahouses moved to new locations, but most of them closed down for good. These days people flock to Lin Heung for a glimpse of the past, or the smarter Luk Yu teahouse nearby in Central. Luk Yu, named after the Tang Dynasty scholar who wrote a treatise on tea in the eighth century, was founded in 1933 and retains its old wooden panelling and atmosphere of edgy glamour. In 2002 it was actually the scene of a triad killing: a local property tycoon was shot in the head as he ate his breakfast. Here, in the mornings, you can still find waiters carrying snacks on trays slung around their necks, a style of service that predates the trolley.

After my breakfast in Lin Heung, I wandered out into the streets of Central. In a market, an old woman was stripping the green peel from tangerines, releasing their sharp, citrus fragrance into the air. Nearby, the sweet, heavy scent of freshly baked custard tarts drifted out from a small bakery. Cured meats and sausages hung over market stalls; butchers worked with cleavers on wooden blocks. Behind every shopfront, red lamps glowed before shrines to protective deities. Hong Kong Island may have one of the world's most hyper-modern skylines, and an infrastructure so efficient it makes you think cramming over a million people on to a tiny piece of land in the South China Sea is a great idea, but at street level, away from the designer shops and the grand hotels, you can still find the grit, the intense physical sensations, and the echoes of a much older China that give the city-territory its enduring appeal.

It was a soggy, sultry day. Rose had texted me the address of the restaurant. It was hard to find, hidden among the cafés and bars of the entertainment district. There was nothing around the nondescript entrance to suggest that this might be a place to eat: just a street number, and a dank concrete hallway leading inside. But the address seemed right, so I stepped inside, and took the small, dark lift to the fourth floor as instructed. There, I stumbled into a florist's workshop, where a Chinese woman was trimming leaves from the stems of roses. 'You here for the restaurant?' she asked. I nodded, and she pointed me towards an apartment door covered by a steel grill. A sign above bore the name of a company importing household goods. It didn't look promising, but the number was correct so I rang the bell.

A few seconds later, the inner door opened, and a man's face appeared behind the bars, looking blankly at me. 'Is this the right place for lunch?' I asked, doubtfully. He clicked open the grill for a second, and invited me in. The walls of the small, scruffy apartment were lined with cabinets filled with files and stacked boxes of napkins and tablecloths. More boxes were piled up on shelves near the ceiling, just as you'd expect from a company importing household goods. If it hadn't been for the tempting aromas and sizzly sounds coming from the tiny kitchen, and the three round tables set for lunch, I would have imagined I was in an office, not a restaurant.

Soon, Rose and her Cantonese girlfriends arrived, and we were all seated around a table in what appeared, from the built-in wardrobes, to have once been a bedroom. A few other guests arrived, and then the man who had let us in began to bring food out from the kitchen. There was braised duck with beancurd, an omelette with oysters, deep-fried prawns with white mugwort leaves, Chinese broccoli with dried fish, and a chicken soup with salted lemons. It was all rather delicious, and tasted even better because of the atmosphere of secrecy and adventure that surrounded our lunch.

The restaurant – I wouldn't tell you its name, even if it had one – was just one of the so-called 'private kitchens' (*si fang cai*) of Hong Kong. These illicit, small-scale eateries first sprang up in the wake of the Asian economic crisis of 1997. They were a way of making a little money without the interference of the taxman and government bureaucrats, and won their trade by word of mouth. Some were so popular that you had to wait months for a table.

Since those early, heady days, the government has tried to rein them in, and many of the private kitchens have become legitimate restaurants. But if you know the right people, like Rose, you can still find the odd speakeasy, like the one we lunched at, which really is run illegally in the offices of an import company.

Why would a sophisticated businesswoman like Rose want to dine in a cheap hole-in-the-wall restaurant like this? It's partly because of the thrill of the chase. Tracking down one of these rumoured establishments and bagging a table makes you feel ahead of the crowd. For the locals there's also, no doubt, a certain pleasure in cheating the government out of its taxes, and getting a slap-up meal at a knock-down price. Most of all, though, there's that slim but tantalising possibility of finding really marvellous and authentic Chinese regional food.

Hong Kong is a city obsessed with eating. Everywhere you go, there are people slurping noodles, devouring dumplings, picking up a skewer of deep-fried sparrows at a street stall. Sounds of frying and delicious smells emanate from all around. And if you start a conversation about food among Hong Kong Chinese friends, be warned that you will unleash a runaway train of food reminiscences, cooking tips, and hot restaurant recommendations.

And because the object of all this passion really is *eating*, rather than glamorous décor or being seen in the right places, people aren't snobbish at all. They know that you will very likely find the best beef noodles in Hong Kong at a shabby *dai pai dong*, or a sensational Muslim pastry in a shack in Kowloon. It's not uncommon to find rich men cracking open seriously expensive bottles of wine in some cramped backstreet café with chipped formica tables. And if you wander through the Wanchai wet market, you can be sure to see chauffeur-driven Mercedes parked nearby, their motors running as the *tai tais* (the Hong Kong equivalent of Ladies Who Lunch) buy impeccably fresh vegetables and seafood for their Thai or Filipina housekeepers to cook. So if word gets around that a good 'private kitchen' has opened, its phone will ring off the hook. Rose only got a table that day by the skin of her teeth.

The private kitchens tend to have their charming eccentricities. One I vis-

ited was billing itself as Hong Kong's answer to El Bulli, and my evening there
was a riot of fusion experiments such as 'steamed foie gras, sticky rice, and
caramelised green daikon purée'. Another had a chef who worked during the
day as a biochemical engineer; his hobby was cooking, so he spent his nights
slaving over a hot stove, producing modernised Shanghainese delicacies such
as a salad of beansprouts and fresh yellow lilies, and braised pork ribs with
honey and vinegar. One of the earliest and most famous private kitchens, Da
Ping Huo, was run by a Sichuanese artist and his wife who had shipments of
chilli and Sichuan pepper delivered every week from Chengdu. She was a
trained Sichuanese opera singer, so every night, after cooking dinner for
twenty or so guests, she would come into the dining room and sing.

On my last-but-one trip to Hong Kong, I was researching a newspaper article
about restaurants and food shops. My editor had asked for 'the ultimate guide
to eating in Hong Kong', and since I am very conscientious but had only five
or six days at my disposal, I had to eat more-or-less non stop from morning
till night. I would begin with *dim sum*, congee and/or noodles, then have a
couple of lunches, spend the afternoon grazing in various food shops and
cafés, and end the day with at least one dinner. I ranged widely in my explorations, from the grand Spring Moon restaurant at the Peninsula Hotel, with
its fine teas and marvellous barbecued pigeons infused with osmanthus, to
Mak's Noodles, where I lunched on prawn wontons in soup.

I ate many delicious things during that week, but the best meal of all was
the last, a late-night supper in Cheung Fat, an old Chiuchow café in the district of Kowloon called Kowloon City. Chiuchow, or Chaozhou, is a region in
the north-east of Guangdong Province with a distinctive cuisine that is little
known outside Asia. In the nineties, when Hong Kong people had money to
splash around, Chiuchow delicacies made with high-class (and high-price)
ingredients like shark's fin or conch were all the rage. To me, however, the folk
cooking of the region is far more inspiring. Chiuchow people specialise in
cold cooked meats and seafoods, which are served with a dazzling array of dips

and sauces. They are also known for their delectable stewed goose. They eat raw crabs and clams marinated in garlic, chilli and coriander; soupy rice with shellfish; delicate sweetmeats; and an addictive preserve made from Chinese olives and salted mustard greens. Chiuchow is one of my favourite Chinese regional cuisines.

Unfortunately I only realised that Cheung Fat was going to be the gastronomic highlight of my trip after I had entered the café, and by then I had already eaten one dinner at another Chiuchow restaurant on the Kowloon waterfront. At the first place, I had intended to order modestly, just for a taste, but the food was so good that I had ended up eating rather a lot of sweet-sour *e-fu* noodles, pigeon casserole, salted radish omelette and green beans with Chinese olive preserve. By the time I reached Cheung Fat, I was already full, and was planning on just having a quick sniff around before going back to my hotel to sleep. But when I saw the crabs hanging in the window and the extraordinarily delicious-looking fare on the tables all around, I realised that this would not be possible. So I tried to impress upon the waiter that neither I nor my Cantonese dining companion was actually hungry, while asking them to give us a kind of tasting menu of all their unmissable specialities.

Thus we ended up with another fourteen dishes for dinner. Of course they were all irresistible. Although Cheung Fat looks like a grotty little café, with its canteen-style furniture, humming fridges, scuffed vinyl floor and walls covered in pieces of paper scrawled with the names of dishes in Chinese characters, it is probably the best place in Hong Kong for grassroots Chiuchow cooking.

We munched our way through various cold, cooked fish dipped in Puning yellow-bean sauce; red-and-white crab with brown rice vinegar; aromatic cold meats that included the famous goose and also cuttlefish; large shrimpy creatures with plum jam; prawn cake with hair fungus and a treacly dip; deep-fried Puning beancurd; an amazing taro cake studded with pork and water chestnut; and a typically Chiuchow soup of bitter melon, soybeans, spare ribs and salted mustard greens. We ended the meal as we had begun it, by drinking tiny bowlfuls of roasted Iron Buddha tea. As you can imagine, by the time I arrived in Taipei the next day to begin intensive gastronomic research for another article, I felt ready to have a heart attack. But that's another story.

After that decadent dinner, I took a taxi back from the run-down ghetto of Kowloon City to the Peninsula Hotel, where I was staying in a four-roomed suite with picture windows overlooking the harbour, a private telescope and its own marble-clad jacuzzi. As always, Hong Kong seemed like a place of almost violent contrasts. There was my own personal seesaw between the pull of China and the longing for home, and between the conflicting desires of my Chinese and English selves; and then there were the contrasts of the place itself, between wealth and poverty, East and West, skyscrapers and street stalls, shrines to the ancient god of wealth and temples to modern mammon. Somehow, I reflected as I lay back in the froth of my jacuzzi, it had been a very typical Hong Kong day.

Steamed chickens' feet with black bean and chilli

豉椒蒸鳳爪

Serve these for breakfast with some nice tea and steamed buns.

18 oz (500 g) chicken's feet
1/3 cup (75 g) white sugar
Oil for deep-frying
1 tsp Sichuan pepper
1 star anise
A piece of cinnamon stick or cassia bark
2 spring onions, white parts only

0.7 oz (20 g) ginger, unpeeled, sliced
3/4 tsp salt
2 tbsp peanut oil
2 tsp finely chopped garlic
1 tbsp fermented black beans, rinsed
3 tbsp oyster sauce
Salt and sugar to taste
One fresh red chilli, cut into thin slices

1. Bring a quart (a litre) of water to the boil in a saucepan.

2. Cut the tips off the chickens' feet, along with the toenails.

3. Add the 1/3 cup (75 g) sugar to the boiling water and stir to dissolve. Then add the feet, return to the boil and blanch for a couple of minutes. Remove and set aside until completely dry.

4. Heat the deep-frying oil to about 392°F (200°C). Add the dried feet and deep-fry until golden-brown. Drain and set aside.

5. Place a quart (a litre) of water in a saucepan with the Sichuan pepper, star anise, cinnamon, spring onions, ginger and 3/4 tsp salt. Add the feet, bring to the boil and then simmer for about 30 minutes until tender. Drain and shake dry.

6. Heat 2 tbsp peanut oil in a wok, add the garlic and stir-fry briefly to release its fragrance. Add the black beans and sizzle for a few seconds more. Add the oyster sauce, stir a few times amd then pour in 100 ml water.

7. Add the chickens' feet, bring the liquid to the boil and season to taste with salt and sugar if necessary. Stir vigorously for a couple of minutes until the feet are covered in sauce and the liquid is much reduced.

8. You can eat them immediately or – in the dim sum fashion – place the feet in a small bowl in a bamboo steamer. Scatter over the chilli slices and then steam them until you wish to eat them.

This recipe is based on one told to me in great detail by chef Zheng of the Royal China Club restaurant in Baker Street, London, with the kind permission of manager Edward Jia.

CHAPTER 12

Feeding the Emperor

'Transmit the viands!' called the young Emperor Pu Yi, imperiously. Dinner time was whenever he felt like eating, there were no fixed hours. 'Transmit the viands!' called the junior eunuchs to the other eunuchs standing in the main hall. The order passed like a Chinese whisper from eunuch to eunuch, until it finally reached the *yu shan fang*, the Imperial Viands Rooms, as the kitchens were called. The cooks leapt into action. Before long, the eunuchs, in procession, were scurrying towards the emperor's quarters with dozens of red lacquered food boxes painted with golden dragons, and the tables on which to serve them. There were no dining rooms in the palace, so they set the tables up wherever the emperor happened to be, six or seven of them: two for main dishes, another in winter for the various soups and stews that sat over flickering flames, one for cakes, one for rice, one for congees, and another for salted vegetables.

Chinese emperors dined off yellow porcelain decorated with dragons, the imperial motif. There were strips of silver on the dishes, and silver chopsticks, because the metal was known to discolour in the presence of poison. (This was just a final precaution, because each dish had already been tasted by one of the eunuchs, who was watched carefully for signs of sickness before the emperor was fed.) The last emperor, Pu Yi, was presented with a mere thirty dishes at a sitting; the Empress Dowager Longyu, dining in her own quarters, with a hundred. The emperor ate alone, scrutinised by the eunuch servants. Whatever he had really eaten, their report to the senior concubines would be the same, dictated by ritual: 'The Lord of Ten Thousand Years consumed one bowl of old-rice viands (or white-rice viands), one steamed breadroll (or a griddle cake), and a bowl of congee. He consumed it with relish.'

These days the Forbidden City is just a museum. Pu Yi abdicated in 1912, at the tender age of five, when Republican forces had overthrown the Chinese imperial system after more than two thuousand years. Yet, under a bizarre agreement with the new government, he remained in the palace with the wife and senior concubines of his predecessor, and a vast staff of eunuchs, for a fur- ther thirteen years, until he was evicted by the warlord Feng Yuxiang's National Army in 1924. During that time, his life continued in all its pomp and ceremony, but his power ended abruptly at the dark-red perimeter walls. After the communist takeover of China in 1949, the palace was maintained as a museum and some of its workers lived within its confines, but later they too were shunted out, because of the risk of fire. Now, when the gates close at night, the citadel known as the Great Within (*da nei*) is deserted.

Although I had been travelling in China for many years, I had never spent much time in the great northern capital, Beijing. I passed through every couple of years on my way to somewhere else, meeting up with journalist friends and eating the odd Peking duck, but I can't say I really knew the city. So, eager to move beyond Hunan and to broaden my culinary horizons, I spent a few weeks there after Christmas one year, researching Chinese impe- rial cooking.

Central Beijing in January is magnificent, with its wide boulevards, stately architecture, and imperial yellow tiles glistening in the pale midwinter sun. At its heart lies the Forbidden City, which is being repainted and refurbished after years of neglect. Parts of it have been restored to gleaming splendour, but in the rest the paint is peeling, and the courtyards are worn and tufted with weeds. I sat, one bright morning, on the steps leading down towards the Inner Court, with the Last Emperor's autobiography in my hands, trying to imagine the smoke rising from the chimneys of the Imperial kitchens; the processions of eunuchs, their feet padding along the drafty colonnades; and the young emperor Pu Yi, surrounded always by his suffocating retinue of staff.

In theory, Pu Yi might have been blessed with the finest of diets. Imperial Beijing, after all, as the more-or-less continuous Chinese capital for 600 years, should have been one of the best places in the world to eat. The sumptuous cuisine of north-eastern Shandong Province, once the home region of Confucius, formed the bedrock of palace cooking. It was grandiose in style, with its fine stocks, rich soups and liberal use of fiendishly expensive ingredients. But it was always augmented by the tastes and techniques of other regions. When, during the Ming Dynasty, the Yongle Emperor moved his capital north to Beijing in 1403, the flood of officials who accompanied him brought with them chefs well versed in the kitchen lore of Nanjing, the old southern capital. During the Qing Dynasty, the Qianlong Emperor enjoyed lengthy sojourns in the southern Yangtze region, where he was seduced by the region's luxurious ways and fine gastronomy. He brought back with him chefs from centres of fine-dining like Yangzhou, who wove their own recipes into the imperial menus.

The Qing emperors were Manchus from the northeast, not Han Chinese. Their ancestors had been nomads, eaters of bread and mutton, nibblers of pastries and candied fruits that were easy to transport on horseback across the northern grasslands. They drank milky tea, like the Tibetans and Mongols. After their conquest of China in 1644, the Qing ruling class never entirely lost their taste for such barbarian fare, and ensured that roast meats and certain sweet pastries became part of the repertoire of palace cooks. They also introduced Manchu dining customs, combining them with the more delicate eating habits of the Han Chinese: they carried knives in sheaths that had a pocket for chopsticks, so they could slice off chunks of meat and then eat them in the Chinese fashion. The blending of Han and Manchu culinary cultures at court reached its peak in the 'Man-Han' imperial banquet, a legendary three-day extravaganza of feasting that is said to have included more than 200 different dishes and snacks.

Into Beijing's melting pot of regional and ethnic foodways poured the finest produce from every corner of the empire. Tealeaves came in tribute from the hills of Zhejiang and Yunnan in the appropriate seasons; candied ginger from Yangzhou; Sichuan pepper from Qingxi in western Sichuan; and exotic delicacies like dried mushrooms and seafood ('treasures from the mountains and the seas') from far and wide.

Outside the palace, civil servants from all over China, working on rotation in Beijing and elsewhere, kept grand official residences. Highly educated, and often with discerning palates, they developed their tastes as they travelled, and goaded their private chefs to innovate at the stove. And so evolved a number of individual culinary styles that blended the flavours and cooking arts of different regions: some of them became so well known that they have survived until the present day, like the Tan Family Cuisine (*tan jia cai*) served in a restaurant of that name in the Beijing Hotel.

The emperor himself normally took two main meals a day: breakfast early in the morning, and the so-called 'evening viands' at around one o'clock. And then at six in the evening or thereabouts, he had an 'evening snack'. Every menu had to be formally approved by the Imperial Household Department before it could be cooked, and each was filed afterwards in the palace archives. (One, dating back to the reign of the Jiaqing Emperor records, for a day in 1799, a light breakfast served to the emperor's father at the start of the Lunar Year. It lists more than forty dishes, including soups made from bird's nest, duck, chicken, deer's tail and pork, vegetables, little steamed buns, New Year's cake, and 'all kinds of pastries and snacks'.) While the main Imperial kitchens supplied the emperor's grand daily provisions, smaller tea-kitchens provided informal refreshments, and pastry kitchens were at hand for buns and cakes.

If the emperor's daily meals were lavish, state banquets were arranged on an improbable scale: at the inaugural feast of the Jiaqing Emperor, for example, the kitchens laid on 1550 hotpots. When the British government first attempted to make contact with the Chinese court in 1793, the Qianlong Emperor entertained the British envoy Lord Macartney and his party to a 'sumptuous banquet'. Small tables, one for every two guests, were stacked with a 'pyramid of dishes or bowls piled upon each other, containing viands and fruits in vast variety'. The serving and removing of the dinner was conducted with such silence and solemnity that the Englishmen likened it to 'the celebration of a religious mystery'.

Sometimes the grand eating habits of the palace spilled out into the life of the common people. It was ex-palace chefs of Shandong origin, for example, who joined a man named Yang Quanren in setting up a roast-duck venture in Beijing in 1864. Roast duck had been around for centuries, but the traditional way of making it was in a covered oven (*men lu*) with a fire beneath it. Yang introduced the people of the capital to the roasting techniques of the palace kitchens, in which the birds were suspended over a fruitwood fire that gave their skin the most delectable crispness. His restaurant, Quanjude, became a national institution, and gave the world Peking Duck as we know it today.

That January in Beijing, I set myself a mission to find the old kitchens of the Forbidden City. Several times I went there, buying my ticket at a booth in the outer courtyard, walking through one of the inner gates, a mousehole at the foot of towering red walls. I spent my first few visits exploring the grand halls, losing myself in the limitless lanes and the vast, abandoned courtyards.

The imperial kitchens were marked on my map as lying just to the east of the Outer Court, but when I eventually found them – two long buildings with tiled rooves – they lay in forbidden parts of the Forbidden City, closed to visitors. After a while, my curiosity overcame me, and I ignored the signs and slipped through a gate. The guards either didn't see me or turned a blind eye. In the end, however, the kitchens were still unreachable in their locked, walled compound. I stole through an open door into a neighbouring building that was filled with steam and fantastical pipes, the nerve centre of an old-fashioned central-heating system, but there was no way through. Walking deeper into the private office areas of the Palace Museum, I fell into conversation with a member of staff, and before long found myself drinking tea with a friendly and knowledgeable expert on the Forbidden City named Professor Luo. His office, at the side of a traditional courtyard, was stacked messily with books and periodicals.

We talked for a while about imperial dining habits, and then, in an act of spontaneous kindness, he took me on a tour of the imperial collections in the museum. We saw the ritual bronzes of the Shang and Zhou dynasties, patterned with stylised beasts and birds; the heavy jars that were once filled with grain and sealed into tombs; the delicate white ceramics of the Sui. We walked through galleries that explained the ritual of imperial wedding feasts. Most intriguingly, Professor Luo told me that some of the palace storerooms had never been cleared, and were still filled with dried foodstuffs and medicinal herbs from the early twentieth century, when the Last Emperor still lived within its walls.

Pu Yi ascended the throne on 2 December 1908, when he was not quite three years old. The formidable Empress Dowager Cixi, who had ruled at court since 1898, had suddenly decided to make him heir to the throne as she lay on her deathbed in November. So the young boy was wrenched, howling, from his family and installed in lonely splendour in the Forbidden City.

It was just the start of a strange and turbulent life. Pu Yi ruled, with his father as regent, for barely three years before his abdication in 1912. When, at the age of eighteen, he was rudely expelled from the palace, having continued to live there until then under the terms of his abdication agreement, he took refuge in the Japanese concession in Tianjin. In 1934 he became the puppet emperor of the Japanese vassal state of Manchukuo in northern Manchuria – an ill-fated collaboration that led to his being branded a war criminal at the end of the Second World War. Following the armistice, he spent five years in a Siberian prison, and then travelled back to China by train in 1950, where he was imprisoned for another decade in an attempt to 'reform' him through labour and ideological indoctrination. In 1959, Pu Yi was formally pardoned by the communist state, and spent the rest of his life as an ordinary citizen in Beijing, working as a gardener and, later, a researcher in the imperial archives.

In his autobiography, Pu Yi condemned the excesses of the old imperial court, and said the Republican government had allowed him and his household to continue 'our prodigious waste of the sweat and blood of the people in order to maintain our former pomp and continue our parasitic way of life'. But he wrote his autobiography under communist supervision, and the communists clearly wanted to play up the wasteful extravagance of the Qing and the Republicans who succeeded them.

But was it even necessary to exaggerate? Pu Yi quotes the imperial records of food expenditure for a single month of his reign, when he was a mere four years old. Apparently, the tiny emperor, the empress dowager and four high consorts together consumed about two tonnes of meat and 388 chickens and ducks in that month alone, of which about 400 kilogrammes of pork and 240 chickens and ducks were destined for the emperor himself. That's about 14 kilogrammes of meat and nine birds every day, for a tiny child! Even in my wildest and most excessive periods of 'research' in China, I haven't come close to this. Needless to say, most of this extraordinary food budget must have been wasted, or siphoned off by the eunuchs, who were notorious for their embezzlement of imperial funds.

After my tour of the palace museum with Professor Luo, fantasising about deer's tail soup for breakfast, I became more and more hungry. But I couldn't find anything to eat. The chimneys rising from the old tea kitchens were cold, the imperial kitchens boarded up and empty, and there weren't even any modern snack bars for the tourists. In the end, my energy fading, I came across a few tables and chairs set up outside the hatch of some kind of stall. I laid down my heavy bag. Through a gate in the dark-red walls, I could see the end of the old imperial kitchens. But the only hot food being sold on that freezing January afternoon was pot noodles, cooked in water poured from a thermos flask. So I sat down with my lists of imperial delicacies, and my books about the lives of the emperors, and ate instant noodles with beef-flavoured sauce out of a disposable plastic bowl.

Food has always been of exceptional importance in Chinese culture. It is not only the currency of medicine, but of religion and sacrifice, love and kinship, business relationships, bribery and even, on occasion, espionage (legend has it that the Chinese organised a rebellion against their Mongol conquerors in the fourteenth century by hiding messages in mooncakes). 'To the people, food is Heaven,' goes the old and oft-repeated saying.

Once, when I was visiting the National Palace Museum in Taipei, I came across a rather peculiar exhibit. There, in a glazed display cabinet, on a deli- cate plinth tooled with cloud patterns in pure gold, sat what appeared to be a chunk of tender cooked pork. The skin was a rich, glossy brown, flecked with the dots of hair follicles. The flesh, layered unevenly with fat, drooped succu- lently over one edge of the plinth. It looked delicious, like a piece of belly pork that had been braised for hours in a clay pot with soy sauce, rice wine and sugar. My mouth watered... but the label on the cabinet was a stony reminder that the 'meat' was made from a piece of cold, hard agate.

This pork chunk is one of the most prized imperial treasures, spirited away from the Forbidden City when China was consumed by war. The Nationalist authorities loaded their pick of the precious objects in the palace onto a convoy of lorries, and drove them deep into the Chinese hinterland. As battle raged around them, and Japanese bombs fell, the custodians of the museum skirted the areas where the fighting was worst, and ultimately shipped their cargo over the straits to Taiwan, where the Nationalists were setting up their exile government. Incredibly, not a single object was damaged or broken in the course of this long and tempestuous journey.

A piece of pork fashioned out of precious stone, displayed on a golden plinth. I tried to imagine a golden joint of roast beef, studded with diamonds, rubies, emeralds and pearls, sitting amid the coronets and sceptres of the

Crown Jewels in the Tower of London. But it was absurd, unimaginable. Only in China would you find a piece of common meat fashioned out of a precious material by master craftsmen and displayed among the treasures of the nation. It seemed like a metaphor for the seriousness of the Chinese approach to food, as well as its wit, its levity and its joy.

In ancient China, food was not only a pleasure but a grave matter and one of the main concerns of government. Edible sacrifices made to gods and ancestors sustained the social and political order: neglect them, and chaos would surely follow. That was why the Zhou Court of the first millennium BC, according to later historians, assigned more than half its staff, or two thousand people, to matters related to food and drink. There were dieticians and chefs; game hunters and butchers; meat-dryers and turtle-catchers; picklers and icehouse attendants. Some were responsible for preparing sacrificial offerings, others for feeding the king and his consorts.

Political power was symbolised by the *ding*, a cauldron used for cooking meat for sacrifices. In the distant reaches of Chinese history, the number of *ding* a nobleman was allowed to possess depended on his rank. Steal a man's *ding* in a military campaign, and you took away his lordly authority. The ceremonial *ding* themselves, cast in bronze, covered in geometric patterns, were at the heart of ritual life. These distinctive cooking pots are still one of the most potent symbols of Chinese civilisation: the Shanghai museum that opened with a great fanfare in 1996 takes the form of a *ding*.

Sages often compared the art of government to seasoning a stew. You had to balance the different flavours, the vinegar and pickled meats, the salt and sour plums, to achieve perfect harmony. 'The cook blends the ingredients,' said the statesman Yanzi in a text compiled more than 2000 years ago, 'and equalises them by taste, adding whatever is deficient and decreasing whatever is excessive. His master then eats it and thereby composes his mind. The relationship between lord and vassal also is like this…'

Others offered serious advice in culinary terms. The Taoist philosopher Laozi, author of the *Tao Te Ching*, warned that governing a state was as delicate a matter as cooking small fish, while Confucius, who lived in the fifth century BC, was as cultivated in his eating habits as he was in other aspects of his life: 'his rice is not excessively refined, and his sliced meat is not cut excessively fine. Rice that has become putrid and sour, fish that has spoiled, and meat that has gone bad, he does not eat. Undercooked foods he does not eat, and foods served at improper times he does not eat. Meat that is improperly carved, he does not eat, and if he does not obtain the proper sauce, he will not eat.' In China, knowing how to eat properly has always been a metaphor for knowing how to live.

The emperor himself ruled by divine appointment, and his first duty was to ensure that his subjects were fed. Droughts, bad harvests and famine were signs that the gods had tired of him, and that his mandate had expired. So every spring he ploughed three furrows at the Temple of Agriculture, and every winter solstice he fasted for three days before the annual sacrifice to Heaven. This was the most solemn religious ceremony of the year. A bullcalf, a sheep, a pig and a deer were killed in the sacred abbatoir of the Temple of Heaven in the southeast of Beijing. And then the emperor mounted the great stone altar, where he made offerings of wine and food, and banged his head on the cold marble floor.

If the best food the Forbidden City itself could offer in the post-imperial era was instant noodles, I'd heard of a Beijing restaurant that specialised in palace cooking. One evening I persuaded my Sichuanese friend Xun, who was also staying in the capital, to accompany me there for dinner.

A gentle wind stirred in the trees as we passed the great red gateway, and crossed the hump-backed stone bridge into Beihai Park. Red lanterns glowed along the edge of the dark, rippling lake. We walked through a curved colonnade, beneath a roof of richly painted rafters, watching the shifting, silent waters. The traffic and general mayhem of the city were forgotten. From here, the skyline appeared mysteriously bereft of high-rises.

Soon the grand entrance of the Fangshan restaurant beckoned. We passed the fierce stone lions, crossed a cold flagstoned courtyard lit by lanterns, and entered the dining room. It shimmered in a haze of yellow and gold, almost hallucinatory. Yellow curtains hung behind tables draped in yellow cloths and laid with yellow plates and bowls. Waitresses in embroidered yellow robes bore trays of yellow teabowls. Golden dragons curled up golden pillars, and writhed on the painted ceiling. The old-fashioned lanterns dripped with yellow tassels. It was overwhelming, this golden evocation of the imperial past. ('When I think of my childhood,' said Pu Yi, 'my head fills with a yellow mist.')

Fangshan specialises in Chinese imperial cuisine, with an emphasis on dishes derived from the repertoire of the great Man-Han banquet. When Pu Yi left the Forbidden City, four or five of the former palace chefs opened this restaurant, then on the northern edge of the lake in Beihai Park, on the advice of a former palace eunuch, Zhao Renzhai. 'There were no recipe books in those days, and most chefs were illiterate,' the manager Wang Tao told us, 'so all their skills were passed from generation to generation by word of mouth. During the Cultural Revolution, for about ten years, this place was not open to the general public, although it continued to serve political insiders; later it was opened to important state guests; and finally in 1989 to the public once again. So although the original chefs were all dead by the sixties, we have an unbroken chain of teaching and tradition that extends right back to the Forbidden City.'

Xun and I began our meal with a selection of delicate palace appetisers. There were small blocks of a paste made from peas, subtly sweetened and ice-cold on the tongue; and slices of a roll made from sugared haricot beans stuffed with red-bean paste and crushed sesame seeds; cold meats and vegetables. Naturally, we were then offered a parade of showy delicacies: shark's fin soup, slices of gelatinous camel's foot in a dark, velvety sauce; soft-shelled turtle; sea cucumber and abalone. Some of the snacks were of particular imperial interest, like the small sesame flatbreads with a minced-pork stuffing. The Empress Dowager Cixi is said to have dreamt of these one night, only to find them served for breakfast the following morning, to her delight. Cixi is also associated with small steamed cones of maize flour: she was given these *wo tou* by a peasant when she fled to Xi'an after the Boxer Rebellion in 1900, and enjoyed them so much that her cooks recreated them in a more elegant fashion on her return to Beijing.

Sadly, Xun and I didn't have three days and three nights available for the full Man-Han banquet experience, so we had to content ourselves with a mere seventeen or so dishes and snacks. We emerged at the end of the evening lost in yellow, well-fed, and rather enchanted with the whole palace dining experience. But of course I was aware that the dishes at Fangshan bore as much relation to the real foodways of Beijing as the menu of a restaurant with three Michelin stars does to the diet of a dustman in Peckham. And while I was in the capital, I wanted to experience the local food at its grittiest. The secretary of the Chinese Culinary Association had told me that, if I really wanted to taste the city's street food, I should try *lu zhu huo shao*, which loosely translates as 'flatbread in broth'. He warned me that it was not for the fainthearted, but I brushed off his words with a breezy smile.

Over the next few days, I kept an eye out for *lu zhu huo shao*. And when, one frosty morning, wandering in the *hutongs* that run alongside the eastern edge of the Forbidden City, I stumbled across a grungy snack shop that had a sign outside advertising ths dish, as well as other local 'small eats', I strode right in and, with my usual bravado, asked them to serve me with their most important specialities. It was a decision I regretted almost immediately.

After all my gastronomic adventures, there is only one thing that I really dislike eating, and that is the digestive apparatus of the pig and other large animals. I've eaten tripe and chitterlings enough times to feel that I am not *prejudiced* against them – I eat them with an entirely open mind, and still I hate them. Their textures don't bother me at all. What I find loathsome is their rank, stealthy taste, that insidious reek of digestive juices that no amount of garlic or coriander can dispel. It stirs up in me a profound, visceral anxiety that I cannot quite explain.

On that freezing morning in Beijing, the cheery staff of the café brought forth their finest dishes and laid them on the table. The steaming stench of offal rose up and engulfed me. Here was the stuff of all my worst food nightmares lined up before me in a gruesome parade. There was a tangle of slivered sheep stomach with a sesame dip; a vile mess of pig's liver and chitterlings in a thick, gloopy sauce; and a murky broth in which floated pieces of sheep's liver, tripe, heart, lung and intestine. Most ghastly of all was the proud centrepiece of the feast, *lu zhu huo shao*, which one of my Chinese food books renders in English as 'Boiled pig's entrails with cake bits'. Beads of oil quivered like sweat on the surface of a dismal broth that was a casket of animal extremities: chunks of purplish pig's lung, pale tubes poking out of their sponginess; pieces of stomach and liver; slices of wobbly intestine... A fetid aroma emanated from the squashy tubes and chambers. This was hardcore streetfood, fuel for the bellies of tough working men.

I felt faint and nauseous. It would have been bad enough at any time of day, but for *breakfast*... I found myself reverting to the kind of disdainful thoughts you'd expect of an adopted Sichuanese like me. 'The diet of these northerners is so rank and stinky! What muttony brutes they are!' I swallowed a few foul-smelling slices of gut and liver and fled to a dumpling shop across the way.

When I first began thinking about the emperor's banquets, I have to admit that I felt a little envious. Imagine, whenever you were hungry, being able to snap your fingers and summon a procession of eunuchs bearing seven tables laden with food! Imagine being followed at all times by servants from the Imperial Tea Bureau carrying boxes of cakes and other delicious titbits, teacups and flasks of hot water.

But Pu Yi says in his autobiography that he never touched the food from the main imperial kitchens. Those thirty dishes had all been prepared long in advance, since they had to be ready to be whisked into the imperial presence at a moment's notice. They had sat around for hours on the stoves, sagging.

According to Pu Yi, the eunuchs set up these official meals some distance away from him, where presumably the fats in the thirty dishes congealed, the soups grew cold, the vegetables wilted, and the pastries staled in the open air. Some of the dishes may even have been fake: one of my sources in Beijing told me wooden roast chickens and other models were used to heighten the impression of plenty.

Meanwhile, the young emperor actually ate from a quite separate selection of dishes produced in the Dowager Empress Longyu's own private kitchen. Like the eunuchs, many of whom had their own catering arrangements, she knew better than to trust the central palace kitchens. The chief imperial cooks, according to Pu Yi, were aware that their food had not been eaten for more than a decade, since the reign of his predecessor Guangxu. Did they even care how it tasted? The food Pu Yi ordered the cooks to send to the High Consorts on their birthdays was, he says, 'expensive and showy without being good… neither nutritious nor tasty.' One can imagine the apathy, the creeping negligence of the chefs, after years of producing these untouched feasts.

The grand state banquets can have been little better. Think of food cooked in enormous cauldrons, on a vast scale, and then transported long distances across lanes and courtyards, before being laid out in front of state guests seated according to a rigid hierarchy in the drafty halls. Imagine the endless toasts, the stifling ritual. How cold and dreary the food must have become. Sometimes, it's true, they set up chafing dishes to keep some of it warm. But it was all show food, fusty and bombastic, a pageant of expensive delicacies to flaunt the wealth of the Chinese empire.

I wondered if anyone had really enjoyed their meals in the Forbidden City. It is a solemn, intimidating place, especially in winter, its beauty austere. From outside, you see only roofs and watchtowers, bounded by faceless walls and a wide, frozen moat. It looks more prison than palace, forbidding as well as forbidden. The hearts of the newly selected imperial concubines must have sunk as its gates clanged shut behind them.

The diets of the concubines were strictly regulated, like everything else in their lives. They were graded by rank: in the Qing period, first below the empress was the imperial consort, then there were two high consorts and four ordinary consorts, eight so-called *gui ren* (another lower rank of consort), and any number of lesser concubines. They were only allowed to eat really well when, or if, they fell pregnant, because it was thought that in normal circumstances a rich diet would breed lustful thoughts. So at other times they were assigned quotas of meat, poultry, vegetables and grain foods according to their status. The imperial consort, for example, might get 12 *jin* (about 6 kilogrammes) of pork and ten aubergines a month, and a chicken or duck every day; but a woman at the bottom of the heap would be given only six *jin* of pork and six aubergines, and a mere ten birds every month. (Imagine the bickering, the bitchiness, as the top concubine savoured her piece of succulent pork at the end of the month, while lesser concubines were left with vegetables and beancurd!) The chance to eat more richly would have been just another incentive to get pregnant, an achievement that might enable a low-ranking concubine to rise up the sexual pecking order: a secondary concubine who produced a son might even end up as empress dowager, like the formidable Cixi.

Life in the palace was ridden with filthy intrigue, whoever you were. Even emperors could be its victims, like Pu Yi's predecessor Guangxu, who was humiliated and imprisoned by the Empress Dowager Cixi after a virtual coup d'etat, and who later died in suspicious circumstances. Many of Cixi's enemies came to sticky ends: suicide, decapitation, imprisonment and exile. She disliked one of her daughters-in-law so much she deprived her of food and drink until she died, had one imperial consort drowned in a well, and was also suspected of poisoning a rival dowager empress with some tainted soup. At one point, Pu Yi himself was so terrified of being murdered that he was unable to sleep, and he says in his autobiography that theft, arson, murder, gambling and opium-smoking were common within the palace walls.

Supposedly, the emperor could have eaten anything and everything. The world was his abalone, in a golden shell. Yet, as a child, Pu Yi had no appetite.

He was taken from his mother before he was three, and the grandmother who had doted on him had a breakdown when he left. He didn't see either of them again for seven years, and his father only visited him for a couple of minutes every two months. Eventually his mother committed suicide, with an overdose of opium. His wet-nurse was the only person who awakened in him feelings of empathy for other human beings, and she was dismissed when he was eight years old. The high consorts of the two previous emperors officially became his 'mothers' when he was adopted into the palace, but it was a formal relationship and he says he never knew any motherly love. The heart of the empire was a cold-hearted place. Starved of affection, Pu Yi developed a stomach ailment.

It probably wasn't just a lack of love that contributed to his digestive problems. Pu Yi's diet was tightly controlled, because the health of the emperor was paramount. 'Your Majesty's body is a sacred body,' Pu Yi remembers his mother telling him when she finally did visit him in the palace. And as Professor Luo explained to me, when we met for tea one day in a café just outside the Forbidden City, 'in those days they thought fever was a symptom of inner fire, which would be exacerbated by the consumption of rich and highly seasoned food. So whenever children in the imperial family fell sick, they were given only congee to eat, to cool them down. Of course such a diet was inadequate, and many of them, over the years, actually died of malnutrition.' Pu Yi himself describes how once 'I stuffed myself with chestnuts, and for a month or more afterwards the empress dowager… only allowed me to eat browned rice porridge; and although I was crying with hunger, no one paid me any attention.' He was so desperate to eat, he says, that he snatched a little cold pork that some princes had sent in tribute to the empress dowager, to the fury of his minders.

Pu Yi's sexual life was no more successful than his gastronomic life. Of course he was provided with a wife and concubine when he came of age (a mere two 'dishes', compared with the hundreds of some of his predecessors). Later, he took another consort and another wife. But sex for an emperor wasn't meant to be enjoyable, any more than dinner. The Chinese have long memories, and no one had forgotten the dissipated life of the Xuanzong Emperor of the eighth-century Tang. He fell badly in love with his favourite concubine, Yang Guifei, and when his reign collapsed after a bloody rebellion, his romantic infatuation was blamed. After that, the sexual lives of the emperors were strictly regulated. Bedmates were not allowed to stay the night, lest they exhaust the Son of Heaven. Whispering eunuchs kept an eye on things, to make sure no dangerous attachments developed.

With Pu Yi, they didn't have to worry. Professor Luo, sipping his jasmine tea in the café, lowered his voice as he told me that the last emperor was impotent. 'One of my grandmother's closest friends was his concubine,' he told me, 'and she wrote many letters to my grandmother. In them she said how lonely and miserable she was, and made veiled allusions to the emperor's incapacities. Of course no one could speak of this openly, but his lack of "face" made him bitter and tormented, and he mistreated his wives.'

Pu Yi himself confessed to a 'taste for cruelty' in his autobiography, and wrote that he abandoned his new empress on their wedding night in 1922 because he preferred to sleep alone. Though he married four girls, he said 'they were not real wives, and were only there for show [and] they were all my victims.' Rumours of homosexuality dogged him when he lived in Changchun under Japanese protection in the thirties and forties. He never had a son, or a daughter for that matter, which rather neatly solved a potential problem for the communists who took over in 1949. There were no loose ends for the Chinese to tie up, as there had been, with such bloody consequences, in Russia.

It was the emperor's duty to feed the people, but his own personal appetites were irrelevant. 'Appetite for food and sex is nature,' the philosopher Gaozi once said. But the emperor wasn't an ordinary man, he was the Son of Heaven, and for him food and sex were political events. Eunuchs watched him eat, and they waited by his bedroom door. All in all, the last emperor was a pitiful figure. Like his ancient imperial predecessor, Shi Huang Di of terracotta-army fame, he was incarcerated in an opulent tomb, provided with endless servants, riches beyond imagining, and every delicacy in the empire. The difference was that, when he was incarcerated, Pu Yi was still alive.

MENU FOR THE WEDDING FEAST
OF THE GUANGXU EMPEROR IN 1889

Spit-roasted Pig

~

Spit-roasted Sheep

~

Two kinds of 'Sons-and-Grandsons' Cakes

~

Bird's Nest 'Double Happiness' 'Eight Immortals' Duck

~

Bird's Nest 'Double Happiness' 'Gold-and-Silver' Duck Slivers

~

Two kinds of Soup of Fine Pork Slivers

~

Bird's Nest 'Dragon' Smoked Chicken Slivers

~

Bird's Nest 'Phoenix' Gold-and-Silver Flowery Pork Knuckle

~

Bird's Nest 'Present' Five-Spiced Chicken

~

Bird's Nest 'Auspicious' Gold-and-Silver Duck Slivers

~

Two small dishes

~

Two kinds of soy sauce

~

Two kinds of 'Eight Immortals' Bird's Nest Soup

~

Two kinds of Old Rice Viands

CHAPTER 13

Guilt and Pepper

The air in the orchard has a mesmerising, citrussy smell. The pimpled green berries, just beginning to blush pink, cling in ones and twos to the thorny stems of the trees. Despite the drizzle and the grey sky, I'm elated. I pluck a pair of peppercorns and rub them in my hands. The fragrance comes quickly, perfuming the air around. It is overwhelming, so fresh and zesty, so redolent of wood and wildness. I close my eyes. And then I put some pepper between my lips. In its green astringent newness, it puckers my tongue immediately, and then, a few seconds later, the tingling hits. That incomparable tongue-numbing sensation of Sichuan pepper, a fizzing that starts stealthily and rises to a mouth-streaming, breathtaking crescendo that can last for twenty minutes, before it slowly, gradually dies away. It is stronger even than I expected, and I laugh in surprise. For years I have dreamt of tasting Sichuan pepper on the tree, and here I am, in Qingxi itself, my lips singing.

Sichuan pepper, flower pepper, prickly ash, *hua jiao*... It is the original Chinese pepper, a native spice used long before black pepper stole in over the tortuous land routes of the old Silk Road. It is also the space dust of the spice world. An unexpected first encounter with it can be disconcerting, to put it mildly. I offered some to a stranger, once, at the annual Oxford Food

Symposium, without a word of warning: he thought I was trying to poison him, and hasn't spoken to me since. Actually, I should have been more careful, remembering my own first experience of Sichuan pepper, during a visit to Chongqing in 1992. 'The dishes were all flavoured with a particular spice which I found utterly unpalatable,' I wrote in my diary. 'It tasted like a powerful combination of aniseed, lemongrass and chilli and numbed my mouth with an unbearable taste. I ate very little other than soup and rice.'

I smile to read that now, knowing how the gentler cooking of Chengdu turned me into a Sichuan-pepper addict. And I have developed a better strategy for introducing it to other people. Psychological preparation is essential ('Are you sitting comfortably? Then let me explain…'). Instructions must be followed precisely. 'Put this pepper husk into your mouth, chew it *two or three times* at the *front of your mouth* and then spit it out immediately! Do not carry on chewing, wondering why nothing is happening, or it may overwhelm you (the tingling sensation takes a good ten seconds or so to develop). Now sit back and wait!' This more subtle approach tends to win people over, if only because of the wild novelty of the sensation, and I've seen many of my friends succumb to its charms.

In all my years of research for my Sichuanese cookery book, I never actually saw a Sichuan pepper tree. For that, you have to go to the high, dry slopes of various places in northern and western Sichuan. But of all the pepper grown in the province, none is better than that of the remote county of Hanyuan in the southwestern mountains, and within Hanyuan County itself, nothing compares to the sumptuously aromatic pepper of Qingxi Township. Even within Qingxi there are finer distinctions for aficionados: if you want to reach the very pinnacle of peppery perfection, you must accept nothing less than pepper harvested from the trees of *niu shi po*, the Ox Market Slopes, at the village of Jianli just outside Qingxi itself. Once, this pepper was sent in tribute to the imperial court. 'Qingxi Tribute Pepper', they still call it here.

I'm not sure why it took me so long to go to Qingxi, when I'd wanted to for many years, but I only made it there, for the first time, in 2001. Most of my Chinese acquaintances would have baulked at the idea of accompanying me on a gruelling journey into the impoverished backwoods of the province, but one old friend, Mu Ma, was game. So, one morning in June, we set off from Chengdu by long-distance bus on the hard eight-hour ride to Hanyuan County.

I met Mu Ma in the course of my food investigations in Chengdu, and we hit it off immediately. He's an academic who spends his time travelling around remote villages in south-west China, researching and documenting traditional crafts and rituals before they disappear. Since knowing me, he's taken more of an interest in beancurd workshops, kitchen ranges and bakeries. Mu Ma's shaggy black hair always looks untidy, even if it's just been cut. He speaks in Chengdu dialect, and teaches me local nursery rhymes, like the Sichuanese equivalent of 'Jack Sprat and his wife':

Cai ban shang	*On the chopping board*
Qie la rou	*Slicing the bacon*
You fei you you shou	*There's fat and there's lean*
Ni chi fei, wo chi shou	*You eat the fat, I eat the lean*
Yao mei ken gu tou	*Little sister can gnaw on the bones*

Mu Ma doesn't give a damn about karaoke and fancy restaurants. When he's on the road, he takes very little with him besides a toothbrush, and stays in the most basic kind of guesthouse. He seeks out archaic teahouses and restaurants, old-fashioned printing houses and dilapidated monasteries; and spends hours in conversation with pedlars, peasants, and artisans.

When we finally arrived in Qingxi, we were accosted by a band of raggedy children, who, excited by this outlandish visitor who said she'd come in search of pepper trees, whooped and laughed as they led us through the lanes. The village houses were ramshackle, higgledy-piggledy, their wooden gateways leading into courtyards stacked with old pots and pans. Sun-bleached corncobs and dried chillies hung from the eaves. Beyond the last houses lay the pepper orchard where I had my first taste of the fruit.

In another month or two, the children told us, the peppercorns would be dark pink all over, dried by the hot sun, and they would split open to reveal their seeds, black and shiny like the eyes of birds. The young men would then strip the peppercorns from the branches, gather them in bamboo baskets, and lay the split, pimpled berries out in the sun to dry. When they were ready, the local girls would sit on their doorsteps, woven bamboo baskets on their knees, tossing the peppercorns to shake out their tasteless seeds, saving the aromatic husks.

Sichuan pepper is one of the spices mentioned in the ancient *Book of Songs*, where its shiny and abundant seeds are a symbol of fertility (a seed and a son sound the same in Chinese: *zi*). 'Pepper houses' (*jiao fang*), they used to call the chambers of Han Dynasty imperial concubines, because the spice was mixed into the mud used to plaster their walls, in the hope that the women would produce sons and heirs. Rural people exchanged bunches of Sichuan peppercorns as love tokens; the spice is still imbued with erotic symbolism because of the way its berries hang in pairs, like testicles. Even today, in remote parts of Sichuan Province, peppercorns are thrown over brides and grooms, an aromatic confetti.

The pepper is also a medicinal herb. It was unearthed in the grave of the Han Dynasty noblewoman found at Mawangdui; accompanying prescriptions written on silk advised its use in treating ulcers. It is thought to be a stimulant and diuretic, good also for relieving flatulence and encouraging digestion. Moths and other destructive insects shy away from the pepper's powerful aroma, so it is traditionally used as an insect repellent in wardrobes and granaries. Ingested in large quantities, it is severely toxic – which is why several ancient texts mention its use as a means of forced suicide.

After my first, striking taste of the fresh pepper, Mu Ma and I left the orchard with our retinue of children, and entered the gates of the Confucian temple opposite, a derelict timber-framed mansion. Once, it must have been splendid; now, it barely whispered of its former glory. A little bridge led over an ornamental pond, but the heads of the statues on its stone balustrades had been knocked off by Red Guards during the Cultural Revolution. The old temple hall had been brutally boarded up and carved into utilitarian rooms, and there were faded revolutionary slogans on the walls. Moss and weeds grew among the flagstones, and the paint on the buildings was peeling. We discovered it was being used as a social centre for the elderly, and on that day they were having a feast, so a dozen round tables had been laid in the courtyard.

As I entered, a flock of old ladies and men rushed up to me, beaming. 'Miss Rose, welcome!' They behaved as if they knew exactly who I was. At first I was perplexed by their familiarity before it dawned on me that they must be thinking I was Rose Acock, an Englishwoman who had been running poverty-relief projects in rural Hanyuan for years. I had never met Rose, but we had been in email contact once or twice. There clearly hadn't been any other Englishwoman in Hanyuan for a while, let alone another named after a flower. 'I'm not Rose, I'm Fuchsia,' I found myself explaining a hundred times. The villagers were astonished to hear this, but no less friendly.

Mu Ma started inspecting the few temple relics: a worn stone tablet inscribed with Chinese characters; an elaborate, dragon-coiled basin for burning incense. Some old ladies stood around him, telling stories of the place. After a while I became aware of a couple of khaki uniforms mingling with the villagers in the temple. They loomed closer, and soon I had a policeman at my side, studiously casual. He watched me as I scribbled in my notebook. Then he asked me for my ID. I rummaged in my bag for my passport. He made a big deal of his scrutiny, giving me a sly, disconcerting smile. I began to feel nervous. As far as I knew, there was no reason why I shouldn't be there. But the policeman was intimidating, and long years of experience of such things had taught me that it was best, in such situations, to play humble.

'What are you doing here?' he asked.

'I've come to see the Sichuan pepper trees.'

I realised as I said this how absurd it must sound. Sichuan is internationally famed for its tourist attractions: the giant Buddha at Leshan, Mount Emei with its 'sea of clouds', and the coloured lakes of Jiuzhaigou. Two hundred years ago, Qingxi was a flourishing transport hub on the *cha ma dao*, the 'tea-horse way' that connected inner China with Tibet and India; now it was a forgotten backwater. What would the policeman make of a foreigner who chose, instead of Jiuzhaigou, a trip to a shabby town in one of the most impoverished counties in the province?

'What are you doing here?' he asked me again, with a pointed glance at my notebook and pen.

'This isn't a closed area, is it?' I asked. He just gave me a hard glance, handed back my passport, and continued to observe me as I walked, self-consciously now, around the temple. He assigned a young policeman to watch over me. Barely more than a teenager, lanky and awkward in his uniform, this boy was plainly unsure what to do with the dangerous alien in his charge. I led him out of the temple and back into the village streets, and he stayed within a metre of me at all times, following me into courtyards, up lanes, and into fields.

I couldn't understand the senior policeman's paranoia. Perhaps he was being defensive in that faintly nationalistic Chinese way, reluctant to let a foreigner see the 'backwardness' of rural China. Perhaps he was just a product of his education: thirty or forty years ago, every foreigner was seen as an imperialist spy, intent on subverting the Maoist political system. When we had finished exploring the village, he insisted on giving us a lift in his police jeep back to our hotel in the nearby county town, Jiuxiang. He warned us not to go out.

Of course, as soon as he had dropped us, we left the hotel and went off in search of supper in the old town centre. The main street was an alley of wooden houses with panelled fronts and low-tiled roofs. Some were already boarded up for the night, others were still open for business. A seamstress leant over her puttering sewing machine at a table in the street. There were makers of funeral wreaths, vendors of incense, cigarettes and snacks. Night was falling by the time we stumbled upon the old *pai fang*, an amazing memorial gateway covered in a froth of extravagant carvings.

We ate rice and vegetables in a crumbling restaurant where the cook shook his wok over the flames of a coal-fired stove. When we finally made it back to the hotel, the police were waiting for us. They left me alone, but interrogated Mu Ma for an hour. They took down the details of his work unit. They asked him, again, what I was doing there. 'It's for her own protection,' they claimed. Some time ago, they told him, a Japanese tourist ran out of money here, stayed 'outside' in a farmhouse, and was murdered. 'It's for her own protection.' I slept uneasily, the sound of the frogs like a ghostly chorus outside.

Before I left Qingxi, I persuaded a villager to give me a small pepper plant, which I planned to take back with me to England. It was a slender thing, bedded in a little earth, swaddled in a plastic bag. I carried it back with me to Chengdu, where I cared for it tenderly, and then to Beijing. But at Beijing airport I had a sudden crisis of conscience. Britain was engulfed in the foot-and-mouth epidemic, and there was a crackdown on the import of fresh foods and agricultural products. I was afraid of being caught with my pepper plant. And so I left it, forlorn in its wrapping, on a table in a Beijing airport cafeteria. I thought about it all the way home, and for weeks afterwards.

Five years later, Mu Ma and I returned to Hanyuan in midwinter, just before the Chinese New Year. I had been in Shanghai for a few months, exploring the tastes of eastern China, and was hankering for mountains and wild open scenery. And I'd wanted for a long time to go back to Qingxi, to find out more about my most beloved spice.

The roads were as bad as I remembered. We took a comfortable modern bus from Chengdu to Ya'an, 'The City of Rain', but after that it was juddering country buses and potholed roads. The landscape was soft and amorphous. The sun shone vaguely through the mist. We crawled up mountain roads, the bus horn honking incessantly, through a landscape of steep terraced fields, green with winter vegetables, bordered by bamboo and pine. Little frothy cataracts spilt down from the heights to the boulder-strewn river bed, far below.

Higher and higher we climbed, the bumpy road clinging to craggy hills. There were precarious patches of cultivated green on even the highest slopes, farmhouses nestling amid plumes of bamboo. In the coal-mining area near Yingjing, we passed a ramshackle workshop open to the street. Everything in it was covered in a thin layer of coal dust, including the old man working there with pieces of metal. It looked like a scene from an old black-and-white film, except that there amid his grimy pots and pans, on a grimy chopping board, was a single lettuce, so vividly green that it appeared to glow. We juddered past, honking. Processions of lumbering trucks passed us. Some old men in army-issue greatcoats and fur hats with ear-flaps played Chinese chess outside a teahouse.

As we drove over the last pass before Hanyuan, the mountains were frosted with snow, the pine trees heavy with it, and then we were engulfed by a freezing white mist, dream-like. Finally we emerged into the arid Hanyuan landscape. Barren in winter, the fields were filled with battalions of spiky pepper trees. Just before we reached Qingxi, the way was blocked by a multiple pile-up, so we had to leave the bus, walk past a crumpled mess of lorries, and hitch a lift in the loaf-of-bread van belonging to an insurance company. 'Are you Miss Rose?' asked the driver as he rattled at dangerously high speed over the potholed road.

The following morning we rose early and went to the bus station, where we haggled for a lift to the village of Jianli where, on the Ox Market Slopes, the finest Sichuan pepper is said to grow. Eventually we agreed a price with the driver of another loaf-of-bread van, a jovial man with round spectacles that echoed the roundness of his face. As he waited for a last passenger to fill up the van, we chatted for a while. 'To look at you,' he said to me, 'one would imagine that you are not Chinese. Are you a foreigner?' Later, talking to Mu Ma, he referred to the *ying guo xiao huo zi*, the 'young English lad'. Staring at him in amazement, I told him that I was actually a woman, and no longer particularly young. The other passengers laughed at him. 'Sorry, my eyes aren't that good,' he said. I sighed as I thought of him driving us along a rutted track into the mountains. But it couldn't be helped. Finally we set off, crammed into the tiny van with a pepper farmer and his daughter, who carried agricultural supplies in baskets on their backs.

The valley was flooded with the cool blue-green of winter garlic. Every household around here once reared oxen to plough the land, and the Ox Market Slopes, where we were headed, was where all the beasts from the surrounding area were bought and sold. 'But now people use machines to till the earth,' said the farmer's daughter, 'so they don't keep oxen. It's too expensive to feed them all year round when they are only used for occasional work.' Still, there were a number of specialist beef restaurants along the road, cashing in on their local history.

The Ox Market Slopes lie at 1700 metres above sea level, 200 metres higher than Qingxi itself. And that, said the farmer, along with the dry climate and the sandy soil, was the secret of the famous tribute pepper. We left the van outside the local government office, where a man was practising Tai Chi in the yard, and a black hen pecked. The village head, warming his hands over a charcoal brazier, offered us tea, and then asked a woman who worked with him to take us around. So we tramped through the crunchy snow, and walked through an orchard of pepper trees. 'This area produces about ten tonnes of pepper a year,' said our guide, as we surveyed the prickly trees and the snow-blurred terraces of the valley. 'And it's the finest of all. They call the tribute pepper *wa wa jiao*, "baby pepper", because each pair of peppercorns also has a pair of tiny, embryonic peppercorns, or "babies" (*wa wa*) at its base.'

Back in the village, we were invited into a run-down farmhouse by some old women, a great-grandmother and a grandmother, who were looking after a two-year-old child while the wife of the household was out working. They gave us some of their home-grown pepper. 'If you have a stomach ache,' said the grandmother, 'take ten peppercorns in your hands, rub them, and then swallow them with cold water. You'll find it very effective.'

Our driver was still waiting outside the government offices, and there was one more sight to see before we returned to Qingxi. High above Jianli, just off the main road, stood a concrete post proudly emblazoned with the slogan: 'Hanyuan County, the home of flower pepper'. Just below it, less conspicuous, there was an old stone tablet engraved in Chinese characters. This stone is known as the *mian gong bei*, the 'Tribute exemption stele'. When we had visited Hanyuan five years before, it had lain, in pieces, under a bed in the local government offices, but a dawning awareness of the county's history and its tourism potential had seen it repaired and brought to this prominent spot.

Its worn characters told the tale of how the pepper farmers of the region won protection from the extortions of corrupt local officials in the last days of the Qing Dynasty. At that time, the imperial court demanded an annual quota of pepper in tribute, and its representatives in Qingxi were harsh in their exactions. They squeezed the peasants dry, driving them into desperate poverty. Eventually the peasants could bear it no more, and they petitioned the higher levels of government for mercy. In an act of imperial benevolence, the tribute tax was abolished, and the stone was set up in Jianli as a guarantee of the government's promise.

We piled back into the van and juddered our way to the main road, talking about pepper. And the local official, our guide, let slip that, in a modern version of the old tribute system, 40 *jin* of the choicest Jianli pepper is bought each year by the Ya'an government, and sent as a gift to Zhongnanhai, the Communist Party leadership compound in the heart of Beijing. 'All these shops,' she said, waving a hand at the rows of little booths along the main road, 'they say they sell tribute pepper, but you can't really find it around here. The best stuff is bought up by officials and people with the right personal connections. Most of what you see on sale here is grown in other parts of Sichuan, and wrapped up in Qingxi packaging.'

Mu Ma and I had lunch at one of the beef restaurants on the main road: a bubbling hotpot that rang and sang with Sichuan pepper. Later, we drove back down to Qingxi. Outside the Confucian Temple that we'd visited five years before, a crowd of peasants in brightly coloured clothes were milling around, negotiating prices for sacks of seed corn. Soon there was a tap on my shoulder. A stocky man told me to accompany him into the government offices, which I suddenly noticed were directly opposite the temple gate. 'Actually, I want to go and look at the temple,' I told him. But it was clear that refusal was not an option. He frogmarched me into the building, and up some concrete stairs into a freezing, smoky office overlooking the seed market. He invited me to sit down, and brewed me some green tea with water poured from a thermos flask.

I braced myself for the usual tedious interrogation. Would he keep me there for hours with his paranoia and political innuendoes? Would he make me write a self-criticism, signed with a fingerprint, like that jittery policemen I'd once met in a Tibetan area of northern Sichuan? Would he assign a teenaged policeman to watch over me? But it turned out that my host, the Secretary of the Qingxi branch of the Chinese Communist Party, was a new kind of party man.

When I explained to him that I was a food-writer and researcher interested in Sichuan pepper, his plump, generous face lit up. 'Welcome, welcome!' he said, and immediately disappeared into an adjacent office, re-emerging moments later with a glossy, full-colour calendar celebrating Qingxi tribute pepper. Proudly, he pointed out its features: the poems, the account of Qingxi's 1346-year history as a county seat, the close-up photographs of the famous *wa wa jiao*. 'Look,' he said, pointing, 'Can you see the "babies", the *wa wa*? That's the sign of authenticity.' He was keen, he told me, to spread the word about Qingxi and its pepper to the outside world.

I was surprised and delighted. He was the first Communist Party cadre I'd ever met who understood that he might make a better impression on a foreign writer by being hospitable than by treating her like a criminal or a spy. Had he been on some new Party PR course, I wondered?

I asked the Party's Secretary's advice about buying Qingxi pepper. 'I've heard that it's not always genuine,' I told him, 'And that some dealers import pepper from other places, and pass it off as the real thing.' 'No problem,' he said, and stabbed out a number on his mobile phone. Minutes later someone else came into the room. He turned out to be the Mayor. 'Look here,' the Party Secretary said to the Mayor, 'Can you get a *jin* or so of Qingxi Tribute pepper for Miss Fu? Make sure it's good stuff.' The Mayor rushed off on his errand.

Half an hour later, he was back with two paper bags, proudly emblazoned with a printed history of Qingxi tribute pepper. The Secretary seized a bag and we smelled the pepper, which was wonderful. The skin of the peppercorns was dark pink and pimply; inside they were silky white. 'Do please show me the *wa wa*,' I said. He looked closely at one pair of peppercorns, then another, and another. Then he shouted in rage. 'This is not real *wa wa jiao*! You see, some of them have the *wa wa*, but others don't, they must have mixed them up, diluted them!' He was fuming. The Mayor was summoned again. 'Look, this is no good, go again, don't ask in the shops, go and find some peasant who has kept by a small supply of the best stuff. There must be some around.' (No wonder it was hard to find the real thing, if even the mayor of Qingxi was fobbed off with fake tribute pepper. I tried not to smile.)

Eventually the Mayor returned with an unlabelled plastic bag of pepper. The peppercorns were still attached to tiny fragments of twig. Their scent was overwhelming, it flooded the room. So we scrutinised the peppercorns, and indeed they all came with their *wa was*. Everyone was happy. 'Thank you so much,' I said. 'And now perhaps I will go and look around the temple.' 'Yes yes,' said the Secretary. 'But please won't you join us for dinner a little later on?' So he gave me his phone number and we arranged a time and a place.

Back at the temple, I met up again with Mu Ma. In the main gateway a small band of naughty boys were sitting around a table, gambling and smoking cigarettes. The ringleader appeared to be about eleven, and was puffing away on his cigarette like an old roué, dealing cards and shuffling piles of banknotes. The others all looked wildly delinquent as they shouted and laughed, and chucked their cards and cash about the table. The ancient temple custodian looked on, quiet and resigned.

After a while a number of rather smartly dressed adults entered the court-yard. The bad boys melted away with their cards and cigarettes. The adults stood awkwardly around, looked at us for a bit, and then left. I guessed that they were government officials, but they left Mu Ma and me alone.

Since our last visit the main temple hall had been opened up and gaudily restored. A huge statue of Confucius in bright, primary-school colours loomed overhead. Outside, the crumbling stele and stone incense burner stood as they had for centuries. The elderly custodian of the temple pointed out the chicken feathers that were stuck to the side of the stele in a clotted, bloody mess. 'Students,' he said, 'killing chickens as sacrifices to Confucius before their exams.'

It was *la yue*, the month of winter sacrifices. Almost every household had been rearing a pig in preparation for the New Year, and now it was time for the killing. By the roadside, fires burned under communal stoves. Steam rose from huge basins of simmering water. We watched a man rounding up his family's pig in the courtyard of his house in the centre of town. The animal grunted, bristly with apprehension. Inside, the butcher was waiting, with his sharp willow-leaf knife.

It took five strong men to manhandle the struggling pig into the yard, and pin it down on the slaughter bench, where it shrieked and wailed like a stricken human. Then the butcher plunged his knife deep into its throat, and the blood gushed out in a torrent of purplish red. The pig continued to scream and writhe for what seemed like ages. Finally, it was dead, and the courtyard ran crimson with blood. The butcher made a cut in its hind leg, and poked in the nozzle of a bicycle pump. Then he stepped on the pump, and the pig plumped up ('Easier to butcher,' he said).

The strong men hauled the great flabby beast on to the stove bench, where they dipped each part of its body in turn into the basinful of steaming water. Another man stoked the fire underneath with pieces of wood. The pig's face, pale and lifeless, stared out at strange angles as they manipulated it on the bench. The blanched body parts were scraped clean of hair. The men were quiet and earnest as they went about their work.

One man sliced off the pig's head with a large knife, and then they hung the decapitated carcass from a wooden frame. They carved it up, there in the yard, ready for salting. A woman with wet hands unravelled yards of looping intestines on the bench while a little boy ran around with a pair of trotters dangling from a piece of string. Inside the house, the women were salting chunks of fatty meat and packing them into waist-high clay jars. A few days later, they would cook them in lard, and lay them down in jars for the rest of the year.

Mu Ma was busy taking notes as dinnertime approached. I reminded him that we were supposed to be meeting the Party Secretary before six. 'I'll join you later,' he said. So I left on my own. I hitched a lift on the back of a young bloke's motorbike, and almost flew down the hill, wind flicking through my hair, gazing at a sun-drenched landscape of peppered slopes and mountains salty with snow.

In the Mountain Villa restaurant, all the Party and government officials of Qingxi were assembled around a large, circular table in a private room. I recognised among them the smartly dressed people I had seen earlier in the temple. (So I had been right.) The Party Secretary was warmly welcoming, and raised repeated toasts to my health. 'Welcome to Sichuan! Welcome to Hanyuan. Even more welcome to Qingxi!' he cried. One or two other officials made attempts to be friendly, but it was clear that the rest of them harboured some lingering doubts about my presence. They glanced uneasily at my notebook as I scribbled. Although I listed the names of the dishes we ate in Chinese characters, my copious notes were in English, so they couldn't tell for sure if I was writing about more than just the food.

'Actually this is the first time the Qingxi government has received a foreign visitor,' said the Mayor, at my side, a little abashed. (Even the famous Rose, it seemed, had not yet dined with him and his colleagues.)

'Well, thank you,' I told him, 'I am honoured.'

The dinner was scrumptious, Sichuanese rustic cooking at its best. We began with slices of wind-dried sausage, tingly with Sichuan pepper and chilli, and chunks of delicious corn-fed chicken dressed in chilli oil. There was *jia sha rou* (slices of fat belly pork with glutinous rice and sweet red-bean paste, turned out of a steaming bowl and sprinkled with sugar); tea-fragrant salted greens stir-fried with minced pork; a whole pork knuckle, dressed in a lavish fish-fragrant sauce and sliding lazily off the bone; stewed brown beans with Sichuan pepper oil; a magnificent chicken stew with *tian ma*, an expensive medicinal tuber; and a slow, hearty stew of beef with carrot. The ingredients were locally produced and they tasted stupendous. It was the best Chinese meal I'd had in months, better than anything I'd had in the glamorous restaurants of Shanghai, and I couldn't stop eating. Rosy with wine and exhilarated with pleasure, I too proposed a toast: 'May the outside world understand and adore your Qingxi *hua jiao*!' The officials were delighted, and raised their cups in unison.

Mu Ma wandered in when the meal was almost finished, rudely, I thought, but I didn't say anything. We all rose from our seats, and Mu Ma used my camera to take a picture of me standing at the centre of two rows of officials, smiling, with the pepper trees and the mountains in the background. A local law officer offered us a ride back to our hotel in his police jeep, and the Party Secretary invited me to join him later at the bar of his own hotel, for drinks and karaoke. We parted on friendly terms.

Mu Ma was still hungry, so we had to find a place to eat. But he was behaving strangely: he wouldn't look me in the face and would barely speak to me. 'What's going on?' I asked, eventually. He wouldn't say. But when I pressed him, all his fears flooded out.

'What are you doing, accepting the hospitality of these local officials? You think they are generous, but I bet as far as local people are concerned, every-thing they give you, all that meat, all that wine, all that precious pepper, is paid for with money that they have screwed out of the peasants. I suspect they are just using you, trying to win you over. How can the local people see these officials as anything other than blood-suckers, greedy and idle? Look at them, running hotels and karaoke bars, hosting dinner parties at public expense. You've seen how poor people are here. When you said, at the pig slaughter, that you were going for dinner at the Mountain Villa, the family we were with all exchanged meaningful looks. And after you'd gone, they told me that's the place where the officials go, where they spend public money on food and drink. They hate the officials, and now they think you are one of them. As far as they are concerned, you have been eating and drinking at the expense of all the poor peasants of Qingxi.'

His words hit me like a thump in the stomach. It was true that corruption was rife all over China. Indeed, in the autumn of 2004, Hanyuan County itself had hit the international headlines. Venal local officials tried to evict tens of thousands of local farmers from their land to make way for a hydroelectric dam, and then to cheat them out of their compensation funds. The outraged peasants rose up against them, staging a sit-in by the dam construction site, just a few miles upriver from Qingxi. The central government, nervous at any sign of unrest, sent in top-ranking officials to reassure the populace, and para-military police to crush the riots before they spread. There were days of rioting, with mass attacks on government offices. Farmers were shot and killed: no one knew how many, because of the news blackout imposed on the whole county. Reading about this, I'd remembered about that paranoid policeman I'd met in 2001, and his vigilance had made more sense.

I was upset by Mu Ma's outburst, but angry too, and defensive. 'What was I supposed to do?' I asked him. 'I'm not like you, able to blend into the back-ground. I'm a foreigner, I'm totally conspicuous. People in these remote places treat me like a visiting dignitary – or a spy. What do you expect me to do when the local party secretary orders me into his office? Cause a scene by resisting? Anyway, I'm a writer, I have to see all sides of Chinese society. I want to know how things work here.' There was truth in my excuses, but I knew perfectly well that I had revelled in that dinner. Corruption and poverty had been the last things on my mind as I sipped my soup and let the steamed pork belly melt in my mouth. Grumbling, Mu Ma accepted that it was different for a foreigner. 'But I still think you should avoid these people.'

He didn't need to mention the riots of 2004. Had any of the officials I'd met been involved in the forced evictions, the compensation scam, and the violence? The Party Secretary had seemed genuinely warm and friendly, and had only recently been assigned to this job, perhaps in an attempt to clear the bad air after the riots. He certainly hadn't been around at the time. And the centre of the troubles had been a few miles away. But less than three years ago, this whole county had been under paramilitary control. After the turmoil, one local man, charged with killing a policeman, was secretly executed before he could appeal. The people of Hanyuan county, if not Qingxi itself, had even more reason to hate their local leaders than most Chinese peasants. A century after the pepper farmers had won their battle over tribute tax, some of them were again struggling to protect their livelihoods from the extortions of their leaders. And I realised that I had been so absorbed in the food that I'd forgotten all about it.

We stopped at a small restaurant where Mu Ma dined simply on bean-curd, vegetables and rice, exchanging friendly banter with the owners in Sichuan dialect. My belly felt uncomfortably full of chicken, pork, and beef. I was torn between gratitude at the kindness of the Party Secretary, whom I'd instinctively liked, and a feeling of guilt provoked by Mu Ma's words. In the end I called the Party Secretary and told him that I was tired and wouldn't make it to his karaoke bar.

The next morning, we woke early, and packed our things to return to Chengdu. The pepper in my bag had scented all my clothes, and the room. We walked to the bus station in a haze of its aroma, as the roosters were crowing, and the street vendors kneading dough for their morning buns. The first ramshackle bus to Ya'an was just leaving. 'Are you Miss Rose?' asked the conductor, as I bought my ticket.

A week after leaving Hanyuan, I was woken abruptly in the vagueness of the night by a bad dream involving a pig.

234 · *Guilt and Pepper*

I was taking care of the pig. It was enclosed in a sty at one side of an out-house with high ceilings and whitewashed walls. One day I came in to tend to it and discovered it at the far side of the room. This was alarming, as it was supposedly penned in, and I realised it must have leapt over the wall of its sty. Then I climbed on to a thin ledge because I needed to reach something. It was a precarious position, but I clung to a little cupboard attached high up on the wall to help me balance. But then the pig reared up on its hind legs and tried to attack me, snarling and snapping. Dark, hairy, and vicious, it leapt into the air like a dog. I seized a thin bamboo cane and hit it in the face several times, but it was strong, and the cane was flimsy. Slowly the cupboard started coming off the wall, and I became desperate, knowing that I couldn't hold myself up for much longer, thrashing at the pig.

Then I woke up.

And I wondered, was I dreaming of *the pig* at all?

Qingxi red-braised beef hotpot

紅燒牛肉

You will need a tabletop burner to make this recipe authentically.
Serves 4–6

2 lb 3 oz (1 kg) beef chuck steak
3 tbsp rapeseed oil or beef dripping (or a mixture of the two)
5 tbsp Sichuan chilli bean paste
0.7 oz (20 g) ginger, unpeeled, sliced
1 tbsp whole Sichuan pepper
1 tbsp ground chillies (optional)
2 tsp dark soy sauce
To serve:
18 oz (500 g) Asian white radish (daikon)
3 Chinese leeks (or 2 celery sticks)
Half a Chinese leaf cabbage
8.8–10.6 oz (250–300 g) beancurd
A good handful of coriander

1. Cut the beef into bite-sized chunks and blanch in boiling water. Drain.

2. Heat the oil and/or dripping in a pan over a medium flame. Add the chilli bean paste and sizzle until the oil is red and fragrant. Add the ginger and Sichuan pepper and stir-fry briefly until you can smell their rich fragrances. Add the ground chillies (if using) and fry for a few moments more. Add the beef to the pan.

3. Add hot water to generously cover the beef, with the dark soy sauce and a little salt, if necessary. Bring to the boil and then simmer over a low flame for a couple of hours until tender.

4. Peel and slice the radish, and trim the leeks or celery and cut into batons. Lay them in the base of a large metal serving bowl. Slice the Chinese cabbage and the beancurd, and place in two small serving dishes.

5. Switch on the tabletop burner. Add a little more water to the beef if necessary (it should still be immersed in liquid). Place the serving bowl on the burner and pour the beef stew over the vegetables. Scatter over the coriander.

6. As the hotpot bubbles away on the table, let your guests help themselves to beef, and the radish and leek when they are cooked. Encourage them to dip the Chinese cabbage and beancurd into the hotpot to cook.

7. Offer steamed rice separately.

If you do not have a burner, omit the leek or celery, the cabbage and the beancurd: simply add the radish to the stew when the beef is nearly cooked, and simmer until tender. Serve as a stew, garnished with coriander.

CHAPTER 14

Journey to the West

At seven o'clock on Sunday morning, the market was already coming to life. Bakers were hooking the first batches of *nan* bread out of tandoor ovens. Snack-sellers were lighting fires under their stoves, setting up cauldrons of soup to boil, and chopping piles of vegetables and hunks of mutton. The rising sun spilled through the poplar trees bordering the field, marking out long fingers of light on the ground. And already the first market-traders were arriving, steering donkey carts laden with produce, or driving flocks of bleeting sheep into the great livestock enclosure. Hungry after an early start, I bought a *nan* from one of the bakers. The golden, onion-speckled crust yielded to fluffy white dough: it was magnificently tasty.

By noon the field seethed with people and livestock, heat and dust. Buyers squeezed the flesh of sheep, haggled over cows, donkeys and goats. Alongside, the snack stalls were doing a roaring trade. A baker with an ear-splitting yell invited customers to taste his piping hot *samsa*, small pastry parcels of lamb and onion that he plucked from the domed walls of his tandoor oven. Young men lolled on ironwork benches under a canvas shelter, eating ice cream with a spoon as they watched noisy Kung Fu films on a propped-up television. Everywhere, people were slurping fruit juice or cool jellies in spicy dressings. The crowds milled around, talking and shouting in a melodic, guttural tongue that sounded like Turkish. The air was filled with the punchy scent of cumin from sizzling kebabs.

I found it hard to believe that I was still in China. The only reminder was the occasional street or shop sign, with Chinese characters alongside the local, Arabic-based script. Kashgar, the Silk Road town where this famous Sunday market draws trade from far and wide, lies in the desert province of Xinjiang, at the westernmost tip of the country. This vast region occupies a sixth of China's territory, and is home to myriad ethnic groups, including the Turkic Uyghur people, the largest minority, Tajiks, Kazakhs, Kyrgyz, Russians and, increasingly, Han Chinese.

I had wanted to go to Xinjiang for some time. Although I hadn't completed my research project on China's ethnic minorities, I'd always been attracted by the diverse cultures of the western regions, and their grasslands and deserts – wide open spaces that offered respite from the crowded intensity of China proper. As a student I had hitchhiked around the Tibetan provinces of Amdo and Kham, but I'd never made it as far as Kashgar. Years later, it wasn't just the thirst for adventure that drew me to Xinjiang. As a food writer, I had a particular desire to explore a region that lay at the culinary crossroads of Asia.

More than 2000 years ago, trade began along the perilous overland routes between China and the West that later became known as the Silk Road. Camel caravans carried silk and other luxuries out of China, bringing back spices, precious stones and the sacred texts of Buddhism. Kashgar was one of a string of thriving oasis towns that lay on the route from Central Asia to the glittering Tang Dynasty capital Chang'an (at the site of modern Xi'an). It was only after the opening of the sea routes in the late fifteenth century that the region lost its vitality, and many of the towns were reclaimed by the desert sands.

In Xinjiang one still senses this ancient connection between the Chinese and Eurasian worlds. At the market that day, I wandered among the farmers' stalls, where fruits and vegetables were laid out on the ground. The produce itself was a living record of the region's multicultural history. When the Han Dynasty Chinese envoy Zhang Qian passed through this area in the second century BC on his missions from Chang'an to the kingdoms of Central Asia, legend says he returned with new foodstuffs that were to have a lasting impact on Chinese cuisine: grapes, alfalfa, coriander and sesame, all of which are still of vital importance in the Uyghur diet. Still, you see carts of alfalfa and dried grapes in the markets, and the scent of sesame hangs over freshly baked bread.

Other foods such as carrots, cucumber and onions also found their way into Xinjiang, and then China, along the desert roads. The names of fruits and vegetables in the Uyghur tongue carry echoes of languages from all over Asia: the Turkic *piaz* for onions and *uzum* for grapes, Chinese words for garlic stems and Chinese cabbage, *turup* like the Persian *torobcheh* for scarlet radishes. And, alongside the crops that entered this region along the ancient land routes are sold the New World tomatoes, potatoes and chillies that revolutionised the diet here as in so many other countries.

For me, all this was fascinating. In my early twenties, during that long, hot summer when I stayed with a Turkish family in Anatolia, learning a little Turkish and Turkish cookery, I had stood on the brink of Europe, looking east; and here I was, a decade later, on the edge of China, looking back in the direction of Istanbul.

As usual, I was hovering around the food stalls that day, watching the cooks at work and pestering them with questions. The ice-cream vendor presided over a juddering machine that whipped up ice-cream in a copper cauldron surrounded by ice. At the back of the stall, enormous blocks of ice lay out on a table, melting slowly. 'How do you make ice on that scale, in September?' I asked him. 'We cut it from the frozen lakes in winter, and haul it back to Kashgar on a donkey cart,' came the unlikely reply. But it was true, the ice was mud-streaked and threaded with reeds to prove it. 'We can keep it all summer,' he told me, 'wrapped up and stored in underground pits.'

At another stall, young men in embroidered caps pulled noodle dough into lengths that they swung and looped in the air, stretching it into strands as fine and even as spaghetti. I persuaded them to let me try. It was an impossible task. In my hands, the dough stretched unevenly, the noodles snapped and shrivelled. Again and again I tried. Occasionally I found my rhythm, and the noodles spun out evenly for a moment, but then they disintegrated, collapsing into a jumble on the wooden board. The boys laughed at me.

I chose to eat a bowlful of their noodles rather than mine, sitting at a table in the sun with a motley assortment of Uyghur sheep-traders. The boiled pasta was topped with a colourful stew of mutton and vegetables: red and green peppers, garlic stems, onion, tomato and cabbage. I plunged in with my chopsticks. The noodles were fresh and springy in my mouth, utterly delicious.

The cooking of the Uyghur people, too, has echoes of both east and west. Their noodles and dumplings link with the band of pasta-eaters who live across northern China as far as Beijing, and they eat them with chopsticks in the Chinese style. The Kashgar spice stalls sell the familiar aromatics of Chinese cookery – Sichuan pepper, star anise, Chinese cardamom and fennel – but they also dispense herbs and flavourings redolent of Persia and Central Asia: saffron, green cardamom, safflower and rose petals. And while the Uyghur drink tea, constantly, like the Chinese, they show their nomadic heritage in their liking for yoghurt and other dairy foods.

For the Chinese, of course, this was always a barbarian land. In the past, they thought civilisation itself ended more than 1000 miles east of Kashgar, at the Jiayuguan fort in Gansu Province, where the last garrison of the Great Wall marked the boundary of the Chinese empire. From the eighteenth century onwards, however, the Manchu Qing state consolidated its grip on this outlying desert region, and a Muslim rebellion against Chinese rule in the 1870s was brutally crushed. In the 1930s, as China fell apart under the stress of warlordism, revolution and foreign invasion, the local people seized their moment and proclaimed a republic, East Turkestan. But it was short-lived. And then in 1949, Mao's victorious communists swept in with their peculiar brand of 'liberation', which actually meant, as it did in Tibet, de facto colonisation.

The Xinjiang Uyghur Autonomous Region remains an anomaly in the Chinese empire. The Uyghur people have even less in common with the Han Chinese than do the Tibetans: they are Central Asians in almost every sense, part of the great family of Turks that extends from Xinjiang through Uzbekistan and across central Asia, as far as modern Turkey itself. They speak a variant of Turkish and eat kebabs, and their faith is Islam.

In recent years, the Chinese state has pursued an aggressive campaign to develop its impoverished western regions. Han Chinese settlers have poured into Xinjiang, lured by economic opportunity, and Chinese white-tiled buildings have sprung up in every county town. The new part of Kashgar looks, by now, like anywhere else in China, with its dull apartment blocks and shopping malls, its karaoke bars and mobile-phone stores. But when I visited, you could still escape into the narrow streets and bazaars of the old Muslim town, and feel that you were in another world.

Coppersmiths beat their gleaming metal into the curves of cooking pots and kettles, while knife merchants lurked amid rows of bejewelled daggers. Shopkeepers sat cross-legged in the doors of dim Aladdin's caves hung with carpets or old porcelain and trinkets. Dark alleys shimmered with multi-coloured Atlas silks. The men wore Muslim skullcaps or fur hats, the women mixed workaday clothes with peacock finery. Some shimmered through the crowded bazaars in glittering ankle-length skirts, their sparkling slippers kicking up dust as they walked.

On many afternoons in Kashgar, I sat on the verandah of a teahouse somewhere behind the Idkah mosque, watching the donkey carts mingle with shoppers in the marketplace below. Ensconced on one of the carpeted platforms, birdcages hanging above me, I ate *nan* bread and sipped my black tea. Sometimes, one of the old Uyghur men would take a newspaper wrap from his jacket pocket, and offer to tip some of its contents, black pepper, safflowers or mysterious herbs, into my teapot.

There was an almost Mediterranean warmth about the Uyghur. The men clasped hands when they greeted each other; people laughed freely and moved

sinuously. All this was delightful to me, and such a contrast to the emotionally reserved Chinese. Even better, Xinjiang was the one place in China where
a Western woman, tall, with brown hair and green eyes, could disappear into
the crowd if she chose to, and walk through a market without attracting attention. Most of the Uyghur had Caucasian features; some of the local people
were fair-haired and green eyed. After the relentless scruniny to which I had
become accustomed in China, it was a sweet relief to be so inconspicuous.

One day, out in the Xinjiang countryside, somewhere near the Pakistan
border, I left the car I had hired and climbed up a hillside in search of a discreet
place to pee. I had been in the region for a week or two, and was dressed modestly in cotton clothes. I had a few scarves wrapped loosely around my head and
shoulders, to fend off the ferocious late-summer sun. On my way back down
the hill, I was surprised to run into a middle-aged Han Chinese tourist with a
long-lensed camera. He gave me a kindly and patronising smile. 'Hello, young
lady,' he said, 'So what national minority are you?' He clearly thought he'd discovered a member of a semi-forgotten tribe of nomads, and I didn't like to
disappoint him. (Perhaps even now I appear in his photo album as a specimen.)

As students in the nineties, intent on venturing into forbidden parts of
China, my classmates and I had found the mere existence of Xinjiang fantastically useful. Most of us had never been there, but we had all run into
Uyghurs in other parts of China, and been told by Chinese people how much
we looked like them. We were well aware that in the backwoods of places like
Tibet and Gansu, no one would expect in their wildest dreams to run into an
actual Westerner. If we concealed our cameras, fancy sunglasses and conspic-
uously Western clothing, we could easily pass for 'Xinjiang people', with our
big noses and strangely accented Chinese.

I remember once sitting on a shaky old bus somewhere in the bleak Gansu
countryside. I knew that the area I was in was closed to foreigners, so I had
tucked my hair into a pair of black knickers and swathed my head in a great
black scarf, which I imagined gave me a slightly Arabic air. My eyes were concealed behind a pair of crude, wonky Chinese-peasant sunglasses, my

backpack was hidden in the kind of white plastic sack that people used for carrying grain, and I was dressed in jeans, a padded jacket and some Chinese army boots. After buying my ticket from the driver, I sat silently at the back of the bus, trying to avoid conversation with my fellow passengers and to be as unobstrusive as possible.

I did, of course, look bizarre by anyone's standards. Not only did I stand out like a sore thumb on that bus full of Chinese peasants, I looked like no one you would ever run into in Xinjiang or anywhere else in China. Nonetheless, as I knew perfectly well, everyone on the bus would dimly remember some middle-school textbook that rambled on about the colourful, singing-and-dancing ethnic minorities of China, with their outlandish styles of dress and quaint social customs. Some of them might even have seen a few of the colourful minorities on TV. And sure enough, as I listened to the muttered conversations around me, I heard the word 'Xinjiang' crop up a few times. No one had the remotest suspicion that I might be an actual foreigner.

The people of Xinjiang were also useful to the foreign students of Chengdu in other ways. All over China, Uyghur migrants, most of them young men, set up portable grills on busy streetcorners, and offered lamb kebabs, scattered with chilli and cumin, to passers-by. So strong was the association between these people and the scent of kebabs that you had only to catch a whiff of cumin on the air to know there was a Uyghur nearby. But when I lived in Chengdu, a number of these kebab-sellers had a second line of trade, in cannabis resin, so the smell of kebabs became a kind of sensory analogy for the smell of smouldering hash.

Because of the link between the kebab sellers and the hash trade, you could always tell when a police crackdown on drugs was in progress. Suddenly, with no warning, the aroma of sizzling lamb and cumin vanished from the streets, and you couldn't find a kebab anywhere, however hard you looked. But then, slowly, the Uyghurs would re-emerge from the shadows, the good folk of Chengdu would start eating kebabs again, and the foreign students would resume their habit of getting stoned on Saturday nights.

In a Kashgar backstreet, I watched Ähmät and his family at work in their bakery. People said their *nan* bread was the best in the district, and in ceaseless demand. Ähmät tended the fire, raking the fierce embers in his tandoor oven, which was set into a platform outside a tiny workshop. Inside, his wife and sister rolled the dough into large rounds, and pricked a pattern into it with a gadget made from chicken's quills. They smeared each round with mashed onion and oil, and flipped it, upside-down, on to a padded cushion. Ähmät then thrust the cushion into the oven, and pressed the dough on to its heated wall. Ten minutes later, when he hooked it out, the bread was a ravishing golden brown, patterned elaborately with quill-pricks and morsels of roasted onion.

The *nan* is the staff of life for Uyghur people; it has an almost sacred significance. It is used in wedding ceremonies, where the imam invites the bride and groom to share a piece of *nan* dipped in salted water as a sign of their intended fidelity. It is also part of the visible landscape of the region. As you drive through the countryside, through irrigated fields lined with trees, and villages of adobe homes, there are bread-stalls at every turn. Sometimes a sleepy vendor sits behind a stack of half a dozen small *nan*; sometimes a stall is laden with dozens of flatbreads of different shapes and sizes. There are large *nan* the size of dinner plates; small *nan* like bagels with the hole filled in; shiny glazed *nan*; *nan* scattered with sesame seeds or onion; greenish *nan* made from dough mixed with chopped Chinese chives; sweet *nan* sprinkled with sugar and chopped nuts or seeds. The *nan* is a bread with many uses. It can serve as an edible platter for kebabs or juicy steamed dumplings; or be used to wrap food for a takeaway. It is eminently portable – perfect for a long, gruelling trip across the desert.

The Uyghur share their *nan*-baking technology with the Persians (who probably invented it), Afghans, Uzbeks, northern Indians and Turks, among others, and it has ancient roots in the region. The museum in the regional capital, Ürümchi, displays fragments of an actual *nan* from the eighth century, which looks very like those baked in Kashgar today. The Uyghur still treat their everyday bread with reverence. They never throw it away: even stale bread can be resurrected by a dipping in tea. One afternoon, as I walked through an avenue of poplars on the outskirts of Kashgar, a very old lady came up to me and clasped my hands in greeting. Then she rummaged in her pockets until she found a small piece of *nan*, which she pressed on me as a gift. I still have it in my flat in London.

Soon after my arrival in Xinjiang, I followed my usual practice and went to a bookshop, where I searched for material about the local cuisine. There were the recipe books I'd expected, and one or two volumes about food tradition, but it was a grainy colour photograph in a book on local customs that really caught my eye. It depicted a group of local dignitaries in traditional Uyghur costume standing around an entire *roasted camel*! On my way to Kashgar, in the nightmarket of the regional capital, Ürümchi, I had seen whole roasted sheep with curly horns, fresh from the tandoor oven, ready to be carved. But a camel? It was enormous! Had they built a special oven?

Of course I spent the rest of the trip asking everyone I met if they knew where I could find a roasted camel. Most of them looked at me as if I was mad. No one had ever heard of such a thing. Although you see camels grazing in the foothills of the Pamirs, to the south of Kashgar, the ubiquitous meat of Xinjiang is the fat-tailed sheep, also prized by the Iranians and other Central Asians. Outside every kebab shop and butcher's stall in the region, sheep carcasses hang, their football-sized lumps of tail-fat obscenely exposed. The fat itself is a delicacy, marvellously aromatic, which is why it is always threaded on to kebab skewers alongside the chunks of lean meat. Whole sheep are slaughtered and cooked for the major Muslim festivals.

I never did find a roasted camel. But one day when I was wandering through the Sunday market in southern Khotan, I almost tripped up on a camel's head, lying in the dust beneath a butcher's stall. Its feet were standing up nearby, like a pair of riding boots in an English country house. Above, amid the bulbous chunks of sheep's tail-fat and the strips of fatty mutton, hung tranches of a darker meat. The butcher told me it was indeed the flesh of the camel, so I bought some, and took it to a nearby kebab stall to be cooked. I retired to a teahouse nearby, and a few minutes later a Uyghur boy made his way through the crowd, bearing my steaming camel kebabs on a *nan* bread platter. It was good meat, rich and flavourful, and more tender than I had expected.

There were other fortuitous encounters on that trip. Sitting in a Kashgar teahouse one day, eating fresh figs, I fell into conversation with Memet Imin, a lively man in his fifties with a charming manner and sparkling eyes. He told me he played in a troupe of musicians who performed at Uyghur weddings. 'There's one tomorrow, come with me,' he said. So I did.

We met at the teahouse the following day, and soon he was leading me towards the old city. We passed the great square outside the Idkah Mosque where the Han Chinese were wreaking their usual architectural carnage. The lovely old Uyghur houses at the side of the square had recently been demolished, and those behind them hung in ruins, their courtyard gardens and wedding-cake plasterwork rudely exposed. The square itself was now fronted by tiled, concrete buildings, Chinese monstrosities covered in a thin veneer of Islamoiserie.

We hurried past this sad sight and dived into what was left of the Uyghur citadel. It was more like Marrakech than Beijing, with its a maze of blank, adobe-walled alleys, their wooden doorways opening into cool courtyards alive with vines and fruit trees. The scents of rice and mutton mingled around the entrance to the bridegroom's house, where a few men were preparing food in an ad hoc kitchen. A vast wok was filled with the essential wedding food, *polo*, a rich pilaf made with pearly rice, chunks of mutton and strips of yellow carrot; in another wok simmered a hot-and-sour vegetable stew.

On an upstairs verandah, Memet Imin and his band set up their instruments and began to sing and play, filling the air with rousing, passionate music. Little children ran up and down the stairs, and soon a girl brought me a bowl of *polo*, to eat with my fingers in the traditional way. 'It's very heavy and rich,' warned Memet Imin as he sipped his tea between songs, 'so you should never eat it in the evening, or you won't sleep soundly.'

As the musicians played on in the bridegroom's house, a young girl led me through the lanes to the home of the bride. Surrounded by her girlfriends, she was posing for photographs in a white, Western-style wedding dress, her hands patterned in henna, her hair glittered. In the next room, the older women of the family sat around a tablecloth on the floor, feasting. They helped themselves to deep-fried pastries served with sweetened *qaymak* cream; almonds, sultanas and dried apricots; *samsa* parcels of mutton, sponge cakes and dough twists; watermelon slices; and some of the literally hundreds of *nan* breads that were piled up in towers all over the cloth.

Amid the merriment of the wedding, I couldn't help thinking of those ruined houses by the Idkah square. Would there be anything left of the old Uyghur town the next time I visited, I wondered? There were no Chinese guests at the wedding, of course: there is little social intercourse between the Uyghur and the Han. Many Chinese people dismiss the Uyghur as *luo hou*, 'backward', that most damning of Chinese adjectives. 'Filthy as hell,' said one Chinese man who gave me a lift in his car, of the Uyghur, 'They don't know anything about hygiene.' Like most Han Chinese, he saw his people as a force for civilisation, bringing modernity to the benighted natives of the western regions.

As a 'barbarian' visitor to China proper, I am occasionally affected by these echoes of the age-old Chinese racial superiority complex, for example in the hints that Westerners are sexually decadent and somehow unclean. Yet this is so often mixed with such toadying because of the relative wealth of my home nation that it's never a disadvantage. But in Xinjiang, I saw what it was like to be a poor 'barbarian', without the weird kudos of an early industrial revolution and the victorious opium wars, without the glamour-by-association of the American Dream. In Xinjiang and Tibet, I witnessed the spectacle of 'Great Han Chauvinism', unleashed on people for whom I felt an instinctive sympathy.

It wouldn't be so bad if this was Tang Dynasty China, a shot-silk, jewelled, perfumed, star-spangled civilisation, the world's legend. But this is early twenty-first-century China, and the 'civilisation' it bestows on its colonies is often a tacky, off-the-peg outfit of wide roads, sterile concrete high-rises, karaoke bars and brothels. Chinese modernity is bad enough in a Chinese city like Chengdu. In Kashgar it is an outrage.

It's strange for me to hear myself saying such things. I've devoted years of my life to China, and I love the country in so many ways. For more than a decade I've been arguing its case. Yet give me a week or more in Xinjiang or Tibet and I see its uglier side. Unlike many of my compatriots, I've never thought of Chinese popular attitudes to Xinjiang and Tibet as malicious. Most Chinese people, after all, have little access to objective information about either place, and have had no social contact with either Uyghurs or Tibetans. Even Chinese policy-makers, I suspect, consider the demolition of old Kashgar to be an improvement, and wonder why anybody minds. I doubt that Chinese chauvanism in Xinjiang is any worse than racism in Europe or the colonialism of my own ancestors. But it's painful to see.

The Uyghur, of course, burn with resentment against the Chinese. It's dangerous for them to express this openly, but in every private situation, the anger and bitterness flood out. Once I was exploring a biscuit shop, marvel-ling at the similiarities between the chrysanthemum-shaped pastries within its glass cabinets and the well-preserved eighth-century pastries on display in the Ürümchi museum, when the owner started jabbering at me in Uyghur. I could understand only the two forbidden English words that he said, again and again, referring to the fragile independence movement and the failed Uyghur republic of 1933.

'Blah blah blah East Turkestan,' (he mimed a razor blade, slitting his throat), 'Blah blah blah blah East Turkestan' (slash). The door of the shop was open and he was almost shouting.

'Yes, yes,' I said, trying to quiet him, knowing that this kind of talk could lead him into serious trouble, but he wouldn't stop. I left the shop.

In the nineties, anti-Chinese sentiment in Xinjiang erupted into riots, bombings, and the assassination of Chinese officials. Many Han Chinese people were afraid to travel to the region. But the flood of Han immigrants that has come in the wake of the economic reforms and a brutal crackdown on dissent have stifled most resistance. People are afraid, on the whole, to talk of political matters.

One afternoon a young middle-school teacher, Ali, and his wife invited me for tea at his parents' house. We knelt around a large, low table covered in the nibbles and sweetmeats known as *gezäklär*. There was *nan* bread, with sugary preserves made from local apricots and shredded carrot; deep-fried dough twists dredged in sugar; crisp, flaky pancakes the texture of pappadoms; all kinds of sweet biscuits cut into ornamental shapes; and a silver tray of dishes filled with tiny almonds, dried jujubes, sultanas and paper-wrapped sweets. We chatted happily about the life and customs of the Uyghur and the British. But then I asked an innocent question about family size, a sensitive issue in China's minority regions, and Ali thought I was straying into political matters. He froze instantly, and the atmosphere did not recover.

Later that evening, as I wandered with my camera among the pool tables and snack stalls of the Kashgar nightmarket, I was shadowed by a secret policeman, who spoke both Uyghur and English. 'Hello, pleased to meet you,' he said with feigned warmth (his eyes hard, unsmiling), before interrogating me about my travel plans. 'Where have you come from, where are you staying, where are you going, are you working for a newspaper…?' I was deliberately vague in all my replies.

He trailed me for an hour. Infuriated, I took my revenge by using him as a free translator whenever a stall-holder did not speak Chinese. 'Please can you ask this man what exactly is in his dumplings?' I asked him. 'Is it sesame seeds or peanuts?' The spook was irritated, but as he was pretending to be my best friend he had little alternative but to oblige. 'How many spices are in this pigeon stew? And what kind of flour does she use in these fritters?' I went on and on and on, giving him none of the information that he wanted but filling my notebook with recipes. It was deeply satisfying. Eventually he gave up, and melted back into the crowd.

I wasn't followed by the police again, but I did become more sensitive to signs of ethnic tension. And I began to notice how often the Uyghurs' loathing of the Han Chinese coalesced around the matter of pork.

For the Chinese, of course, pork is the staple meat. They eat it on its own or stir-fried with vegetables, they wrap it into dumplings, they use its bones for stock and its fat to flavour almost everything they eat. When the Chinese say 'meat', they mean 'pork' unless otherwise specified. To the Uyghur, as Muslims, the mere idea of eating pork is abhorrent. One taxi driver, cocooned with me in the privacy of his cab, assured me that 'if a true Muslim eats pork, his skin will erupt into blood-spouting boils that can be fatal'. Others spat out that old adage about the Chinese 'eating everything' with expressions of visceral disgust.

Han Chinese have occasionally used the pork taboo in ways designed to inflame Muslim sensibilities. During the Cultural Revolution, Chinese Muslims were reportedly forced to eat pork and to drink water from wells contaminated by pigs. More recently, in the early nineties, a spate of offensive publications showing Muslims with pigs or pork triggered street protests in four Chinese provinces. Violent clashes between Muslims and Han Chinese in 2000 were sparked off by the hanging of a pig's head outside a mosque.

Although the Chinese authorities in no way condone such crass behaviour, many Uyghurs feel the government does not try hard enough to protect their feelings. 'In the eighties, there were more sensitive policies on ethnic minorities,' a teacher told me, 'and Han Chinese had to be discreet about their consumption of pork. It was actually illegal to display it in shops or markets, and anyway they would not have dared to flaunt it, because they knew they would be beaten up or knifed immediately. But now the Chinese have tightened their control of the region, and they are no longer afraid of us. They don't care anymore what we think.'

The Muslim taboo on pork reinforces strong social divisions between Uyghur and Han. Most Uyghurs won't patronise Chinese restaurants, even those that claim to serve food prepared in accordance with Muslim dietary laws. 'You can't trust the Chinese not to use any pork products, whatever they say,' a Uyghur shopkeeper told me. As for the Han Chinese, they tend to see Uyghur restaurants as dirty. And so the two ethnic groups dine separately, and don't talk to each other.

Revulsion at the pork-eating of the Han Chinese is the focus for general anxieties about cultural assimilation and contamination. A few years ago, a rumour that pigs had trampled all over Chinese black tealeaves earmarked for sale in Xinjiang spread like wildfire. It was widely believed that this had been done as a deliberate affront to Uyghur sensibilities, and moreover that the Uyghur chairman of the Xinjiang Uyghur Autonomous Region had published a notice in a newspaper warning Muslims not to drink Chinese tea. 'So everyone stopped buying tea produced in inland China,' one young Uyghur told me, 'and now we buy Indian tea instead.'

As the days drifted by, I found myself developing an unexpected aversion to pork. Perhaps it was all those taxi-drivers, ranting about the omnivorous Chinese, filling my head with visions of pustules and sickness, but I couldn't bring myself to go into Han Chinese restaurants. They started to acquire the dangerous aura of the early English Chinatowns: dark, mysterious, risky places, where you might end up drugged or abducted. Chinese butchers' shops reeked of rapacious carnivorousness, perhaps even cannibalism (those Chinese eat *anything*). If I ate pork myself, would the Uyghur be able to sense it, just as the Chinese say they can sniff out a dairy-eater in a crowd, from the smell of her sweat?

So I stopped eating pork. Except for once, in Khotan, on the Southern Silk Road. Magnificent though the Uyghur traditional foods were – those delightful noodles, rich *polos*, crisp *nans* and spicy kebabs – after a few weeks they were becoming a little repetitive for a European barbarian nurtured on the 'hundred dishes, hundred flavours' variety of Sichuanese cuisine. Like most travellers to Xinjiang and Tibet, I had found myself starting to dislike the Chinese, but I was still fantasising about their food. So one night I stole into an upmarket Chinese restaurant in the new part of Khotan. The food was stupendously good: the roast pork, the stir-fried duck, the sizzling chives... It was clearly a place for serious Chinese gourmets, aimed at wealthy jade dealers and local officials. Guiltily, I had to admit that it was the finest meal of the trip. But it left a bad taste in my conscience, a kind of rancid, oily shame.

The Uyghur may not be as omnivorous as the Han Chinese, but some of their traditional foodstuffs are just as imaginative. In a courtyard in one of Kashgar's Uyghur districts, a street vendor named Qurban and his wife laboured over a favourite local street snack: sheep's lung, and sheep-intestine sausages. The scene in their outhouse on the morning I visited resembled a surrealist installation. Two pairs of sheep's lungs, gleaming in the bright sunlight which shone in from the courtyard outside, lay on the ground, their obscene, glistening windpipes attached to the wooden nozzles of dangling cloth bags.

While I watched, Qurban filled the bags with a pale starchy liquid. As the liquid sloshed through the windpipes, the lungs themselves hissed gently and began to expand. They blew up extravagantly as Qurban filled them with almost unbelievable amounts of liquid. After the lungs had quadrupled in size and looked fit to burst, he bound the windpipes tightly with pieces of cloth. Then, one at a time, he lifted the immense, bulging sacs, hauled them across the yard, staggering under their weight, and hurled them into a vast wokful of simmering water on a brick stove by the gateway.

Later, down by the market in a Kashgar backstreet, I tasted the strange fruits of Qurban's labours. On his stall, the great ivory lobes of boiled lung were steaming away, topped with the rice-stuffed intestines made by his wife the same afternoon. He lopped off a few chunks of lung and a few slices of sausage and piled them up in a china bowl, drizzling over a good ladleful of stock. A gaggle of hungry customers were seated at benches around his stall, tucking in.

The texture of this delicacy is hard to describe. The pale lungs are smooth as custard, floury as a white sauce, chubby as a cheesecake. In fact, with a little added sugar you might imagine you were eating an English pudding, if it wasn't for the odd tube poking out...

In late summer and autumn, the bazaars of Kashgar are piled high with fruit. Men crouch over baskets of ripe, juicy green figs cradled in their fragrant leaves, or pull barrows filled with watermelons, pears, or mottled brown-and-green jujubes. There are dried fruits too, as there are all year round: dark, treacly apricots from the Kashgar area, green sultanas from the vines of Turpan, and melons from Qumul in the northeast. But while the region is famous for its fruit in general, it is the pomegranate that has the strongest resonance in Kashgar. In the shady carpet shops around the Idkah mosque, it appears as a motif, woven into the intricate patterning of the local rugs. And in the orchards, large, exotically beautiful pomegranates hang amid dark leaves, their skins glowing yellow, orange and ruby-red.

It was late afternoon, and two Uyghur businessmen had invited me to join them on their carpeted platform under the pear trees. The teahouse garden was dappled with sun. They sat on either side of a low table, propped up by cushions covered in brightly coloured, shot-gold brocade. There were teabowls on the white tablecloth, and a waitress brought platters of grilled lamb chops, sliced melon and pomegranates. The men were in an easy, expansive mood.

Both of them, they told me, were traders, running companies that were flourishing with the resurgence of economic ties between China and Central Asia. One of the men, Ismail, was keen to inform me about the nutritional benefits of the Uyghur diet. 'The onions we grow here are very pungent,' he said, 'so they counteract the fattiness of the mutton, and keep the blood pressure low.' The other, Husseyn, explained how the climate of the Kashgar oasis, with its cold nights and scorching days, brought forth the sweetest fruits. We broke open the pomegranates and devoured their sweet, dark juices, warmed by the late summer sun.

After a while, to my surprise, their conversation drifted into sensitive political matters. 'We Uyghurs are basically the same as the Uzbeks and Turks,' said Ismail. 'We were a great people once, under the Ottoman Empire, but it all ended with the First World War. The problem with the Uyghur is that they are too simple and pure, too trusting. They are easily abused, and now they are angry.' He went on in the same vein.

A slight breeze stirred in the trees; birds twittered in their branches. No one could hear us, but I still felt uneasy on their behalf. Perhaps they felt protected by their wealth and powerful connections, yet I couldn't help thinking of Rebiya Kadeer, the prominent female Uyghur entrepreneur and philanthropist, who was once held up by the Chinese authorities as a role model for the country's Muslims. In 1999, the political winds changed and she was detained for 'endangering state security' because she had sent some newspaper clippings to her husband abroad. She was imprisoned for six years before she was allowed to go into exile in the United States.

But Ismail was still speaking freely. 'The Han Chinese, they are a greedy race. Look at them, with their Kitchen God, and their shrines to the God of Wealth. They are a greedy race. I ask you, what *kind* of people worship food and money?'

Kashgar kebabs

1 lb (450 g) lamb shoulder meat
Salt
Pepper
1 small egg
3 tbsp cornstarch
Ground cumin
Ground chillies

1. Cut the lamb into ³/₄ inch (2 cm) chunks and sprinkle with salt and pepper. Combine the beaten egg with the cornstarch in a small bowl and add to the lamb. Mix well and set aside for half an hour or so.

2. Heat the grill or prepare the barbecue.

3. String the lamb chunks onto flat metal kebab skewers.

4. Grill or barbecue the kebabs. As they cook, sprinkle them generously with salt, cumin and ground chillies to taste.

5. Serve with fresh bread.

Note: if you have access to the flesh of the fat-tailed sheep, alternate the chunks of lean meat with chunks of tail-fat.

CHAPTER 15

Of Paw and Bone

As I began to explore new culinary regions of China beyond my old stamping grounds of Sichuan and Hunan, I found my thoughts drifting towards Fujian Province. Fujian lies on the south-eastern coast of China, sandwiched between Guangdong and the southern Yangtze region, and although it is now little known abroad, it was once at the forefront of Chinese international trade. In the Song Dynasty, Arab merchants sailed their galleys into the Fujianese ports of Quanzhou and Xiamen or Amoy, where they exchanged their cargoes of East Indian spices and luxury goods for Chinese porcelain and silk. Europeans traded at Xiamen from the sixteenth century until the mid-eighteenth. Later, the Chinese closed it to foreigners, but the British forced its re-opening as an international treaty port in 1842, after the first Opium War. As an entrepôt, Fujian has long exerted a steady, though rarely recognised, influence on the outside world: it is one of the most important sources of Chinese tea (the word 'tea' itself, and all its European variants, derive from Amoy dialect), and Fujianese immigrants, though less conspicuous than the Cantonese, are a powerful economic force in Western Chinatowns.

Fujian, like most provinces, has its own style of cooking, which the Chinese call *min* cuisine. Xiamen and the Fujianese coast are known for their oyster pancakes and other seafood delicacies; the mountainous areas of the north for wild foods that include bamboo shoots, mushrooms and all kinds of creatures. Fine oolong teas, including Tie Guanyin or 'Iron Buddha', and 'Big Red Robe' (*da hong pao*), are produced in many parts of the province. Living in Hunan, I had acquired a taste for Fujianese teas, and I'd sampled *min* cooking in the new Fujianese cafes of London's Chinatown, but I was hungry for more. And so I arranged to visit the scenic area of Wuyishan in the north with some old Sichuan University classmates who were living in Shanghai, before travelling to southern Fujian on my own.

We had set off along the Nine-Bend River in blazing sunlight, on a bamboo raft, the soft plish-plash of the poles in the water lulling us into a stupor. The famous karst limestone peaks of Wuyishan loomed up on either side. 'We call that one the tortoise,' said our young guide, pointing to a low bank of rock rising out of the water, 'and that's the Great King's Peak.' He improvised too, for fun: 'Over there we have the *han bao*, the hamburger' (of a fat stack of slabs), 'and that's the Titanic' (of a mighty prow of rock, facing downriver). But the clouds gathered quickly, the rain spat, and then a torrential deluge began. Briefly, we took shelter under a vast overhanging cliff, but it was nearly nightfall, and we had to press on. By the end we were all sodden, shivering. Our guide dropped us off in pitch darkness by the bank. We clambered up to the road, and flagged down a lift in a passing vehicle.

That evening I was more in the mood for shepherd's pie than an extreme gastronomic experience, but it was my last night in northern Fujian and I felt I had to eat snake. Restaurant owner Mrs Liu had a few, coiled slinkily, in cages out the back, by the kitchen. Her husband stubbed out his cigarette and lifted the lid of one of the cages. A poisonous snake reared up angrily, hissing. He slammed the lid down again. When the snake had calmed down, he raised the lid more gently and grabbed it by the neck with a long pair of tongs. It lashed and writhed until he snipped off its head with a pair of scissors. He had two shot-glasses of strong rice vodka at the ready. The blood he shook into one of them, and then he pierced the ripped-out gall bladder and let it leak its greenish juices into the other.

'Drink them immediately,' he told me. So I put my lips to the rim of each glass in turn, and drank the traffic-light cocktails, the blood swirling scarlet in the first, the second bitter and invigorating. The strong liquor scorched my throat and brought tears to my eyes, while the sight of the raw swirling blood made me feel a little queasy. Then I watched Mrs Liu's husband slip off the snake's skin easily, like a piece of silk underwear, eviscerate and chop its carcass, and throw it into a pot of boiling water, with a handful of wolfberries.

Mrs Liu's restaurant looked out over teabushes towards craggy mountains. In daylight the view was spectacular; at night it was a dark and peaceful place. The picture windows were unglazed, so you heard the loud hum of the insects as you ate, and felt that you were part of the landscape. Mrs Liu specialised in local ingredients, many of them wild. Her fridges were stocked with exotic fungi: finger-like 'dragon's claws', golden trumpets, grey 'thousand hands', slices of a large mushroom named locally after the Great King's Peak. Wildflowers with bright pink petals sat on the shelves alongside bamboo shoots and clawlike bulbs. There was another fridge too, for the meat. It contained some run-of-the-mill pork, but that wasn't really why people went to Mrs Liu's. The customers who frequented her establishment wanted the wild muntjac, wild rabbit, wild pheasant, wild turtle, snake…

The kitchen was a simple affair, clean, white-tiled, with a sink and a couple of gas burners. The cooking was straightforward too, but the ingredients so fresh and fine that it all tasted magnificent. Our snake soup was refreshing, the flesh tender and savoury on its snagged, spiny nuggets of backbone. We ate sliced muntjac with fresh red chilli and onion, robust and gamey; wild mushrooms; pheasant red-braised with carrot and chilli; rabbit with sweet peppers, ginger and garlic; and a wild green known as 'ginseng vegetable'. Mrs Liu had run out of eggs, so when we ordered some egg-fried rice, she sent her son out into the live, twittering darkness to find a villager who kept hens.

As a foreigner who had made a decision, long before, to eat everything, I should have been in my element. But ethical dilemmas were creeping up on me, more and more. By now I knew that some species of muntjac were endangered. How was I to know whether the one on the table was among them? It was the same with almost everything in Mrs Liu's fridge, when I thought about it. I hoped that the snake whose blood and gall I'd just drunk was not a wild five-pace snake (the long-noded pit viper is known in Fujian as the *wu bu she*, because you'll drop dead after five paces if it bites you), but I was no expert on snake markings, and Mrs Liu was open about her sale of endangered species.

'*Bao hu dong wu* (protected animal),' she said in a stage whisper when she showed me a dead turtle in the fridge. She had one live five-pace snake in a cage, and a cobra curled, dead drunk, in a jar of spirits and medicinal herbs. 'Isn't it risky selling these things?' I asked her. 'Don't you get raided?'

'Oh, they carry out inspections from time to time,' she rattled away, with a vague smile, 'but we usually know when they're coming.' Once she was caught red-handed with a fridgeful of illegal wild creatures, and the inspectors wanted to fine her 50,000 yuan. But she buttered them up by inviting them for dinner, and got away with paying just five thousand. 'Anyway,' she went on, 'local officials themselves eat endangered species. Of course they daren't do it publicly, in fancy city places, but in a quiet, out-of-the-way spot like this, it's okay. And there are different grades of protected animals. There are heavy, heavy penalties for killing Grade One State-Level Protected species, like the panda.' She mimed a knife slitting her throat. 'For Grade Twos, you're looking at six months in prison. But Grade Threes are sold openly on the market, like the muntjac you just had for dinner.' (A sharp pang of guilt.)

'You won't find bear's paws in anyone's fridge, that's for certain. It's too dangerous. But you can have anything if you set your heart on it. Want a bear's paw? Let me know the day before, and I'll make sure I get it. You'll have to give me a deposit of a thousand *yuan* upfront, and another thousand after dinner. I get that kind of stuff from a middleman, so we don't have to keep it hanging around.'

'What kind of person spends two thousand *yuan* on a bear's paw?' I asked Mrs Liu.

❧

'Oh, you know, rich company bosses and Party or government officials,' came the reply.

The next day my friends returned to Shanghai and, alone, I hitched a ride on a motorbike up a wildly beautiful valley. My driver and I passed terraced fields neat with tea bushes, bamboo groves, and stubbly ricefields where a few water buffalo grazed. At the foot of a mountain, we left the bike and climbed stone steps to a Buddhist temple, high, high above, that clung to the ragged rock of a sheer cliff-face.

Like most Chinese peasants, my driver was a walking *materia medica*, eloquent on the edible and medicinal properties of the countryside. 'This herb,' he said, stopping to pluck a leaf or two, 'can be infused in water as a treatment for heatstroke.' In the late summer he worked as a mushroom picker, supplying the tables of local restaurants. The most valuable, he said, was the 'red mushroom', which dyes a soup broth pink.

'What about wild animals? Snakes and bears?' I asked him.

'Well, there aren't many left!' he laughed. 'I mean, snakes are good money if you can catch them, and as long as no one sees you, it's fine. But you won't find any bears around here, at least in the wild. There's a farm down the road where they rear them for their bile.'

A couple of hours later, our small motorbike puttered back along the road, and we turned up a steep driveway which brought us into the courtyard of a modern concrete building. This was the farm my driver had talked about. We dismounted, and he led me through a smart, well-appointed hall with a display of boxes and jars of pharmaceutical products made from snakes and bears, and into a long room where snakes lay around in glass cages. A few sightseers were peering at them through the glass. 'These are five-pace snakes,' said my driver, pointing out the markings on their skin.

In an inner courtyard, a viewing gallery had been constructed above a deep concrete chamber, where three enormous black bears shambled around. Tourists were invited to buy whole cucumbers and steamed buns to feed them. The bears reared up on their hind legs to catch the food. This was not the kind of place where foreigners were normally welcome. The rearing of bears for their bile is a sensitive subject: the medicinal bile is drained from the gall bladders of live animals, and animal rights activists regard it as an abomination. I half-expected to have my way barred, or to be thrown out by an officious manager. But nobody stopped me, and the staff members who caught sight of me were shy with surprise. Was this where Mrs Liu sourced her bear's paws for high officials' tables, I wondered.

There has always been an appetite in China for rare culinary exotica. Bear's paw was a courtly delicacy in the Warring States period; until then only emperors were allowed to touch it. One early Han Dynasty text refers to a primitive 'red-braised bear's paw', cooked with medicinal peony root and fermented sauce. And nearly two and a half millennia ago, the Confucian philosopher Mencius used it as an allegory for virtue in a disquisition on the inherent goodness of human nature:

> I desire fish, and I desire bear's paw; but if I may not have them both, I will forsake the fish and have only the bear's paw. I desire life, and I desire righteousness; if I may not have them both, I will forsake my life and choose righteousness.

Bear's paw was only one in a pantheon of ancient delicacies that included owl, jackal and leopard foetus. Later, more modern exotica like shark's fin and bird's nest (the dried nests of swifts, made from their saliva, which are eaten in soup) attained the highest culinary status. The first written mention of bird's nest as an ingredient is in a Yuan Dynasty text; shark's fin was eaten widely from the Ming. Both were among the indispensible luxuries of the Qing Dynasty court.

Although leopard's foetus appears to have gone out of fashion, many rare and exotic ingredients are still widely eaten by the rich and privileged in

China, or they were until very recently. One cookery book in my collection, a compendium of state banquet recipes published in the mid-eighties, includes lavish colour plates of the famous delicacies served to national leaders and foreign dignitaries. And there, among the shark's fin, bird's nest and abalone, is a photograph of a hairy black bear's paw arranged on a ruched tablecloth, next to a dish bearing another, red-braised, paw, with an elaborate vegetable sculpture in the background.

One book of recipes for the fabled Man-Han imperial banquet makes for eye-popping reading, even for me. Not only does it tell readers how to prepare well-known extreme delicacies like sheep tendons, shark's lip, camel's hump, deer penis, bear's paw and the ovarian fat of the Chinese forest frog, it includes a recipe for *dried orangutan lips*. And this book was published in 2002! Fortunately, in a gesture to emerging environmental concerns, it offers readers the alternative of cooking deer lips in a similar sauce, and of using skin-on mutton squashed into a paw-shaped mould as a substitute for bear's paw. (A note at the foot of the real bear's paw recipe reminds them that bears are a National Grade Two Protected Species, and may not be served at dinner without official approval.)

Theoretically, much of the appeal of these rare delicacies lies in their tonic properties, and their luxurious mouthfeels. Shark's fin, for example, is rich in protein, contains some minerals, and is thought to combat arteriosclerosis; it is also prized for its strandy silkiness in the mouth, and its gelatinous bite. Bird's nest has a pleasantly slithery crunchiness and contains several minerals, as well as glycine: it is one of the most important *yin* tonics in Chinese medicine. The ovarian fat of forest frogs is a snow-white cloud of diaphanous slipperiness. Other banquet ingredients such as bear's paw and camel's hump, and presumably dried orangutan lips, subside, after a long, slow cooking, into smooth, soothing, rubbery waves.

Yet however much one pontificates about their nutritional benefits, or waxes lyrical about their textures, in the end, one has to admit that much of their appeal lies in their snob value. After all, a simple pig's foot or a bit of seaweed would be just as rubbery, and just as rich in nutrients. As the editor of one food magazine told me, 'People want to eat delicacies like shark's fin just because they are rare and expensive, and because they are the kind of thing emperors used to eat!'

In the past, one imagines, when bears ran wild in the Fujianese mountains, sea cucumbers wriggled in vast numbers in the East China Sea, and turtles swam in lakes and streams, the traditional Chinese gourmet's penchant for eating such things wasn't too much of a problem. Only the richest and most well connected could afford them: just eating meat was a privilege. But the Chinese economic boom of the late twentieth and early twenty-first centuries has put a new strain on the market for exotic animals, as the aspirational middle classes seek to join in the feast.

Food and drink are at the heart of Chinese social relationships. Plying friends and business associates with expensive delicacies not only shows respect and conviviality, it also binds them into a web of mutual back-slapping (or *guan xi*) that might last for decades. Serve a whole shark's fin at a feast, and your guests will know that you are a person of substance. Offer one to an influential official and, with a bit of luck, he or she will feel sufficiently indebted to remember you for future favours. The exchange of fine foods is well established as a system of subtle bribery.

In the nineties, the entrepreneurs of the Special Economic Zones in the Cantonese south were the first to get rich in the wake of the Chinese economic reforms, and they revived the old art of conspicuous consumption, splashing out on exotic animals and imported brandy. Later, as businesspeople in the rest of China caught up, they followed the Cantonese lead. Suddenly, the *nouveaux riches* all over China were ordering shark's-fin soup just as English footballers order magnums of Cristal champagne – to show everyone how rich they were.

The rapacious appetite of the Chinese elite is now not only threatening wild creatures within the country's borders: it has become an international issue. The Chinese, for example, devoured almost all their own freshwater turtles some time ago; and most of those served in restaurants are farm-bred. But wild turtles are still held to be more potent in taste and tonic properties. For years they were imported from mainland Southeast Asia, until the Chinese gobbled up most of the turtles in that region too. Now they are being brought in from North America. It's a similar story with the pangolin, and the sea cucumber: sea cucumbers, commercially extinct in China, are being harvested as far afield as the Galapagos Islands.

The threat to sharks from the insatiable hunger of the Chinese market for their fins has received most international publicity, partly because of the practice of 'finning' (where fishermen reportedly slash the valuable fins off a live shark, and throw the rest of the fish back into the water, bleeding and disorientated). Shark's fin is *de rigeur* at Cantonese wedding banquets; half the global trade in sharks' fins is conducted in Hong Kong, where entire shops are devoted to them. The notorious traffic in fins is, however, just the tip of the iceberg, the fin of the fish. The Chinese are the world's most rapacious consumers of endangered species in general. Wild creatures from every corner of the planet fetch up in Chinese hotpots and medicinal brews.

The Chinese authorities make sporadic attempts to crack down on the illegal trade in endangered animals. The SARS crisis of 2003 lent an urgency to their efforts, because the epidemic was thought to have been caused by the virus leaping from wild civet cats (a traditional tonic food) into the general population. But it is hard to change an age-old culture of exotic eating. The officials nominally in charge of the heralded crackdowns are often those who like to slurp snake soup and turtle stew on the sly. And as for the peasants – well, if you were a Fujianese peasant living on 2000 *yuan* a year, struggling to pay for your children's education and your parents' healthcare, and you saw a five-pace snake curled innocently in the bracken, what would you do?

In May 2007, a rickety wooden ship was found floating off the coast of Guangdong Province, a cross between the Marie-Celeste and a gruesome Noah's Ark. It was stacked with wooden crates in which wild animals languished, most half-dead with dehydration in the tropical sun. There were 31 pangolins, 44 leatherback turtles, nearly 2720 lizards, 1130 Brazilian turtles, and 21 bears' paws wrapped in newspaper. All of them rare and threatened creatures, they were on their way from the jungles of Southeast Asia to the dinner tables of the Cantonese south. The engine of the ship that carried them, stripped of identifying marks, had run out of power. Local news reports did not explain why its crew had abandoned such a valuable cargo.

The animals, thirteen tonnes of them, were taken into the custody of the Guangdong Wild Animal Protection Centre. 'We have received some animals,' a staff member at the centre was quoted as saying by the local media. 'We are waiting to hear from the authorities what we should do with them.' Given the appetite of Cantonese officials for rare animals, the high market-prices for such delicacies, and the corruption endemic all over China, one hopes that the creatures were allowed to remain in the protection centre rather than eaten. Mr Fox, will you take care of my poor lost chickens?

That night at Mrs Liu's restaurant, I had sat back and sipped my tea after dinner as frogs and insects sang in the velvet darkness outside. Apart from from my moral doubts over some of the delicacies on the menu, it was the kind of place I love to find in rural China: a family business where the food is local, seasonal and freshly cooked. The kitchen was plain but spotlessly clean, the warmth of the welcome genuine. But despite its rural simplicity, of course, it owed its existence to the patronage of tourists like me. Local people, living in their gracious but dilapidated courtyard houses, growing and processing oolong tea for a living, couldn't afford to dine there. That snake soup alone had cost more than 300 *yuan*, a seventh of the annual per-capita income of a peasant in a poor place like this. But these days there's a growing market in China for 'rustic' eating.

The first time I heard the phrase *'nong jia le'* was on one of my earliest return visits to Chengdu, a year or so after I had finished my course at the Sichuan cooking school. My old friends Zhou Yu and Tao Ping, always a good barometer of trends in local food habits, had invited me out for dinner:

'Let's go to a *nong jia le*!' cried Tao Ping. I had no idea what she was talking about ('*nong jia le*' literally translates as 'the happiness of peasant homes', but might be rendered more loosely as something like 'place of rural good cheer').

The *nong jia le* turned out to be a kind of pseudo-rustic restaurant catering to the Marie-Antoinette tendencies of the new Chengdu middle class. We piled into Zhou Yu's small van and drove a few miles out of the city, until we spied a bamboo gateway festooned in bunting. Driving in, we pulled up outside a bamboo shelter that had been erected next to a concrete farmhouse. Several groups of people were seated at bamboo tables under the shelter, cracking open sunflower seeds with their teeth and playing Mah Jong. Some of them had already begun to eat.

Everything about the place was studiously bucolic. The sunflower seeds were served on the kind of chipped enamelled trays with stencilled flower patterns that you find in peasant homes. Raincoats made of straw and woven bamboo hats hung on the walls. We were invited to catch our own fish for dinner, in a pond by the door, and to select a live rabbit for the pot.

For a slightly older generation of urban people, the countryside is a place of bitter memories. After the chaos of the early Cultural Revolution, the Red Guards, (teenagers who had gone wild in their vicious attacks on Chinese tradition and so-called 'capitalist roaders', were rusticated, en masse, to 'learn from the peasants'. For the young Red Guards, it was like a penance for the thrilling freedoms they'd enjoyed, travelling ticketless all over China to spread revolution, waving their Little Red Books at Mao in the rock-concert hysteria of Tiananmen Square.

Many were sent to remote areas where they lived in dire poverty for years. One friend of mine shared a disused storehouse in the mountains with some female friends, and had to eke a precarious living from the rocky soil. They slept on beds made from cornstalks and leaves, had no electricity or running water, and were always hungry. This friend returned to Chengdu after three years, but other, unfortunate girls married village men and were *never* allowed to go home, condemned for the rest of their lives to hardship and deprivation.

The younger generation to which Zhou Yu and Tao Ping belong was never forced to live the grinding life of a Chinese peasant. Newly mobile, with their private cars and vans, they have begun to see the countryside as a playground, and a refuge from the pollution and hurly burly of city life. *Nong jia le*s have sprung up all over the country to cater for them. Some are straightforward restaurants, others tourist farms where you can stay for a few days and try your hand at digging the land, grinding soybeans for tofu, or gathering fruit. Real peasants, more accustomed to being viewed with withering disdain by urban-ites than romanticised like this, must be amazed at such a turn of affairs. The more 'backward' the village, the more primitive its conditions, the more attractive it is to city-dwellers! Furthermore, city people are willing to pay good money for the kind of wild ferns and weeds that real peasants only eat if they are starving to death!

Some *nong jia le*s offer a ridiculous pastiche of rural eating. One night in northern Fujian, before we stumbled upon the delicious haven of Mrs Liu's, my Shanghai friends and I asked a taxi driver to help us find a restaurant serving local specialities. We imagined a Fujianese version of a Tuscan *agrit-urismo*, a tranquil farmhouse in a bamboo grove. Of course we should have known better. The driver's face lit up: 'Yes, I know a place, it's very rustic, you'll love it.'

We pulled in at the most horrendous Disneyland version of rural simplic-ity you can possibly imagine. 'There you are!' said our driver proudly, gesturing towards a vast sprawl of covered walkways and private dining rooms, jerry-built out of wood and bamboo. My heart sank, but it was late and we were hungry. A waitress dressed in a fake peasant tunic made of flower-printed cotton led us to our private dining room. I glanced through the open doors of the other rooms as we passed. Each one framed a scene of greed and devasta-tion. Round tables were piled with plates, bowls, claypots, miniature woks on tabletop burners. The food left on them was ruined, but unfinished, and the filmy plastic that covered each table was scattered with detritus: spat-out chicken bones, fishy fins and prawn shells, pools of spilt *bai jiu* spirits and beer. And around the tables, rows of red, dishevelled faces, bleary with alcohol, lolled at various angles.

The restaurant tried to spin out the illusion of farmhouse eating by making us give our order in a kitchen ante-room where fish and eels swam in tanks, 'wild' vegetables filled enormous fridges and bee larvae squirmed in the remains of their nest. But this was rustic catering on an industrial scale. After a desultory meal, we returned to our hotel, a mountain-villa complex that was a favourite among the ruling classes. That weekend it had been invaded by junketing officials who were pretending to hold a conference while savouring the pleasures of rural life. They wandered around drunkenly in the small hours, shirts untucked, shouting in the corridors, knocking randomly on the doors of our rooms. Dolled-up young women from the massage parlour in the grounds hurried to and fro, giggling.

I had hoped to find more genuine rural simplicity in southern Fujian. My path took me through Xiamen, where I stayed for a few nights on the small island of Guliangyu, just off the coast, once the home of the foreign treaty port residents. It was still clustered with colonial buildings, and home to China's largest collection of pianos – another legacy of its cosmopolitan history. My destination, however, was not coastal Fujian, where the snakeheads run their illegal immigration rackets, and the friendly people eat sea worms in aspic with mustard sauce, sharkballs stuffed with minced pork, and all manner of delicious seafood snacks. Instead I was headed for an area near the border with Guangdong Province where the Hakka people live. The Hakka, which roughly translates as 'settler households', are traditionally the wanderers among the Han Chinese. Centuries ago, they migrated south, in several stages, from their homelands in northern China, to avoid insurrection and war. In the early years of the Qing Dynasty, many of them put down roots in the mountainous areas of Guangdong and Fujian, because others had already claimed the more fertile, low-lying lands. They became known for their preserved vegetables and robust peasant cooking. And there is one area of south-western Fujian that I had longed to visit for years, where the Hakka clans still dwell in their ancestral clanhouses.

Having left Xiamen by bus in the afternoon, I arrived in the village itself after darkness had fallen. It was a slow, winding drive from the nearest county town, along a hilly road littered with the aftermath of landslides. My driver was mostly silent, but whenever he answered his mobile phone he shouted into it as if his voice might otherwise be drowned out by the silence of the night. Eventually we stopped, and when I left the car I could hear the sound of water tumbling over stones. We picked our way along a path by a river, and through a gateway on to a long terrace, and then he led me through a small doorway in a great wide wall.

The Lin brothers were sitting at the side of their courtyard, drinking Iron Buddha tea. They invited us to join them. Lin the Elder poured hot water from a flask into a small clay teapot, brewed the leaves for a few moments, strained the green-golden liquid into a jug, and then filled four tiny teabowls.

'Drink some tea', he told me, so I did.

The Lins are the great-great-grandsons of the wealthy tobacco farmer who built the mansion in which they still live. It's a magnificent, fairy-tale extravagance of courtyards and grey-tiled rooves, framed by mountains, overlooking the stream. Now, of course, most of the drafty halls are empty and unused; no incense burns in the ancestral shrine. But in recent years, this area has been discovered by tourists and foreign designers, attracted by its distinctive architecture, and the Lins have turned one wing of their mansion into a guesthouse. It's a simple place, with rudimentary plumbing, but I'm not sure I've ever stayed anywhere so enchanting.

The Lins' grand house lies at the heart of *tu lou* ('earth-building') country. For more than ten centuries, until as late as the 1960s, the Hakka who migrated here constructed fortified compounds to protect their extended families from rival clans and marauding gangs. Many of the buildings are roundhouses, a little reminiscent of Shakespeare's Globe Theatre in London.

Their towering outer walls are windowless on the lower floors, punctuated only by a single, easily defended gateway. Inside, tiered galleries rise up around a courtyard, each one opening into a ring of rooms. On the ground floor are the kitchens, the wells, the chicken coops, and the ancestral shrines; on the first floor the granaries; and above them the bedrooms and living rooms. Some of the roundhouses are very small; others have room for dozens of families. Similar clan-houses are built around square or rectangular courtyards, like the Lins'. In times of conflict, the Hakka could simply barricade their gates, and hold out for months with their fresh water and eggs, their stores of grain, tea, and preserves.

The day after my arrival, I rose early, took breakfast in the courtyard, and then wandered out into the village. It was harvest time. Along the riverbanks, old women were peeling persimmons and laying them out to dry on bamboo trays. Fresh, they were fleshy and orange; after a few days they darkened and became toffee-sweet. Hisbiscus flowers also lay in the sun, shrivelled and purple, like witches' hands.

I spent the next few days exploring the clan-houses, first on foot, and then, in the surrounding valleys, by motorbike. Some had been spruced up for the new tourist trade; the majority were falling into dereliction. Like most parts of rural China, the society of the *tu lou* region had been hollowed out by the effects of economic reform. Almost all the young adults had migrated to the cities to work, leaving behind only the elderly and children. Courtyards that had once echoed to the sound of a dozen sizzling woks were desolate. Chickens pecked around the discarded agricultural tools and cooking pots on the ground.

An old crone sat on a wooden chair in one vast, empty roundhouse, over-grown with weeds, scattered with rubbish. She was shelling dried soybeans, hunched up over a bamboo tray, shaking the yellow beans out of their papery pods. She murmured in thick local dialect: too old to have studied Mandarin, she could neither speak nor understand it. In another roundhouse, two elderly men in blue Mao suits showed me around. They had resurrected their family shrine, retrieving the wooden statues of their ancestors from their Cultural Revolution hidey-hole. Their clothes were worn and they looked at me eagerly, hoping for a tip. In the late afternoon, I came across a small, grubby boy wandering around with a ricebowl and chopsticks, eating a supper of noodles without meat or relish.

On my last evening in the village, I had dinner in the Lins' courtyard, with the other two guests, a Eurasian photographer and his British-Chinese girl-friend, both visiting from Hong Kong. We chose from a printed list of Hakka specialities that the Lins had produced for their foreign visitors. They made us a soup from a whole duck simmered with tea-tree mushrooms, and stir-fried chicken with shiitake mushrooms; there was stir-fried musk-melon, and 'blood vegetable', a wild local green. The fowl were inconceivably delicious, as real farmyard birds usually are. And then we had that most famous Hakka dish, steamed belly pork with preserved mustard greens. There was far more than we could possibly eat. The elder Lin brought us a jug of a Hakka home-brew made from glutinous rice, warm and heady like cider. We lingered in the courtyard, mellow with wine, as the candles burned down.

The next day I had to catch the early bus back to Xiamen. As I waited in the courtyard for my lift to the bus stop, the local butcher was doing his rounds. A slight, scruffy man bearing two bamboo trays on a bamboo shoul-derpole, he shouted out 'Meat-for-sale! Meat-for-sale! *Mai rou! Mai rou!*' He paused in the gateway, and I caught a glimpse of his wares. He didn't have much to sell, just a few rather mean-looking hunks of pork, and some bones.

At the entrance to the roundhouse next door, he discussed prices with two elderly men. One of them, frail and dignified in his threadbare Mao suit, ended up coming to a deal, and then walked home, clutching his purchase, unwrapped, in his hand. It was a single pork bone, a small one, with a knuckle at one end, to which clung a few ragged shreds of meat.

I thought back to the vulgar extravagance of the *nong jia le* in northern Fujian, and the easy abundance of our 'rustic' dinner the night before – the plentiful dishes of duck and chicken, the steamed pork that we had barely touched – and my heart stuck in my throat. Then the man disappeared from view as he descended the stony path by the riverside, and the younger Lin brother arrived on his motorbike to take me to my bus.

Stewed bear's paw

扒熊掌

One fresh bear's paw
An old female chicken
2 lb 3 oz (1 kg) pork
9 oz (250 g) ham
3.5 oz (100 g) ginger and 3.5 oz (100 g) spring onion whites, crushed
   slightly
$1/2$ cup (100 ml) Shaoxing wine
1 gallon (4 litres) fine clear stock
3.5 oz (100 g) reconstituted dried bamboo shoots, sliced
3.5 oz (100 g) large reconstituted dried shiitake mushrooms, sliced
Dark soy sauce
Salt and white pepper to taste
Cornstarch mixed with water
1 tbsp chicken fat

1. Singe the bear's paw in a naked flame, taking care not to damage its skin. Soak it in boiling water for one hour and then strip away the fur.

2. Bring a large panful of water to the boil. Add the paw and boil vigorously for forty minutes. Remove and rinse thoroughly under the tap.

3. Place the paw in a large heatproof pot with the chicken, pork, ham, 2.5 oz (75 g) ginger, 2.5 oz (75 g) spring onion whites and $1/3$ cup (75 ml) Shaoxing wine. Heat the fine stock and pour over the bear's paw and other ingredients. Cover the pot with a lid and put it in a steamer. Steam over high heat until the stew has come to the boil; then reduce the heat to medium and steam for 2–3 hours until the paw is tender.

4. Remove the paw from the pot and set aside to cool. While it is still warm, remove its bones.

5. Make crosswise incisions in the paw at half-inch (1.25 cm) intervals, cutting deeply but not all the way through. Place the paw in a deep dish. Place in each incision a slice each of bamboo shoot and of mushroom. Scatter with the remaining ginger, spring onion and Shaoxing wine, and pour over 2/3 cup (150 ml) of the strained cooking broth. Place the dish in a steamer and steam over high heat for 15 minutes.

6. When the paw is ready, discard the ginger and spring onions, drain away the cooking liquid and arrange the paw elegantly on a serving platter.

7. Reheat 7 fl oz (200 ml) of the original cooking broth. Add enough soy sauce to give it a rich caramel colour, and season with salt and pepper to taste. Thicken the sauce with a little cornstarch mixture, and then pour it over the waiting paw. Scatter over the chicken fat, and serve, garnished with carved vegetables if you desire.

Adapted from 'Imperial Dishes of China', China Travel and Tourism Press, Beijing and Tai Dao Publishing Limited, Hong Kong, 1986. Please note that my version of the recipe has not been tested and is included for illustrative purposes only!

CHAPTER 16

Scary Crabs

My steamed crab crouched on the table in front of me in a blaze of sunset-orange, its claws bearded with moss-like fur, its legs fringed with spiky yellow hair. It looked as though it might scuttle away at any moment. I prepared for the attack. Eating hairy crabs is a messy business. You cannot avoid a tussle with shell and flesh: crunch, suck, crack, lick, probe, slurp. The restaurant had provided an array of stainless-steel tools, along with dry napkins, wet napkins, plastic gloves and toothpicks. So I crushed the legs with the crushers and poked out their tender meat, excavated the frondy white flesh of the claws. Then I dipped the meat into a saucer of ginger-infused vinegar before popping it into my mouth.

Oh, it was delicious. The deep savouriness of the crabmeat, combined with the honeyed tang of the vinegar and the arresting sharpness of the ginger, made a sublime chord of flavour. I demolished the rest of the legs. I sighed. Finally, I began to lap up the custard-like meat inside the shell, nature's foie gras, and the yolk-yellow semen, dripping with golden oil. Outside the window, the sun gleamed on the still, blue waters of the lake.

It wasn't surprising, I thought, that the pleasures of crab had been one of the themes of Chinese life and literature for centuries. Every autumn, at the start of the crab season, gourmets from Hong Kong, Tokyo and even further afield flocked to eastern China to eat them. It was a seasonal event, like the Grand National in England, or the Monaco Grand Prix. The female crabs ripen in the ninth lunar month, followed quickly by the males, and from then until the year's end it's a non-stop orgy of crabbery. Chefs in fancy restaurants incorporate hairy crab into extravagant recipes: stewed turtle with crabmeat, silken beancurd with crabmeat, 'soup' dumplings stuffed with pork and crab… Ephemeral crab shops spring up on the streets, selling live crabs burbling away in tubs, panes of glass to stop them running away.

Many Chinese people are obsessed with crabs, yet no one has ever managed to match the crab-induced ecstasies of the seventeenth-century playwright Li Yu. 'As regards the excellence of food and drink,' he wrote, 'there is not one single thing whose exquisiteness I am unable to describe… And yet when it comes to crabs, while my heart lusts after them and my mouth enjoys their delectable taste (and in my whole life there has not been a single day when I have forgotten them), I can't even begin to describe or make clear why I love them, why I adore their sweet taste, and why I can never forget them…

'I have lusted after crabs all my life,' he went on, 'to the extent that every year as the crab season approaches, I save up my money in anticipation. My family tease me so much for treating crabs as though my life depends on them that I think I may as well call these savings my "ransom money". From the first day of the crab season until the last day they are sold, I… do not let a single evening pass without eating them. All my friends know about my craving for crabs, and they entertain and fête me with them during the season; therefore I call the ninth and tenth months "crab autumn"… Dear crab, dear crab, you and I, are we to be lifelong companions?'

The best crabs in China, everyone agrees, are those reared in the Yangcheng Lake near Suzhou, because of the limpid purity of its waters. That is why I ended up, on that warm October Sunday, making a day trip with friends to the shores of the lake. I was with Gwen, an old classmate from Sichuan University, and our ringleader was Li Jing, a glamorous Shanghainese divorcée in her thirties to whom Gwen had introduced me. The Shanghainese are notoriously snooty and rarely associate with the Westerners who now reside in their city. But Li Jing had lived in France, spoke fluent French and English, and worked for an international company. She was unusually open-minded, and she loved to eat. So she persuaded a rich and well-connected friend to drive us out of Shanghai in his jeep, along the new crab expressway towards Suzhou.

The centre of the autumn crab trade is the lakeside city of Kunshan in greater Suzhou, but these days it's a nightmare of commercial tourism. Coaches disgorge their parties of proles at tacky restaurants, where they gorge on crabs and have their photographs taken. Someone as cosmopolitan as Li Jing wouldn't dream of going to a place like that. Instead, we turned off the main road and drove through fields of cabbages to a restaurant perched on an unspoilt stretch of the lake's shore. We left the jeep and pattered over a zig-zag of bamboo walkways to a dining room propped up on stilts in the shallows.

As I savoured the last, tantalising morsels of meat in my crab, I glanced over at Li Jing. Dark hair falling about her shoulders, she was sucking at the coral-red ovaries of her own, female crab, her fingers shiny with its most intimate juices. Everyone in the dining room was locked in silent concentration, the only sounds the determined crunching of shells and a gentle, pervasive slurping. Once, our taciturn companion, the son of a Chinese admiral, aloof with his own self-importance, broke his silence to say, 'Remember that the crab is very cooling (han), you should drink some wine with it, otherwise you'll get a stomachache.' He nodded in the direction of the warm Shaoxing wine, infused with heating ginger. I took my wine cup in fingers stained yellow by crab semen, and raised it to my lips. The warm alcohol went straight to my head.

By the time we had finished our lunch, the trays on the table were piled with crab debris. We sat around for a while, drinking wine and chatting. 'This is one of the best hairy crab restaurants in the area,' said Li Jing. 'It may look plain, but the crab they serve here is a "green food product", not like the industrialised crabs you find in Kunshan. They are reared outside, just over there, on a diet of fish and snails rather than artificial feed. Even national leaders come here to eat.'

Gwen and I left Li Jing and her friend at the table, and wandered out to look at the crab farm. Over the entrance, a large signboard showed a photograph of the former General Secretary of the Chinese Communist Party, Jiang Zemin, gazing into a basket of live crabs at the restaurant. Inside, the crabs lived in large cages suspended in an inlet of the lake. One of the crab-keepers showed us around, and pulled out a great hairy crab in his hand. He grinned as it waved its legs around in futile protest. What with the sun, the fresh air and the lightheadedness brought on by the wine, we were in a good mood. Until we noticed the state of the water. An oily scum swirled on the surface, with a mass of grubby flotsam that had drifted in from the lake. The legend of the pure Yangcheng waters, like so many others in China, had failed to keep pace with an industrialised reality. The thought of the crabs we had just eaten, raised amid such filth, was suddenly unappealing.

Soon after we visited the restaurant, a crab scandal blew up in the Chinese national press. Officials from the Taiwanese health ministry had examined a shipment of hairy crabs imported from the Yangcheng Lake, and found them to be contaminated with residues of an antibiotic that has been linked to cancer, AOZ. Yangcheng crab breeders insisted that they didn't use AOZ, and that the problem must lie with crabs from elsewhere that were being passed off as the real thing. According to the official Chinese media, local crab-eaters were undeterred by this cancerous little rumour, and blithely went on eating crabs for the rest of the season. But the story left a bad taste in my mouth. For the rest of my stay in Shanghai, I found myself avoiding hairy crab wherever possible.

Every time I look in a Chinese newspaper these days, it is full of food scares. Ten years ago, such stories were few and far between, and those I did come across seemed almost comical – like that of the Shanghai eel farmer who kept his eels on the human contraceptive pill to make them plumper. Now the tales are nastier, and they come thick and fast: 300 people in Shanghai poisoned by pork tainted by the drug clenbuterol; duck eggs doctored with an industrial dye; fifty babies killed by fake formula milk. It's partly, of course, because the Chinese newspapers are more frank than they used to be when in comes to discussing unpleasant issues. But it's also because of runaway economic growth, poor regulation and widespread corruption.

Three-quarters of the half-million or so food-processing plants in China are small and privately owned. For their owners, it's often cheaper to pay the occasional fine than to invest in safe production. Once I wheedled my way into an illegal factory making preserved duck eggs on the outskirts of Chengdu. It was a small, fly-by-night workshop in a filthy yard. The workers there told me that their eggs took a mere seven-to-ten days to mature rather than the traditional three months: a sure sign, said the friend who accompanied me, that they were 'fast' preserved eggs, speeded-up by additives like ammonia.

The contamination of Chinese food products hit the international headlines in the spring of 2007. Ironically it was concern at the health of animals, rather than people, that started it. When American cats and dogs started dying in odd circumstances, the cause was found to be a Chinese-made ingredient in their food: wheat gluten that had been doctored with the chemical melamine, a cheap protein-enhancer. The world started looking at Chinese imports with greater scrutiny. American journalists dredged up years-worth of US Food and Drug Administration reports documenting rejected imports from China: mushrooms laced with illegal pesticides; prunes stained with chemical dyes; shrimp tainted with carcinogenic antibacterials. The United States had turned back over a hundred shipments of Chinese food products in a single month that spring. And these were just the imports that had been intercepted.

The Chinese government was so embarrassed by the global furore that it sprang into action. Officials announced a crackdown on small, poorly regulated food-processing firms, and conducted a nationwide inspection into food safety. The results were unsettling. Inspectors found illegal industrial materials such as dyes, mineral oils, paraffin wax, formaldehyde and malachite green used in the manufacture of all kinds of ordinary foods: flour, sweets, pickles, biscuits, dried fungi, melon seeds, beancurd and seafood. The scale of corruption in the food regulation system was made clear when the former head of the Chinese Food and Drug Administration was *executed* for taking bribes.

Even before the pet-food scandal, a Chinese official who had once been responsible for controlling doping in sports, Yang Shumin, warned that athletes competing in the 2008 Beijing Olympics might fail their drugs tests if they dined out in restaurants, because so many anabolic steroids were routinely pumped into Chinese meat. In an attempt to avert panic in the sports world, the government hastily promised that all the food served in the Olympic Village would be purchased from selected suppliers, wrapped in tamper-proof packaging and delivered by tracked vehicles. Furthermore, the kitchens would be guarded round the clock, and all the ingredients used in cooking for the athletes would first be tested on mice! Their pledges were hardly reassuring for those of us living outside the sterile, armed-guarded, mouse-tested confines of the future Olympic Village.

So it's not just middle-class paranoia that has made some of my Chinese friends hesitant about eating meat in the last few years, and my Hong Kong friends wary of ingredients imported from Mainland China. My own enjoyment of eating in China has been clouded by growing anxiety about what's actually in the food on the table. Those tempting prawns, stir-fried with black beans and chilli; that sweet-and-sour carp… Fish farms in China seem to slip a lot of banned antibiotics and fungicides into their ponds, so these may well be tainted by residues. Those tender chunks of belly pork with jujubes… growth hormones, anyone? What about the questionable chemicals used in the manufacture of deep-fried doughsticks, or the lead oxide that is a traditional additive to preserved duck eggs? Most chickens now are battery farmed, almost certainly, in conditions that I'd rather not think about in England, let alone in China. Furthermore, I've watched those peasants with cans of pesticides on their backs, drenching their beans and cabbages.

In England I eat as much organic produce as possible, avoid factory-farmed meat and poultry, and steer clear of junk food, mostly. In China, such fastidiousness is impossible. What's a professional omnivore to do?

Aside from the deliberate adulteration of food by corrupt manufacturers, the pollution is so dire in many parts of China that it poses a direct and grave threat to human health. According to the government's own figures, 10 per cent of Chinese farmland is dangerously contaminated with excessive fertilisers, heavy metals and solid waste, and a third of the rural population lacks access to safe drinking water. Many rivers are so filthy that their waters are toxic in contact with human skin. The newspapers are filled with terrifying stories about poisoned lakes and reservoirs, their waters unfit even for irrigation. According to a World Bank report, which the Chinese government tried to suppress, 700,000 Chinese people die prematurely every year because of air and water pollution.

Anyone living in China knows that these are not just abstract statistics. If you go out on to the streets of Beijing on a bad day, you can sense the pollution as you inhale. You will probably choke on it. Often when I go back to Chengdu or Changsha these days, I develop a cough, a headache and an asthmatic wheeze. While I'm in China, I drink Chinese tea all the time, because I adore it. Once in a while, though, when I feel that I've had enough tea, I drink a mugful of *bai kai shui*, plain boiled water, instead. It's usually a shocking experience. In Hunan, one memorable mugful of *bai kai shui* tasted of petrol and God-knows-what other chemical effluents. Even when the taste is not so extreme, the water, unmasked by tealeaves, tends to have a metallic tinge. Often, I want to spit it out immediately – but what's the point, when the same water is used to cook all the food I eat?

One day when I was living in Hunan, I went to visit a friend in Zhuzhou. Zhuzhou is on the World Bank list of the world's most polluted cities (China lays claim to sixteen of the top twenty on that list). It was a terrifying place, a blighted metropolis where the chimneys of the local metallurgy and chemical plants spewed their vile, gaseous excrement over the entire landscape. I waited for my friend in a taxi outside his work unit. The view through the car windows was apocalyptic, trails of white smoke shrouding everything, blotting out the sun. One chimney on a lower slope sent its filthy plume directly into the compound where he worked. The air was so foul that I, an outsider, scarcely dared breathe. I ate very little at lunch, because although the food was delicious, I was thinking of the tainted earth in which the vegetables must have sprouted, the corrupted water in which the fish had probably been farmed. I didn't want to let any of it into my body. How anyone could *live* there I did not know.

The world is currently deeply enamoured of China, and everyone wants to go there on holiday. Flick through any travel magazine and you'll very likely come across an article on the glamorous Shanghai restaurant scene, or perhaps, in the right season, on the delights of hairy crabs. But you don't see much mention of the country's terrible environmental problems. When I was in New York recently, I met up with another Chinese food writer who lived there. She had just returned from China, where she had been flabbergasted by the pollution. 'It's appalling,' she whispered to me. 'Why doesn't anyone talk about it?'

My ex-pat friends in Shanghai and Beijing, particularly those with small children, don't like to think too much about the food, air or water they are forced to ingest. They try to calm their fears by making small adjustments to their lifestyles: not eating at street stalls or more dubious restaurants, for example. Even in fine establishments, there there are certain things they avoid like the plague. Once, when lunching with my Italian friend Davide in our favourite Shanghai restaurant, I was tempted to order the slippery whitefish, a local speciality. Davide raised an eyebrow. 'Have you looked at the water recently?' he said. One top Shanghai chef, internationally renowned, confessed to me that the greatest challenge of working in China was trying to source decent ingredients.

Now, when I'm in China, I find I eat far less meat, fish and poultry that I used to, because I just don't trust them. Of course I *want* to eat everything, because the cooking is as fabulous as ever, and I'm as curious as I always have been about Chinese food. But can I face such a cocktail of hormones and chemicals? My fears are not greatly eased by headlines in the *China Daily* that say: 'Most vegetables safe: official'. The only foods I eat with complete confidence are the wild bamboo shoots, wild vegetables and farmhouse produce I encounter in remote rural areas.

It's as if my gastronomic libido is slipping away. In the old days, in Sichuan, my hunger was a free and joyful thing. The food before me was fresh, free-range and wholesome, and I wanted to devour it all. But in the last ten or fifteen years China has changed beyond all recognition. I've seen the sewer-like rivers, the suppurating sores of lakes. I've read the newspaper reports; breathed the toxic air and drunk the dirty water. And I've eaten far too much meat from endangered species. In China I have to throw all my principles to the wind if I am continue in my vow of eating everything. The only way to recover my wanton old appetites is to draw a deliberate blind over all the evidence, to switch off my brain, and to eat without thinking. And I'm not sure I can do it anymore.

Not long ago, I was back in Chengdu for a lightning visit, to research a couple of articles and catch up with friends. A businessman acquaintance had invited me out for dinner. Our taxi pulled into the driveway of a restaurant on the outskirts of town. A grubby red carpet ran up the wide steps from the street and across the vast empty lobby, stained by the filthy soles of thousands of greedily stampeding feet, rushing in from their taxis and company cars. Girls in red silken dresses stood in rows to welcome us; glittering chandeliers hung overhead. Inside, the restaurant was decorated in the newly fashionable 'European style', with padded, upholstered chairs that looked a bit French.

The rest of the party was already assembled. I took my place at our table, in the main dining hall. None of us was really hungry, but someone was paying for the dinner on company expenses, and it doesn't look good in China to sit before a modest table. My friend therefore ordered a fanfare of scarlet prawns with an elaborate garnish; a whole fish, steamed; crabs smothered in chilli and garlic; a whole knuckle of pork; chicken, duck and beef in great quantities; expensive wild mushrooms; soups and dumplings. To me, it all seemed like vulgar food: garish to look at and taste; enhanced by food colourings, chicken powder and MSG. We toyed with it, but no one was really eating. Most of it would go into the pigswill in an hour or two.

Although few Chinese people would eat like this at home, it was a typical restaurant dinner. '*Hen lang fei* (very wasteful)!' said my host, with an embarrassed laugh. But he had ordered all that food himself, knowing that it was more than we could finish: his apologetic comment was made purely for my benefit, because he sensed that I, as a foreigner, might disapprove. We both knew that at this dinner hour, across the country, tables groaned like this with wasted food. In provincial capitals such as Chengdu and Changsha, there were super-restaurants that could seat five hundred, a thousand, two thousand, even four thousand guests simultaneously. And no one ever finished what was on the table. Even in remote county towns, I had witnessed scenes of such gargantuan excess that they could have been part of a medieval morality play.

In some ways, such decadence is perfectly understandable. Anybody over fifty in China lived through Mao's terrible famine and the ensuing decades of rationing. Not long ago, peasants rubbed pieces of pork fat around their woks to lend a hint of meaty flavour to their vegetables, before putting the fat carefully away so it could be used again. Some people have told me they actually had dreams about pork in the 1960s. In some ways, China is still living through an extreme reaction to those years of deprivation. The profligacy is part of a vast, collective sigh of relief that it's over, that there is meat on the table, and that the puritanical Mao failed to to stifle one of the greatest pleasures of Chinese life.

It is also cultural. The banquet in China is a social institution. If you are hosting a dinner for family members and friends, it's an expression of love and generosity. For clients and colleagues, it might be a demonstration of wealth and power, and a chance to win 'face' – that peculiar Chinese concept that expresses a person's social and professional dignity. In either context, you must overwhelm your guests with food, the best you can offer. The best, of course, is almost always meat, fish and poultry rather than grains and vegetables. At a proper banquet, you may not be offered rice at all.

Many people frown on the traditional style of banqueting. The Chinese authorities, clearly troubled by visions of the nation's wealth squandered in a litter of half-eaten meals, issue occasional circulars urging moderation and banning the holding of banquets at public expense. And for businessmen, the endless round of feasts they must attend in the course of their work can be a torment, particularly because they usually involve forced *bai jiu* toasts and unavoidable drunkenness. One former colleague of mine, an Englishman working as a sales rep in Henan Province, became so sick in the course of his professional socialising that a Beijing doctor diagnosed him as suffering from 'banquet fever'.

The Chinese are also afflicted increasingly with the diseases of plenty that are so familiar in the Western world: obesity, diabetes and cancer. Grandparents who once went hungry stuff their grandchildren with fast food and sweets. I've seen some of my middle-aged friends, dining out almost every night, become plump and pasty.

When I eat in these flashy, extravagant restaurants, I find myself thinking nostalgically of my first year in Sichuan, when I was so moved by the frugality of the way people ate. I remember lunches of egg-fried rice livened up with morsels of meat, or a few simple vegetable stir-fries. I yearn also for the dishes that I lived on as a student, sitting on a stool in the Bamboo Bar and the other small restaurants around Sichuan University: the delicious fish-fragrant aubergines, the duck hearts with chilli, the stir-fried silk gourd, the twice-cooked pork with green garlic. Every so often I still find one of these mom-and-pop places, tucked away in a small street that has somehow escaped the demolition crews, serving unfashionably traditional dishes in a white-tiled shed with formica chairs and tables, and I think I'll be disappointed. But then the food arrives, and tastes as good as I remember, and it warms my heart. I forget, for a while, about the pollution and the hormones. And it reminds me why I fell in love with China, and why my first book about Sichuan cookery demanded to be written.

One evening, I was having dinner with Gwen in a Shanghai restaurant.

'I feel so guilty,' said Gwen, sipping her soup. It was a Shanghainese soup – a pale, slightly thickened broth filled with wisps of something that might have been tofu or eggwhite, but on closer inspection was a mass of tiny, thread-like fish. Each strandy creature had two black eyes on its pin-like head, about the size of specks of black pepper.

'Just think how many lives we are eating,' said Gwen, 'Ten thousand, twenty thousand?'

It was true. Each spoonful of soup was a confusion of dozens, perhaps hundreds, of small fishy lives.

'Somehow it seems worse to eat so many,' said Gwen. 'Much worse than, say, eating a single eel.'

What she said made me shiver, and I, too, finished my soup with a feeling of guilt.

There's a nineteenth-century English engraving called 'Fatal effects of gluttony: A Lord Mayor's Day Nightmare'. Dedicated to 'all the city's gourmands', it depicts a fat London merchant lying in bed, suffering the consequences of his carnivorous self-indulgence. A swarm of animals lay siege to him in a terrifying hallucination: ducks, geese, cow, pig, stag, wild boar, sturgeon, flying fish, they besiege him within the curtains of his bed. A lobster tries to pinch his nose, and an enormous turtle straddles his chest.

Sometimes, when I think of what I've eaten in China, I imagine that I'll end up like this. There's an entry in one of my 1999 notebooks that reads: 'In the last three days I have eaten: snails, frogs, snakes, sparrow gizzard, duck tongues, fish heads, duck hearts, tripe; also half a duck, most of a carp, duck's blood, at least five whole eggs, smoked bacon, and stewed aromatic beef.' I'm ashamed to say that this kind of excess is not unusual. A vegan friend of mine once told me that all the animals I'd eaten in the course of my life would sit in judgement over me after I was dead. 'Most people,' he said, 'would just have a row or two of judges: a cow and a pig, a sheep and a chicken. But you – imagine, them, Fuchsia, they'd be like the audience in a football stadium, tier upon tier: civet cats, dogs, snakes, frogs, fat-tailed sheep, muntjac, eels, etc. etc.'

As a scholarship student in Chengdu, I longed to taste the exotic foods that had graced the tables of emperors. Now, I feel a dawning revulsion. Is there anything a Chinese gourmand will not eat? Alligator flesh, the downy antlers of the young deer, rabbit's kidneys, the palms of chicken's feet, those orangutan lips... a riot of animals, pillaged for our titillation. Sometimes it seems beyond satire, as pretentious as the food served at Petronius' 'Banquet of Trimalchio'.

In the course of my duties as a professional food writer, I am offered such esoteric delicacies at every turn. Often the circumstances make it hard to refuse. A bowl of shark's fin soup placed before me by a generous host; the eyes of the other guests fixed on me expectantly, hoping that I am able to appreciate the honour. We all know that a single bowlful of shark's fin soup costs hundreds of *yuan*. I hesitate. Then, with a guilty conscience, I smile, sip, and praise it for its soft, strandy texture, the subtle savours of the broth.

The bronze ritual vessels of the Shang and Zhou dynasties are among the most ancient and potent symbols of Chinese civilisation. Wine jugs, cooking pots and steamers, they are decorated with geometric designs based on the stylised faces of monstrous animals with curled horns and staring eyes. You can see them in the oriental collections of most world-class museums. On some bronzes, the animals resemble tigers, bulls or birds; on others they are more abstract. No one knows exactly what these menacing beasts meant to the people of the Shang and Zhou, but they are known in China as *tao tie*. This word means, in modern Chinese parlance, 'a fierce and cruel person, or a glutton'; *tao tie* was also the name of an ancient villain known for his voracity, according to one antique text. The fierce animal designs of the sacrificial bronzes, one of the most recognisable symbols of Chinese civilisation, have for centuries been bound up with the idea of monstrous greed.

The influential archaeologist, K.C. Chang, in an essay on ancient Chinese food history, once suggested that those threatening animal designs may have been emblazoned on the ritual vessels used by the Shang and Zhou ruling classes as a reminder of the dangers of gluttony. Like the *memento mori* of medieval Europe – those images of death that were intended to remind people of their mortality – they may have been a warning to the 'meat-eaters' of their day that greed was monstrous and corrupting.

In recent years, as I eat in China, the shadow of the *tao tie* has seemed to loom more and more insistently over the dinner table. It makes me feel sick at heart. The banquets that once seemed to be a glorious perk of my job have begun to feel like an occupational hazard, a minefield of ethical, environmental and health issues. I find myself torn between my old habit of omnivorousness, and a moral loss of appetite. A horned *tao tie* beast watches me as I sip my shark's fin soup, staring at me with its ancient, beady eyes. I can no longer meet its gaze.

My loss of appetite creeps up on me. I soldier on, attending feast after feast, but I'm actually eating less and less. A mulish resistance sits on my stomach. I taste things, pick at them, write my notes. And then I go home to wherever I am staying and fill up on instant noodles because they are the only food I can face. I feel a kind of kinship with that great Qing Dynasty gourmet Yuan Mei, who went home after a forty-course dinner party, appalled at its vulgar excesses, and needed a bowl of rice porridge to assuage his hunger. After each trip, I fly back to England with dull skin and drab hair, feeling rundown, and it takes me a few weeks to recover.

I feel a rising sense of panic. This is my life, my work, to eat in China. I have built a career on it. For more than a decade I have been a professional glutton. My cast-iron digestion has protected me from the immediate risks of eating everything, though I have been reckless in my omnivorousness. My intellectual fascination is undimmed. But I just can't do this anymore. The food-writer has lost her appetite.

Of course I'm aware that, at some level, my distaste is also a metaphor. I'm weary not only of this constant feasting, but also of travelling, and of China. For years I have given everything to this country, and it's wearing me out. I'm tired of always being the perfect diplomat; I'm exhausted by the crazy, peripatetic lifestyle. I'm always missing someone, something. Now I've eaten my fill; I just want to go home. I don't want to spend my life consuming rabbit-heads and sea cucumbers. I want to grow vegetables in my own garden, to cook shortbread and steak-and-kidney pie.

There are pages of despair in my diaries, now, among the recipes and sketches.

As I sit at these debauched Chinese dinner tables, I think of the looming food crisis of which scientists are warning. Climate change is beginning to damage food production; China and India are switching to meat-based diets that demand more land; water tables are falling; and the global population is rising. The era of cheap food and surpluses may be over. How mad this profligacy will seem, in the not-too-distant future, when we are fighting over oil and water, perhaps even grain. These banquets – tables laden with fish and meat, platefuls of shrimp and chicken that end up in pigswill – will seem like an hallucination, echoes of a few greedy, giddy decades sandwiched between periods of rationing and scarcity. Decades when we forgot the value of things.

The *tao tie* beast, with its gluttonous associations, may be a symbol of Chinese civilisation, and the Chinese may do gluttony better than anyone, but I wonder, in the end, aren't we all just as bad? What's the difference, really, between eating shark's fin and caviar? Or cod, or bluefin tuna? They are all, now, endangered species. A third of the food bought by British households ends up being thrown in the bin. And look at us, flying around the world on holiday, eating beef reared on ranches that used to be rainforest, buying unseasonal produce flown in from the other side of the world. Think of the increasing amounts of land being given over to growing grain for ethanol production. If feeding your *car* on grain that could be used to nourish poor African farmers isn't the mark of the *tao tie*, I don't know what is.

The Chinese do seem to eat everything, one must admit. But in a sense they are just a distorting mirror, magnifying the voracity of the entire human race. The Chinese word for 'population' is 'people mouths', and in China there are now 1.3 billion mouths, all munching away. China itself is like a big mouth eating. And it is hungry for more than just *Chinese* ingredients. The Chinese are slurping up the seafood of the world's oceans. And now that they have discovered dairy products, they want our milk, too, to feed their children, and their growing appetite for it is inflating milk prices on global markets. It's the same with timber, mineral and oil, which feed Chinese economic development. China has become the world's largest consumer of grain, meat, coal and steel. It may look rapacious, but the Chinese are really just catching up with the greed of the rest of the world – on a dizzying scale.

Sitting over my instant noodles, late at night after another unsettling banquet, I often find myself thinking about my Hunanese friend Liu Wei. In his modesty and restraint, his compassion, and his vegetarianism, he seems to embody a rather better attitude to eating, and, indeed, to life. Yet although his frugality looks counter-cultural in an era of widespread gluttony, it actually resonates with another, equally rich and ancient strain of Chinese thought.

More than two thousand years ago, the sage Mozi wrote of ancient laws regarding food and drink:

> *Stop when hunger is satiated, breathing becomes strong, limbs are strengthened and ears and eyes become sharp. There is no need of combining the five tastes extremely well or harmonising the different sweet odours. And efforts should not be made to procure rare delicacies from far countries.*

Confucius, living at around the same time, did not eat much, and took care that the amount of meat he consumed did not exceed the amount of rice. His example has been used as a model for generations of Chinese children, urged by their parents to eat up their rice or noodles, and not to be distracted by their appetite for the accompanying dishes of fish or meat. And while businessmen and officials in early twenty-first century China stuff their faces with meat, fish and exotic delicacies, many people live at home on a simple diet of mainly grains and vegetables.

For the irony is that, despite the conspicuous consumption of banquet culture and that grotesque old stereotype of 'eating everything', the traditional diet of the Chinese masses could be a model for the entire human race. It's the way the older generation, the poor and the wise still eat: steamed rice or boiled noodles, served with plenty of seasonal vegetables, cooked simply; beancurd in many forms; very few sweetmeats; and small amounts of meat and fish that bring flavour and nourishment to the table. Unlike the typical diet of the modern West, with its profligate emphasis on dairy products and animal proteins, the traditional Chinese diet is minimal in its environmental impact, nutritionally balanced, and marvellously satisfying to the senses. After all my gastronomic adventures, I don't know if I can think of a better way to live.

Perhaps, for the privileged in China, as in many other places, life has always been a struggle between the gentleman and the glutton, restraint and voracity. Liu Wei and me, sitting at dinner, he with his bowl of rice and beancurd, I with my shark's fin soup and stir-fried duck tongues, are just a continuation of this age-old tradition.

And strange though it may sound, after all these tales of greed and omnivorousness, sometimes I think I'll end up becoming a vegetarian.

Rice porridge, or congee

Rice porridge or congee, according to the Qing Dynasty gourmet Yuan Mei. The following extract is taken from his cookery book, The Food Lists of the Garden of Contentment.

If you see water and no rice, this is not congee; if you see rice and no water, this is not congee either. The rice and water must be helped to combine harmoniously, in one soft smoothness: only this may be called 'congee'. Officials and men of letters say it is better for a man to wait for his congee, than to make the congee wait for him: this is a well-known maxim. Avoid leaving your congee for too long, lest the flavour dissipate and the liquid be lost to the air. These days people make duck congee, adding meat; and 'eight-treasure' congee, to which they add various fruits. But these all result in the loss of the proper flavour of congee. One should add nothing but mung beans in summer, and broomcorn millet in winter: this is simply the combination of various of the 'five grains', respecting the categories of things rather than harming them. I have often, while dining out, made the observation that although the dishes are numerous, the rice or congee is so coarse and unrefined than I can only swallow it with the utmost reluctance, and then felt ill after my return home.

CHAPTER 17

A Dream of Red Mansions

In January 2007, I went back to China again for more than a month. My heart was not in it. I did wonder if I had reached the end of the road. Would it not be more honest, I asked myself, to admit that the gluttonous China phase of my life was over? It had been an incredible journey, for sure, and one that I wouldn't have missed for anything. But the joy of it had faded. Years before, I had abandoned one career based on other people's expectations of me, and it had been a liberation. Perhaps it was time to do the same thing again. Often, people were asking me, 'Which Chinese regional cuisine are you going to do next, Fuchsia?', assuming that I was planning to write a book about each province in turn. 'Are you crazy?' I wanted to reply. 'Do you know how many provinces there are? Do you know what Hunan did to me?'

But China was a hard habit to break, and I had signed a contract for this book, one that I had wanted to write for a very long time. 'Another month,' I told myself, 'and then you can say goodbye.' So I packed my bags, dragged myself to the airport, and flew to Shanghai, where my kind friend Gwen had offered me a room of my own, in her lovely flat in the French Concession. There, in businesslike fashion, I set about exploring the food traditions of eastern China.

Shanghai itself has become the darling of food journalists, who flock there to scoff 'soup dumplings' at the Nanxiang restaurant in the Yu Garden, and to dine at the celebrated Jean Georges on the Bund. But, by Chinese standards, Shanghai lacks history: it's a modern metropolis, owing its ascendancy to the foreign concessions built there in the mid-nineteenth century, and richer in 'fusion cuisine' than real culinary tradition. My researches were to take me to the more ancient centres of gastronomy, in the hinterlands of Jiangsu and Zhejiang Provinces.

While one might say that northern Beijing is the home of imperial cooking, southern Guangdong of the cuisine of the merchant class, and Sichuan of fiery peasant fare, eastern China is the gastronomic demesne of the cultivated man. It was in Hangzhou that the Song Dynasty poet Su Dongpo encouraged the development of a marvellous stewed pork; and in Nanjing that the gourmet Yuan Mei wrote his famous cookery book. In the twentieth century, the writer Lu Wenfu set his novella *The Gourmet*, the story of the relationship between a reactionary gourmand and a puritanical communist over decades of revolution, in his hometown of Suzhou.

The southern Yangtze region, in which these ancient cities lie, produces some of China's finest ingredients, including Jinhua cured ham, Shaoxing rice wine and Zhenjiang vinegar, as well as those famous hairy crabs. Many of its cities are known for speciality dishes: Hangzhou for Beggar's Chicken, Vinegar Fish and Dongpo Pork (named after the poet), Nanjing for its salted duck, and Suzhou for sizzling eel and a soup of leafy water-shield from the Taihu lake. Yet none of these places can compete with the culinary glory of Yangzhou, the ancient gastronomic capital of the east, and the cradle of what they call 'Huaiyang' or 'Weiyang' cuisine (the names have old geographical connotations).

Yangzhou lies in the fertile southern Yangtze region, long recognised as a 'home of fish and rice' on account of the plenty of its produce. Since the Qin Dynasty it has been an administrative centre, although its roots as a settlement are yet more ancient. It came to prominence with the contruction, during the Sui and Tang Dynasties, of the Grand Canal, a waterway linking Hangzhou, even then a famous producer of silk and tea, with the old northern capitals at Luoyang and Xi'an. Yangzhou lay at the crucial intersection of the Grand Canal, running from north to south, and the Yangtze river, which flows from the mountains of Tibet to the eastern coast. As the transport hub of China, Yangzhou became one of its wealthiest cities. For centuries its name was a byword for luxury and sophistication. But after the railways came in the nineteenth century, leaving Yangzhou languishing on a secondary line, it became a relative backwater. These days tourists flock to Suzhou, for its gardens, and Hangzhou, for its pretty West Lake. But Yangzhou is off the beaten track.

For me, it was the last, vital missing piece of a jigsaw. For fifteen years I had roamed all over China, from the deserts of the west to Shanghai's 'Paris of the East', from colonial Hong Kong to the old imperial capital of Xi'an. My travels had been by no means exhaustive – in China there is always more to explore – but I had covered a great deal of gastronomic territory. Yet although I had glimpsed Yangzhou's cuisine in its influences on the courtly cooking of Beijing, and on the chic new restaurants of Shanghai, I had never actually been there. For a specialist in Chinese cuisine, this was an unforgivable omission.

It was a cool, sunny morning when I took the main Shanghai-Nanjing railway line as far as the old vinegar town of Zhenjiang, a slow-moving place where, even in the early twenty-first century, foreigners were as remarkable as martians; men in Mao suits carried chirruping crickets in their pockets, and a blacksmith, working on the pavement, hammered woks out of red-hot iron. A taxi carried me to the car-ferry port, where I walked aboard. And then I stood on the top deck as we wove our way across a shifting warp of barges and passenger ships on the Yangtze, whose waters glittered in the bright winter sun. When we reached the northern bank, I hitched a lift for the short hop to Yangzhou.

I wasn't expecting much of the trip. So many times I had arrived in a Chinese city that I didn't know, seduced by legends about its lively street life and architectural beauty, only to find that most of it had been demolished and replaced by monotonous concrete. Suzhou had lost most of its canals and old streets; I could find no old lanes in Hangzhou; and they were pulling Shanghai apart by the day. In my writing, I was determined to find beauty in these places, to bring alive their characters and rich culinary traditions, and yet it seemed increasingly like an exercise in archaeology rather than reportage. That's why Yangzhou was such a delightful surprise. From the moment my driver dropped me off near the city centre, I felt that there was something different about it.

As usual, my preparation had been minimal. I had searched in vain for useful books about Yangzhou and its food. I did, however, have the address of the local branch of the Chinese Culinary Association in my notebook, and I knew from past experience that it might be a good place to start. Since it was early and I had little luggage, I simply hailed a bicycle rickshaw.

I gave the driver the address of the association. 'Please will you take me through the old streets?' I asked, expecting him to tell me that they had been knocked down last year. But he didn't – he actually drove me through the old streets. They were everything I had longed to see. We rambled over a canal bridge where a few people were selling pheasants, rabbits, and baskets of fruit, and into a long lane bordered by grey-brick courtyard houses, with alleys running off on either side. Old-fashioned cotton banners emblazoned with the Chinese characters for 'rice' and 'wine' hung outside little shops. There were street vendors too: an elderly man making pancakes on a griddle, a butcher mincing pork with a cleaver on a wooden board, someone selling home-made salted mustard greens, dark and sleek. Pig's ears and chunks of carp and chicken hung on the outer walls of houses, salted and spiced, wind-drying.

Even the busier streets in the old town had retained some character. They were lined with wutong trees and small shops selling kitchenware, clothes and locally made knives; they were busy with bicycles and unruly mopeds. We passed a mother cycling home with her son, his head resting gently on her back; a baker, standing beside an oven, wiping her hot face with a wet towel. This was no pastiche of local street life recreated for the tourists, but a living city. It reminded me of the vanished old quarters of Chengdu that I had known and adored.

The three deputy secretaries of the culinary association who were at work that day were immediately welcoming. I found them in a first-floor office piled with papers. They sat amid cupboards crammed with food magazines and books, looking out over low rooftops. The amiable, chain-smoking Mr Qiu made me a cup of tea, and they all gathered round for a chat. Within minutes we discovered that we had mutual friends – professors of food history in Chengdu. I got along particularly well with the gruff-voiced, talkative Mr Xia, who seemed to know everything about Huaiyang cuisine. When the other two had drifted back to their desks, he and I continued to sip our tea as he taught me about Yangzhou's magnificent past.

The city was a famous trading port, he said, with direct commercial links to Japan, friendly relations with Persia and many other distant realms. Marco Polo supposedly stayed here in the late thirteenth century, and remarked on the 'large and splendid city… so great and powerful that its authority extends over twenty-seven cities, all large and prosperous and actively engaged in commerce'. Above all, Mr Xia told me, Yangzhou owed its wealth and opulence to the salt trade, which flourished during the Qing. Sea salt, evaporated in salt-ponds on the Shandong and Jiangsu coasts, was transported by water to Yangzhou, the largest wholesale salt market in China. It was such a profitable business that Yangzhou salt taxes came to make up a quarter of China's *entire* tax revenue.

On the back of their lucrative trade, the Yangzhou salt merchants grew rich. They built mansions and pleasure gardens, entertained lavishly, and led lives of great refinement. One of them compiled a collection of recipes that is still in print. Men of letters flocked to the city. During the Tang, the prominent poet Du Fu praised the beauty of its people, the wine-loving Li Bai penned lines inspired by local feasting and carousing, and Wang Jian wrote of the thousand lanterns that gleamed in its nightmarkets. The Song poet Su Dongpo also lived here for a while, taking up lodgings in the Stone Tower Buddhist Temple.

During the Qing Dynasty, the Kangxi and Qianlong Emperors were unable to resist the charms of Yangzhou. They must already have had a taste for its delicacies, because Huaiyang cooking had long been influential at court. They lingered in Yangzhou during their lengthy 'tours of the south', idling in its gardens, playing at fishing, and being entertained by the salt merchants to sumptuous feasts. The only extant description of the fabled Man-Han imperial banquet of the Qing era is in a chronicle of Yangzhou life and society, 'Record of the painted pleasure-boats of Yangzhou', written by a local playwright, Li Dou, in the eighteenth century: 'They had bird's nest with chicken slivers, abalone with pearl leaves, a thick soup of crab and shark skin, bear's paw with crucian carp tongues…' Li Dou listed more than a hundred dishes made with every fine ingredient, accompanied by fresh fruits and delicate vegetables.

I left the office of the culinary association, later that afternoon, laden with gifts: glossy cookery books, academic studies of Yangzhou culture, an anthology of poems about Huaiyang cuisine, out-of-print collections of recipes. I was touched by the kindness and generosity of the food researchers I'd met, and captivated already by the magic of the city. Most satisfyingly of all, I left with an invitation to dinner.

'You see,' said Mr Xia, surveying a tempting spread of cold hors d'oeuvres, 'Yangzhou cooking is concerned with the *ben wei*, the essential tastes of things. Here you won't find the heavy sweetness of Suzhou cooking, or the spiciness of your Sichuanese. We like to show off the *natural* flavours of fresh and seasonal ingredients, subtly enhanced by seasonings like salt, sugar, oil, spring onion, ginger and vinegar. Please, eat!'

Under the encouraging eyes of the association's deputy secretaries, I raised my chopsticks. First I tasted the 'four strands of flavour' (*si tiao wei*): tiny, stimulating dishes to awaken the palate. There were fried peanuts, cubes of fermented beancurd stained pink by red wine lees, morsels of pickled cabbage and slices of ginger preserved in soy sauce. Afterwards, I moved on to the appetisers proper: savoury salt-water goose, 'vegetarian chicken' made from marinated beancurd skin, tiny 'drunken' river shrimps, crisp-and-supple sweet-sour cucumber, and a marvellous rendition of Zhenjiang *yao rou*. This was a terrine of shards of pork in aspic served with a dip of aromatic Zhenjiang vinegar. The *yao rou*, whose name might be translated as 'delectable meat', melted, divinely, in my mouth.

The main courses were just as delicately pleasing. We sampled 'hibiscus-flower fish slices', soft white pillows of fish-flesh blended with egg white and starch, tender as a custard but with a slight crispness to their bite; fresh broad beans with straw mushrooms; and a red-braised carp head with farmhouse beancurd, served on a grand blue-and-white china platter (Mr Xia probed out for me the sweet, fatty flesh around the fish's eye). And then there were the famous 'lion's head meatballs', cooked slowly in individual clay pots until they were so tender they yielded at a chopstick's touch.

'Those last dishes were two of the so-called "three heads" of Yangzhou,' said Mr Xia. 'The third was a whole pig's head. But we thought that might be a bit excessive for today, given that there are only six of us. Perhaps another time we can gather a few more people for a full "three-headed" feast?' (Later, I learned the intriguing fact that the most acclaimed producers of the slow-cooked Yangzhou pig's head were *monks* at the Fahai Buddhist temple, who were officially, like all other monks, vegetarian. They would only show off this talent for carnivorous cookery to people they knew and trusted – if a stranger knocked on the door and demanded a pig's head, they would be dismissed with a mischievous smile and a Buddhist greeting: '*A mi tuo fo!*')

The next dish, Wensi Beancurd, also had Buddhist connections. In a dense broth hung filigree strands of silken beancurd, threaded with a few wisps of Jinhua ham. It was invented, so they say, by a Qing Dynasty monk at the Tianning Temple who was renowned for his beancurd cookery (he made a vegetarian version, seasoned with mushrooms). Earlier, at a beancurd stall in the backstreets, I had seen a man cutting curd for this dish. His sharp knife, slicing up and down, moved almost imperceptibly through the block of beancurd, shaving off slices as thin as silk. These he cut, in turn, transforming the slices into a mass of fine threads. It was masterful.

I learned from my dining companions that Yangzhou cooks were known across China for the dexterity of their knifework. The lion's head meatball, for example, owed its irresistible succulence to the fact that the meat was hand-chopped into 'fish-eye' grains, and not minced or puréed. 'The cook's cleaver, of course,' said Mr Xia, 'is just one of the "Three Knives" of Yangzhou: the others are scissors, and the pedicurist's blade. "Foot-repairing" is another of this city's great pleasures. You must try it.' (Later, nervously, I entrusted my feet to a pedicurist who shaved bits off them until they were as soft and sweet as a newborn baby's.)

We sat there, talking in Chinese, of course, discussing the characteristics of Yangzhou cuisine. At one point during the meal, Mr Xia looked at me with sudden concern, and asked: 'I do hope you can take the flavour of Huaiyang dishes, when they are not hot and spicy like your usual Sichuanese food.' I looked back at him in puzzlement, but it was Mr Qiu who reminded him that I was not *actually* Sichuanese, but from England, so it was unlikely to be a problem. We all laughed, Mr Xia at his mistake, I because this curious exchange made me realise how often I did actually find myself referring to other foreigners as *lao wai*, and saying things like: 'In Sichuan, we tend to add a bit of chilli-bean paste to our red-braised dishes' or 'In Sichuan, *we* call it such-and-such' or 'In Sichuan, *we* drink the soup at the end of the meal'.

We finished our dinner, inevitably, with the one dish that the entire outside world recognises as a local speciality – Yangzhou fried rice. On almost every restaurant menu in Western Chinatowns it appears, and finally I was tasting it in its place of origin. The rice was shot with tiny cubes of dark pink ham and brown shiitake, wisps of golden egg, crabmeat, and tiny shrimp. It was rich but not oily, wok-fragrant and utterly delicious. Afterwards, we rinsed our palates with a broth afloat with mushrooms and *cai tai*, a seasonal green, and then refreshed ourselves with slices of watermelon and fresh sugar-cane from the south.

We had been joined for the meal by a young officer from the local government trade office, Mr Liu, and a chef named Chen. When we had finished eating, Liu and I went for a walk along the Grand Canal at the south of the old town. Peach trees and weeping willows grew along the banks. People were ballroom dancing outside pavilions festooned in fairy lights. We caught the last pleasure boat of the night, and as we were the only passengers, we asked the driver to switch off the lamps. So we stood on the prow with the breeze in our faces and tried to imagine that we were emperors, on a visit from Beijing to sample the delights of the south ('and to find a pretty concubine' said Liu, with a laugh).

Over the next few days, I explored the landscaped gardens of Yangzhou. The grandest was the Slender West Lake Park, upon which the salt merchants had lavished their funds to make it fit for the Qianlong Emperor's visit. The curves of the lake were softened by weeping willows; pavilions and ornamental bridges dotted its shores and inlets. I wandered to the end of the spit of rock where the emperor had cast his fishing line. It was like walking in a Chinese ink-and-water painting.

In the more modest He Garden, built in the nineteenth century by a local official, I climbed the steps of a rockery to a tiny pavilion, where I sat and wrote for a while, engulfed by the intoxicating scent of winter plum blossom. Down below, in a two-storey building with a tiled roof that curved up at the ends, two musicians were practising. A middle-aged lady sung a plaintive tune, while an *er hu* player drew his bow over strings. Before me lay a miniature landscape tailored to appeal to a certain Chinese literary sensibility. Every feature had a name of poetic allusion. There were hidden promonteries from which to view the garden, places where a scholar might pause and be inspired to compose a few lines. At the far end of the complex was a pond designed to mirror the moon's reflection. Sitting in my eyrie, writing at a marble table, I felt at peace.

Perhaps Yangzhou had a particular meaning for me because I was in the midst of reading Cao Xueqin's great eighteenth-century Chinese novel, *A Dream of Red Mansions* (also known as *The Story of the Stone*). It is a family saga, the tale of four generations of the Jia clan who live together in two neighbouring mansions in a notional Chinese capital in northern China. Although the novel is set in the north, Cao himself came from the southern Yangtze region, and the life he describes resembles that of the Yangzhou literati. Cao wrote the novel while living in poverty in Beijing, after the collapse of his once-illustrious family's fortunes. Many of the characters are thought to be be based on real people, the friends and relatives of Cao's own youth, and it is generally seen as a nostalgic evocation of his past.

In English translation, it is a novel in five volumes, and for the few months I spent reading it, it took over my life. The story begins in the 'golden days' of the family's history, when the young Jia cousins amuse themselves in the Prospect Garden. They hold poetry competitions, play drinking games, devour hairy crabs and admire chrysanthemums. As the novel progresses, the tale becomes darker. There are suicides, kidnappings and savage betrayals. Eventually the family's wealth is confiscated by the imperial authorities, and the Jias' reputation lost amid a storm of scandal. But I travelled to Yangzhou when I was still absorbed in the first, happier volumes of the novel, the Golden Days, and everything I experienced there seemed to resonate with the gilded life of the Jias.

Somehow the elegance of the city had endured, despite everything. Like almost anywhere in China, Yangzhou had been damaged by the communists, who demolished its ancient city walls, carved up the salt merchants' mansions, and unleashed the chaos of the Cultural Revolution. Its relative obscurity, however, had saved it from the worst ravages of the reform period. In Suzhou, I'd seen how the Xuanmiao Temple was penned in by American fast-food outlets, and the bicycle rickshaws plastered with McDonalds advertisements. No one had bothered to smear Yangzhou with such tacky commercialisation. Slum buildings along the canal had been cleared, and the banks of the canal redeveloped, but local leaders had decided to protect and revive the old city.

High-rises were banned in the historic centre, and they were gradually restoring the salt merchants' mansions to their former splendour.

Perhaps, compared with Yangzhou's heydays in the Tang and Qing, when it was one of the most polished cities in the world, it was now just a shadow of itself. But wherever I went, I found echoes of its legendary refinement and charm: in the gardens, in the food, and above all in the graciousness of the people I met.

Mr Xia had invited me for breakfast at a salt merchants' mansion that had been turned into a restaurant and a museum. A gentle mist blotted the willow trees as I hurried along the canal to meet him. Outside the mansion's long, grey-brick walls, some middle-aged ladies were practising Tai Chi. Inside, Mr Xia was waiting for me, in a grand hall with high ceilings and wooden panelling, wearing a baseball cap and clutching his jar of home-brewed tea. Once, this was part of the inner quarters of the mansion, where the grand ladies of the household would have sat at their needlework, but now it was crowded with working men and women, chatting and laughing quietly over their breakfasts. Waitresses in padded pink silk jackets bustled around bearing towers of steamers.

'The early-morning tea breakfast is an institution in Yangzhou, just as it is in Guangdong,' said Mr Xia. 'The difference is that the Cantonese like to discuss business over their dumplings. Here we just like to relax and have fun.'

Our breakfast was extraordinarily delicious. We ate steamed buns stuffed with radish slivers; with chopped pork, bamboo shoot, mushrooms and tiny shrimps; and with finely-chopped greens. There were juicy steamed dumplings with a sweet, meaty filling; grilled buns with toasted sesame; dry beancurd slivers with soy sauce and sesame oil. 'Look at this *bao zi*,' said Mr Xia, pointing at a bun resting in a bamboo steamer, 'it's beautiful. See how delicately it has been wrapped. The folds are so even. And the flavour, you'll find, is excellent: a rich savouriness balanced by a hint of sweetness.'

Most advocates of Chinese local cuisines insist that theirs is the best in

China, and disparage the cooking of other regions. But in Yangzhou I was tempted to agree with the culinary patriots. Yangzhou food, as they say, combines the strengths of the cooking traditions of northern and southern China. It is about the art of balance, the miraculous transformation of ingredients in the pot that the chef Yi Yin had talked about more than three thousand years ago. Yangzhou cooks are famously particular in their selection of raw ingredients. They insist on the tenderest of spinach leaves, the hearts of cabbages, the crispest tips of bamboo shoots. They have rules on seasonality: no drunken crabs after the Lantern Festival, no hairtail anchovy after the Feast of Clear Brightness. And lion's head meatballs, though available all year round, are cooked with bamboo shoots in spring, freshwater mussel in summer, crab coral in autumn, and wind-dried chicken in winter.

Yangzhou food doesn't jump up and amaze you, like its Sichuanese counterpart. It won't make your lips tingle, or dance jazz on your tongue. It is not a sassy spice girl with red lipstick and a sharp wit, thrusting itself into the limelight. Yangzhou food is an altogether gentler creature. Like one of the Jia cousins in *A Dream of Red Mansions*, it sits in a landscaped garden, ornaments of jade and gold in its hair, composing poetry at a marble table. It seduces by understatement, with its delicate colours (pale pink, green, yellow), fine stocks, soft and soothing textures, and sensitivity to salt and sweetness.

Yet despite their strikingly different characters, the cuisines of Sichuan and Yangzhou are nonetheless related. They are linked by the artery of the Yangtze River, and also by their enviable geographies – the fecund soils and abundant produce that helped to supply their famous kitchens, and which enabled the more fortunate of their people to lead lives of great luxury and refinement. Talented cooks in either place conjure up banquets of unbelievable variety, but they express themselves in different registers. 'Huaiyang cuisine is like Sichuanese cuisine without the spiciness,' as Mr Xia told me once. In the Tang Dynasty, they used to say 'Yangzhou first and Chengdu second', in wonder at the flourishing economies and cultures of these two beautiful cities.

I don't know what it was that made me fall so completely for Yangzhou. Perhaps it began with the sun glittering on the waters of the Yangtze; maybe it was the old streets, which brought back so many memories of my beloved Chengdu. Or perhaps it was the extraordinary kindness of Mr Xia and his colleagues, and their modest pride in Huaiyang culinary culture. I also had the sense there of a city being rescued and reborn from the ashes of the Cultural Revolution, and of hope in a Chinese future that was more than just rampant capitalism.

Two and a half centuries after the Qianlong Emperor had been mesmerised by Yangzhou, the city still had an irresistible pull, and it worked on me like a tonic. Softly and imperceptibly, it melted away my bitterness and exasperation at China. Chef Chen, to whom I had been introduced at that first fine meal with my friends at the culinary association, told me: 'Hunanese cooking, with all those bold and brassy flavours, is the food of war – look at the military leaders it nourished. Yangzhou food is the food of peace. In times of harmony, that is what you should eat.' Somehow his words expressed perfectly my own feeling that being in Yangzhou was, for me, a kind of peace after the war of writing my Hunanese cookbook.

Many Chinese friends have spoken to me over the last few years of a historical progression from 'eating to fill your belly' (*chi bao*), through 'eating plenty of rich food', (*chi hao*) to 'eating skilfully' (*chi qiao*). In the past, they say, food was just about sustenance; starvation was a constant threat. With growing wealth, the Chinese began to eat as much meat and fish as they could, as if to make up for years of deprivation. Now, though, the thrill of plenty is wearing off, and a growing number are trying to eat with more discernment, seeking out 'green food products', reducing their consumption of animal foods, and ordering less gluttonously in restaurants.

In Yangzhou, after my own period of 'eating plenty of rich food' in China, I found myself eating more 'skilfully'. I dined out with the officers of the culinary association on food that wasn't full of colourings and MSG. I ate well, but not excessively, at the old Yanchun teahouse by the canal, famous for its buns and dumplings. And I wasn't offered meat from a single endangered species. Gradually, my appetite returned, and eating became a pleasure once more. I felt my spirits lifting.

In a sense, Yangzhou rescued me, and my Chinese food-writing career. Like a dream of red mansions, it reminded me, not only of the vanished elegance of a certain aspect of the Chinese past, but also of my own lost love for China. Chengdu as I had known it might have been swept away by the tidal wave of real-estate development, but in Yangzhou, with its understated charm, its delicious food, and its exceptionally kind and elegant people, I found something of the same enchantment. Yangzhou rekindled the fire. I knew then that I could, and would write this book, and that there was life yet in my relationship with China.

It was my last day in Yangzhou, and I wanted to visit a mansion near the Grand Canal that had caught my eye, several times, as I passed. It was a vast and imposing complex of courtyards and halls that had just been restored and opened as a museum. So I bought my ticket and went inside. Somewhere in the midst of the house, in a small courtyard with its own well, I was pleased to find an old-fashioned kitchen. The bright, airy room was dominated by an enormous cooking range, built in brick, covered in whitewashed plaster, and decorated with blue line-drawings of a blooming lotus and a fish. On top, a Kitchen God presided in his shrine. There were four 'fire-mouths' on the stove, two with wooden lids covering inset woks, one for the rice-steamer and one for a stack of bamboo steamers to cook buns and dumplings.

It was the only old Yangzhou range I'd seen, and I wasn't sure how everything worked. Luckily for me, the other visitors that day were three elderly men in Mao suits who remembered such stoves from their childhoods. 'When we were young,' said one, 'everyone had ranges like this. You see those cubbyholes at the back, they were for seasonings: you know, the salt, the oil, sugar, soy sauce and vinegar. And those cupboards underneath, you could store your wok brushes there, or put wet shoes inside to dry them out. The hooks hanging from the ceiling were for hams and smoked ribs. And you stacked up the firewood behind the stove.'

As we chatted, I became aware of a man and woman watching me from the edge of the room, and discreetly eavesdropping on our conversation. Eventually, when the old men had exhausted their kitchen memories and bid me goodbye, these two came forward and greeted me. 'Hello, may we trouble you a little?' said the man. 'My name is Zhang Wenjie, and I am the manager of the People's Number One Hospital, which owns this land. This is Yuan Yuan, the manager of the museum.' He seemed friendly and open, and Mrs Yuan had a gentle, soft face and was dressed in a fitted coat, with a mother-of-pearl clasp in her hair. 'Won't you come with us, and drink some tea?'

There was some unspoken eagerness behind his invitation, but I had no idea what it meant. They led me through a labyrinth of courtyards, and then up a little path to an anomalous two-storey building in a walled garden. It was built in the Western colonial style, with red and grey bricks, casement windows and a wooden verandah, and stood awkwardly within the walls of a traditional Chinese mansion. The ground floor had been turned into a teahouse for tourists, but we didn't stop there: they led me up a wooden staircase to the private rooms on the upper storey. The innermost room had been restored in the 1930s 'European' style, with a fireplace, glass-fronted cabinets, and Chinese wooden sofas around a coffee table. In the corner, a wind-up gramophone sat on a table, its brass horn flaring above. 'This is known as the *yang lou*, the foreigners' building,' said Mr Zhang.

We sat around the coffee table, and they offered me tea. Again, I had the sense that there was more to their hospitality than met the eye, but they just smiled and chatted politely. I noticed that there was an old 78 record on the gramophone, and suggested that we play it. To oblige me, Mr Zhang cranked up the machine, and set the needle in the crackly groove. I was expecting a musical glimpse of the thirties, something like 'Nights of Shanghai' by Zhou Xuan. It would have suited the atmosphere so perfectly, the gentle urbanity of my hosts, the delicacy of the tea, and the cosmopolitan atmosphere of this curious room. So it was a shock when we heard the shrill marching tune of a Maoist anthem. It jarred, horribly. We smiled at one another in embarrassment as Mr Zhang lifted the needle and let the gramophone wind down in silence.

'Let me tell you the story of this place,' said Mr Zhang. 'The mansion was built in 1904 by a Yangzhou man named Wu Yinsun, a customs official who was posted to Ningbo, in neighbouring Zhejiang Province. He intended to return here when he retired from official life, so he bought the land, and built the complex mainly in the Zhejiang style. His plan was to start a trading business, so he had this building designed as a suitable place for receiving *yang ren*, foreign businessmen. But Wu never returned to Yangzhou, so the foreign businessmen never came. In 1949, the whole mansion was requisitioned by the new communist government, who gave it to the Number One People's Hospital. They converted it into living quarters for hospital workers: at one time it was home to a hundred families. But this building, the *yang lou*, was left to decay. The verandahs collapsed, and it became unsafe to enter.

'Now we've restored it, as you can see,' he said, gesturing towards the sleek new wood of the verandah, the neat brickwork. Then he smiled, a little bashful. 'In fact, you are the first foreigner who has ever come into the *yang lou*, that's why we wanted to invite you.' He and Mrs Yuan waited, a little nervously, for my response.

I was overcome with a sudden sense of all the time that had passed since I first came as a foreigner to China, and of all that had happened to me in those years. I had learned to speak Chinese, and in some ways to think and feel in the language. I had developed deep ties of affection with my Chinese friends, and had roamed all over the country. I had learned to eat everything, and had even trained as a Chinese chef. Yet however much of an insider I had become, in some ways, it seemed, I would always be a *yang ren*, a foreigner, a *lao wai*. It was a sobering thought, but a sweet one, under the circumstances.

In the *yang lou*, I wanted to hug Mr Zhang and Mrs Yuan, but that's not what Chinese people do. I was moved, and somehow delighted. Finally, after more than a century, the late Mr Wu's occidentalist dream had been fulfilled, and by pure coincidence I was the agent of this fulfilment.

Then Mr Zhang summoned the photographer who had been waiting in the wings, and asked if I would mind if they marked the occasion for posterity. So I posed for photographs by the fireplace and out on the verandah, smiling brightly, flanked by the director and the hospital boss, a token foreigner in the building built for my alien kind.

Yangzhou fried rice

揚州炒飯

Serves 2 as a main dish, 4 as part of a Chinese meal

0.7–1 oz (20–30 g) raw pork fillet
0.7–1 oz (20–30 g) small frozen prawns
0.7–1 oz (20–30 g) cooked ham or salami
0.7–1 oz (20–30 g) cooked chicken
2 dried shitake mushrooms, soaked in hot water for half an hour
0.7–1 oz (20–30 g) bamboo shoot
3 spring onions, green parts only
1 egg
Salt and pepper to taste
5 tbsp gpeanut oil
0.7–1 oz (20–30 g) frozen peas or soybeans
2 tsp Shaoxing wine
7 fl oz (200 ml) chicken stock
21 oz (600 g) cold, cooked Thai fragrant rice (9 oz/250 g when raw)

1. Cut the pork, frozen prawns, ham or salami, chicken, mushrooms and bamboo shoot into very small dice. Finely slice the spring onions greens. Beat the egg with a little salt and pepper to taste.

2. Heat 2 tbsp oil in a wok over a high flame. Add the raw pork and prawns and stir-fry briefly, until the pork is pale. Add the ham, chicken, mushrooms, peas or soybeans and bamboo shoot and continue to stir-fry for a minute or two, until everything is hot and sizzling. Add the Shaoxing wine, then pour in the stock and bring to the boil.

3. Season with salt to taste, and then pour off into a bowl.

4. Rinse and dry the wok. Return it to the heat with 3 tbsp oil. When the oil is hot, add the egg and swirl around the base of the wok. When the egg is half-cooked, add all the rice and stir-fry, using your ladle or wok scoop to break up any lumps of rice.

5. When the rice is very hot and smells delicious, add the bowlful of prepared ingredients in their stock sauce. Mix well, add the spring onion greens and stir briskly for another half minute or so, seasoning with salt or pepper if you wish. Serve immediately.

The Caterpillar

It was a wet day, and I was at home in Oxford for a few days' writing. 'Help yourself to vegetables from the garden,' my mother had said, on her way out of the house. So I did. I walked out into the cool air and plucked carrots and leeks from the dark moist earth, pulled off spinach leaves. Lovingly I washed them, cut them into pieces and laid them in a steamer. At lunchtime, I sat at the table before my plate of steaming vegetables. I sprinkled a little salt, trickled over some olive oil. Then I noticed, upon the lazy tangle of wilted leaves, a small and perfect caterpillar, perhaps two or three centimetres long. It was light-green and delicate, and looked fresh and clean as it lay there, steaming, with its babyish sucker-feet aloft.

I was just about to throw it out of the door, when I stopped myself. Because suddenly I remembered that, only weeks before, I had written a long article about eating insects in China. As part of my research, I had visited a restaurant in Sichuan that specialised in insect dishes, and had munched my way through a creepy-crawly menu featuring, among other things, bee pupae, timber grubs and sand-crawling caterpillars. These were expensive delicacies, too, sold at high prices to discerning urban customers, not just any old rough peasant food. And some of them had been delicious.

So many times I've been confronted by my cultural taboos about eating, only to push them aside. It's become almost a habit. Ten years ago, it took me about half an hour to pluck up the courage to eat a deep-fried scorpion. I held it in my chopsticks, uneasy and afraid, scrutinising its pincers and its sprung tail, before plunging it headfirst into my mouth. These days it rarely takes more than a minute or two to tackle something new, even in worst-case scenarios. And of course, once eaten, the deed is done, the taboo broken, and it's really not so bad after all.

In Taiwan, I made the mistake of getting involved in a game of one-upmanship with a well-known food writer. 'Oh yeah, insects, done them,' I bragged, listing the many bugs and grubs I'd been eating in Sichuan. 'And snakes and dogs, had them many times, no problem.' Mr Chu grinned broadly. 'Well,' he said, drawing a deep breath, 'when I was in this restaurant in Yunnan, the waiter brought me a live caterpillar, several inches long. He dared me to hold its head down on the table with my thumb and then tear its body away with my other hand, and eat it, just like that. It was delicious.' That shut me up pretty quickly. It just went to show that, try as you might, you couldn't beat the southern Chinese at their own game. But I have tried.

My good English table manners, so carefully instilled by my mother, have been ruined by my years in China. When I'm there, I spit my bones out, I raise my rice bowl to my lips; I slurp along with everyone else. In my first years in Chengdu, I even picked up, for a while, the unsavoury habit of spitting in the streets. 'You are half-Chinese,' my friends there tell me. And, as I look at them out of my round Caucasian eyes, I have to acknowledge that, inside me, there is someone who is no longer entirely English. I'm not even sure if I know, anymore, precisely where the cultural boundaries lie.

Sometimes my Western friends catch me in the act of being Chinese – eating something rubbery with murmurs of appreciation, or making unusual noises over my soup. Generally I try to reassure them with a veneer of Englishness, making a joke of my own omnivorousness, or keeping my sounds and my disturbing satisfaction to myself. But occasionally I forget, and the mask slips, with a bone thrown outrageously on the table, or a noise that arrests my companions, who can't believe what they hear coming from the mouth of a nice English girl.

Back in my parents' house in Oxford, I contemplated the caterpillar. Why is it, I wondered, that I would think nothing of eating this in an insect restaurant in China, but I am hesitant to try it here? Even my friends by now expect me to eat all kinds of weird and revolting things in China. My tales of eating insects and snakes seem hardly to perturb them. Dog might strike them as a bit more unsavoury, but because it's in China, it's just part of my exotic travelogue, it adds a bit of colour to my narrative.

I realised, however, that eating a caterpillar from my parents' garden would be a real transgression. There would be no excuse for it: I couldn't justify the act as 'doing as the Romans do' – or '*ru xiang sui su*' (following the customs of the countryside) as they say in China. My English friends would be far more shocked at me if I ate this English caterpillar, freshly steamed and dressed on my mother's willow-pattern plate, than they would be by my most outlandish tale of eating in China. They would look at me askance; they would see me as someone who could, *potentially*, eat their pet dog or cat (perhaps even *them*?).

As I ran my eyes up and down the small green creature on my plate, I admitted to myself that, try as I might, I couldn't really feel shocked at the idea of eating it. Any mild horror I could muster was disingenuous, based on the desire to mollify an imaginary audience of compatriots rather than any true abhorrence. I had to face it: I was no longer simply an adventurous English traveller, pandering while abroad to the strange customs of the natives. Living in China had profoundly changed me, and my tastes. My English friends might think I still looked the same, that I was still one of them, but actually I had crossed to the other side. Whether or not to eat the caterpillar was no longer a question of whether I dared to eat it, but of whether I dared to show so flagrantly that I really didn't give a damn.

You can probably guess what happened. Reader, I ate him. I confess, I bit into that tender green flesh, I felt the little suckers on my tongue, I swallowed. Nothing happened. There was no clap of thunder, no earthquake, no deluge unleashed by outraged local gods. The caterpillar itself had an insipid, watery taste. I felt fine. It was a non-event. So I took another bite from its body, ate the head. And then I simply got on with my lunch, and enjoyed it.

I remember that lunch as a threshold of sorts, a moment of recognition. For weeks afterwards I went around with a sense that I had finally nailed my colours to the mast.

LIST OF THE MAIN
CHINESE DYNASTIES

Xia	c. 21st – 16th century BC
Shang	c. 16th – 11th century BC
Zhou	c. 11th century BC – 221 BC
Qin	221 BC – 206 AD
Han	206 – 220
Three Kingdoms	220 – 280
Jin	265 –
Northern and Southern dynasties	386 –
Sui	581 – 618
Tang	618 – 907
Five Dynasties and Ten States	907 – 979
Song	960 – 1279
Yuan	1279 – 1368
Ming	1368 – 1644
Qing	1644 – 1911
Republic of China (Nationalist Party)	1912 – 1949
People's Republic of China (Communist Party)	1949 - ?

ACKNOWLEDGEMENTS

I couldn't have written this book without Gwen Chesnais, who gave me a room of my own in Shanghai; Zoë Waldie, who is the best agent anyone could possibly have; Mike Finnerty, who let me take six months' sabbatical from my job at the BBC; Rebecca Carter, whose ingenious editing helped me to pull the whole thing together; my US editor Maria Guarnaschelli, whose encouraging emails always seem to arrive at the right moments; and Phil Parker, who gave me so many inspiring ideas. Shao Wei has been an incredibly generous friend and colleague, and Liu Yaochun has helped me to answer countless vital questions. I am grateful also to Sarah Lavelle and Carey Smith at Ebury Press for their enthusiasm for this book.

Mara Baughman, Penny Bell, Bess Frimodig, Seema Merchant and Francesca Tarocco read early versions of the manuscript and held my hand through various book-related crises. My parents, Bede and Carolyn Dunlop, and my brother and sister-in-law Merlin and Charlotte have been supportive as always, and my parents have given me many useful comments on the manuscript. Some of the stories in this book grew out of pieces I wrote for the *Financial Times*, *Gourmet*, *Saveur*, *Observer Food Monthly* and the BBC's *From Our Own Correspondent*, so thanks very much to my various editors, Richard Addis, Lorna Dolan, Tony Grant, Rahul Jacob, Nicola Jeal, Margo True and Jocelyn Zuckerman. I am very grateful to Per-Anders Jörgensen for the use of the photograph on the cover, and to Sebastian Wilkinson for his beautiful illustrations.

I owe more than I can express to the friends in China and in England who have helped me with my writing and my culinary explorations over the years: Bian Jiang, Winnie Chan, Ian Cumming, Volker Dencks, Du Li, Fan Qun, Fan Shixian, Feng Quanxin, Feng Rui, Andrew Flower, Rob and Nancy Gifford, Gan Guojian, Rachel Harris, He Caiping, Aziz Isa, Annabel Jackson, Jiang Yuxiang, Edward Jia, Nikki Johnson, Susan Jung, Nigel Kat, Rob and

Leslie Kenny, Rebecca Kesby, Lai Wu, Lan Guijun, Liliane Landor, Lau Kin Wai, Rose Leng, P.K.Leung, Willie Mark, Li Rui, Li Shurong, Li Xiaorong, Liu Guochu, Michelle Liu, Liu Wei, Liu Xinjun, Liu Yi, Long Qingrong, Lu Maoguo, Luo Jixiang, Luo Leiguang, Luo Suizu, Hugo Martin, Mao Anping, Mao Yushi, Graham Nash, Qin Lingzhi, Qiu Rongzhen, Qiu Yangyi, Davide Quadrio, Sansan, Shi Zhitang, Tang Huaping, Tao Ping, Tian Zhengtian, Wang Tao, Wang Xudong, Sebastian Wilkinson, Wu Xiaoming, Xia Yongguo, Xiao Chang'an, Xiao Jianming, Xie Laoban, Xiong Sizhi, Yu Bo, Yuan Yuan, Zhang Wenjie, Zhang Xiaozhong, Zhou Xun, and Zhou Yu. Thanks also to Mark and Rebecca Bethell and Sam Chatterton Dickson for their comments on various chapters.

In particular, I must thank Liu Wei and Sansan in Changsha, and Xia Yongguo in Yangzhou, for reasons that I think are clear in my narrative!

A BRIEF ACKNOWLEDGEMENT OF WRITTEN SOURCES

In writing this memoir, I have consulted a great variety of sources, most of which are in Chinese. It seemed inappropriate to list them all in a book that is intended to be fun rather than academic. I would however, like to acknowledge a few English-language sources that I have found particularly useful: Anderson, E.N., *The Food of China*, Yale University Press, New Haven and London, 1988; Chang, K.C. (ed.), *Food in Chinese Culture*, Yale University Press, New Haven, 1977; Knechtges, David R., 'A Literary Feast: Food in Early Chinese Literature', in *Journal of the American Oriental Society*, Vol. 106, No.1, Jan-Mar 1986), pp.49-63; Roberts, J.A.G., *China to Chinatown: Chinese Food in the West*, Reaktion Books, London, 2002; So, Yan-kit, *Classic Food of China*, Macmillan, London, 1992

Readers who wish to cook some of the dishes mentioned in the Sichuan and Hunan chapters might like to read my two previous books: *Revolutionary Chinese Cookbook*, Ebury Press, London, 2006, and *Sichuan Cookery*, Penguin Books, London, 2003

PERMISSIONS

INDEX